Field Guide to the
Birds of the
Dominican Republic
& Haiti

Field Guide to the
Birds of the
Dominican Republic
& Haiti

Steven C. Latta, Christopher C. Rimmer & Kent P. McFarland

Principal Illustrator: Dana Gardner

Supporting Illustrators: Cynthie Fisher, Barry Kent MacKay, Tracy Pedersen, Bart Rulon, Kristin Williams

Princeton University Press
Princeton and Oxford

Princeton University Press is committed to the protection of copyright and the intellectual property our authors entrust to us. Copyright promotes the progress and integrity of knowledge. Thank you for supporting free speech and the global exchange of ideas by purchasing an authorized edition of this book. If you wish to reproduce or distribute any part of it in any form, please obtain permission.

Requests for permission to reproduce material from this work
should be sent to permissions@press.princeton.edu

Published by Princeton University Press
41 William Street, Princeton, New Jersey 08540
99 Banbury Road, Oxford OX2 6JX

press.princeton.edu

All Rights Reserved
ISBN (pbk.) 978-0-691-23239-3
ISBN (e-book) 978-0-691-23377-2
Library of Congress Control Number: 2021952293

British Library Cataloging-in-Publication Data is available

Editorial: Robert Kirk, Abigail Johnson, and Megan Mendonca
Production Editorial: Karen Carter
Text Design: D & N Publishing, Wiltshire, UK
Cover Design: Wanda España
Production: Steven Sears
Publicity: Caitlyn Robson and Matthew Taylor
Copyeditor: Lucinda Treadwell

This book has been composed in Museo Sans and Calibri

Printed on acid-free paper. ∞

Printed in Italy

10 9 8 7 6 5 4 3 2 1

CONTENTS

PLATES

OUR SPONSORS

NATIONAL AVIARY

The National Aviary (https://www.aviary.org/) is America's only independent indoor nonprofit zoo dedicated to birds. Located in Pittsburgh, Pennsylvania, the National Aviary strives to inspire respect for nature through an appreciation of birds. The Aviary's Department of Conservation and Field Research works to save birds and protect habitats around the world. Our national and international conservation and field research projects span a range of topics and perspectives, from classical ecological research, to applied conservation, to more traditional zoo-based breeding and reintroduction activities. But all of our projects are founded on the belief that field research, conservation, and education are linked and are best done in concert with the active collaboration of locally based biologists, conservationists, and community scientists.

VERMONT CENTER FOR ECOSTUDIES

The Vermont Center for Ecostudies (VCE) (https://vtecostudies.org/) advances wildlife conservation across the Americas through scientific research, ecological monitoring, and community engagement. VCE biologists study birds, insects, amphibians, and other vulnerable wildlife from Canada to South America, with help from a legion of volunteer community scientists and naturalists. VCE shares its discoveries about wildlife and conservation with fellow scientists, policy makers, conservationists, and the public. VCE publishes its research in peer-reviewed scientific journals and uses its findings to help inform public policy. VCE's growing body of data on biodiversity is a free, openly accessible resource for anyone who seeks to discover and enjoy wildlife.

GRUPO JARAGUA

Grupo Jaragua (www.grupojaragua.org.do) is a Dominican nonprofit organization whose mission is to conserve biodiversity and associated ecosystem services on Hispaniola, working in collaboration with local communities and basing its decisions on the best available science. Its major lines of work are biodiversity conservation, environmental advocacy and education, and support of sustainable, rural livelihoods.

GRUPO ACCIÓN ECOLÓGICA

Grupo Acción Ecológica (GAE) (https://www.facebook.com/grupoaccionecologica/) is a Dominican nonprofit organization founded in 2009 that works to protect biodiversity through field studies and community education. Founded by some of the country's most dedicated conservationists and most capable ornithologists, GAE is focused on the importance of research, education, and conservation to fulfill its mission: "For the birds, the environment, and you." Grupo Acción Ecológica has changed lives by conducting person-to-person education in small communities where GAE finds that residents increasingly *value* birds once they *know* the birds. GAE's primary focus to date has been on studies of birds dependent on critically important riparian habitats, the importance of water quality to biodiversity and human health, biodiversity in organic cacao plantations, and education of students and citizen scientists in field research and conservation techniques.

ASOCIACIÓN DOMINICANA DE FOTÓGRAFOS DE LA NATURALEZA

Asociación Dominicana de Fotógrafos de la Naturaleza, INC
ADFONA

The Asociación Dominicana de Fotógrafos de la Naturaleza (ADFONA), or the Dominican Association of Nature Photographers (https://www.facebook.com/adfonaDO/), uses photography for education, the preservation of nature, and the promotion of good environmental practice in the Dominican Republic. ADFONA records species and ecosystems in a specific time and place to support scientists in their investigations. ADFONA also strives to strengthen measures to protect the environment by documenting practices that negatively impact nature. Since photography is a universal language with the unique ability to highlight conservation needs and knowledge in a graphic way, our images help us to expose environmental abuse, honor conservation success, and celebrate the beauty and wonder of nature.

RUTA BARRANCOLÍ

Ruta Barrancolí (https://www.caribbeanbirdingtrail.org/sites/dominican-republic/) represents the first national birding trail in Latin America and the Caribbean. Consisting of 44 sites spread across five regions of the Dominican Republic, it was designed by Steven Latta and Kate Wallace in 2011. Birding trails are driving and walking routes linking birding locations, and they create access, opportunities, and an economic market for birding. Birding trails demonstrate a community's commitment to environmental protection based on responsible tourism and bird appreciation, and they help foster a conservation ethic. A full-color book, *Ruta Barrancolí: A Bird-finding Guide to the Dominican Republic*, includes site descriptions, maps, driving and walking directions, lists of expected bird species, and recommendations for food, accommodations, and other cultural attractions. In 2014, the Ruta Barrancolí was adopted as the Dominican leg of the Caribbean Birding Trail by BirdsCaribbean.

ABOUT THE AUTHORS

Steven C. Latta

Dr. Steven C. Latta is Director of Conservation and Field Research at the National Aviary in Pittsburgh. A native of Northern Michigan, he was educated at Kalamazoo College, University of Michigan, and University of Missouri. After serving four years as Director of the Latin American Program at Point Reyes Bird Observatory (California), he came to the National Aviary in 2006. Latta has worked extensively on Hispaniola for 30 years, where his research has focused on the winter ecology of migratory birds, and on understanding how migrant and resident species respond to natural and anthropogenic changes to habitat. A focus of current research uses the Louisiana Waterthrush as a model species, evaluating how the degradation of streams across the annual cycle leads to population reductions in this riparian-obligate species. Other work has focused on the ecology and conservation of threatened endemics, and the evolution, diversification, and impacts of avian malaria. He is a cofounder of Grupo Acción Ecológica, has authored several books on the birds of Hispaniola, and published more than 150 research articles. Latta continues to dedicate himself to training young biologists in field research and avian monitoring techniques in the Dominican Republic and elsewhere.

Christopher C. Rimmer

Chris Rimmer is the founding Executive Director of the Vermont Center for Ecostudies, a nonprofit wildlife conservation group based in Norwich, Vermont. He completed undergraduate studies in Wildlife Biology at the University of Vermont and graduate work in Ecology and Behavioral Biology at the University of Minnesota, where he studied Yellow Warblers on the James Bay coast of Ontario. Prior to his graduate studies, Chris was an itinerant field biologist, with stints in Peru, Ellesmere Island, James Bay, coastal Massachusetts (Manomet Bird Observatory), and Antarctica. Much of his work over the past 30 years has focused on conservation research of Bicknell's Thrush at both ends of its migratory range, from New York and New England to the Dominican Republic and Cuba. Since 1994, he has spearheaded multiple avian studies and conservation projects on Hispaniola with local collaborators, most involving birds of high-elevation forest habitats.

Kent P. McFarland

A cofounder of the Vermont Center for Ecostudies, Kent McFarland is a conservation biologist, photographer, writer, and naturalist with more than 30 years of experience across the Americas. Kent has coauthored more than 50 scientific journal articles and book chapters. His writing and images have appeared widely in magazines, newspapers, and mobile field guides. Kent and Chris Rimmer received the Partners in Flight Investigation Award in 1999 for their contribution of outstanding research on Bicknell's Thrush, a migratory bird that led them to Hispaniola. Incredibly, the first thrush Kent captured on the island to band and release turned out to be one that he and his team had banded just a few months earlier not far from his home in Vermont. Migratory birds connect us all—a lesson that he has never forgotten.

ACKNOWLEDGMENTS

This guide is the result of many years of work by the coauthors, with the help and support of a large number of long-time collaborators and friends from the Dominican Republic, Haiti, USA, Canada, and elsewhere. We thank in particular the many birdwatchers who have contributed recent reports and observations of birds, or commented on the status of species on Hispaniola. These include Wayne Arendt, Giff Beaton, Stephen Brauning, Sandra Brauning, Adam Brown, Heather Christensen, Sean Christensen, André Dhondt, James Goetz, Thomas Hayes, Karen Holliday, Marshall Iliff, Tom Kemp, Miguel A. Landestoy, Yolanda León, Danilo A. Mejía, Ivan Mota, Luís Ramón Paulino, Maria Isabel Paulino, Jason Price, Pedro Genaro Rodríguez, Andrea Thomén, Kate Wallace, and Shane Woolbright. We thank the energetic members of the Asociación Dominicana de Fotógrafos de la Naturaleza (ADFONA), who consistently come up with fascinating photos and new bird records. Finally, we also thank the many contributors of eBird checklists and reports, many of whom are unknown to us; by virtue of their contributions, eBird has significantly advanced our knowledge of bird distributions and occurrences.

We thank Andrea Thomén and Yolanda León for their contribution of the comprehensive assessment of avian conservation on Hispaniola. Several people carefully read portions of the text and provided invaluable comments. These included Sean Christensen, James Goetz, Yolanda León, and Andrea Thomén. A multinational team of colleagues helped to standardize Dominican and Kreyòl names for all the birds in this guide. Thanks go out to Francoise Benjamin, Heather Christensen, Sean Christensen, Rene Derocher, Eladio Fernandez, Maxon Fildor, James Goetz, Anderson Jean, Yolanda León, Danilo Mejía, Miguel A. Landestoy, Maria Paulino, Pedro Genaro Rodríguez, and Andrea Thomén.

We appreciate the help of our editors at Princeton University Press, Robert Kirk and Karen Carter, assistant editor Abigail Johnson, production manager Steven Sears, and especially of our copyeditor, Lucinda Treadwell. Madeleine Smith (www.madeleinesmith.co.uk) contributed significantly to preliminary designs of the book. We recognize the generosity of Herb Raffaele, his coauthors, and the artists of *A Guide to the Birds of the West Indies*, as well as Princeton University Press, for allowing us the use of many of the fine plates from that guide in this work. In addition, we recognize Allan Keith, his coauthors of *The Birds of Hispaniola: Haiti and the Dominican Republic*, as well as the British Ornithologists' Union, for permission to publish data and descriptions that originally appeared in their annotated checklist.

Steven Latta's work in the Dominican Republic has been supported by the U.S. Fish and Wildlife Service, USDA Forest Service International Program, USDA Forest Service North-Central Forest Experiment Station, U.S. Environmental Protection Agency, University of Missouri Research Board, National Fish and Wildlife Foundation, Wildlife Conservation Society, National Geographic Society, Association of Avian Veterinarians, The Nature Conservancy, Wildlife Conservation Society, PRBO Conservation Science, and the National Aviary. The work of Chris Rimmer and Kent McFarland on Hispaniola has been supported by the American Bird Conservancy, Blake Fund of the Nuttall Ornithological Club, Carolyn Foundation, Conservation and Research Foundation, National Geographic Society, National Fish and Wildlife Foundation, Stewart Foundation, The Nature Conservancy, Thomas Marshall Foundation, Wildlife Conservation Society, U.S. Fish and Wildlife Service, USDA Forest Service International Program, and Wendling Foundation.

ARTISTIC CREDITS

Cynthie Fisher: 73 (BNST), 75 (AMOY), 79 (except LBCU), 81–9.

Dana Gardner: *iii*, 43 (GADW), 49 (GRSC), 51, 55 (SCPI, WNPI), 57 (EUCD), 59 (except NORP), 61, 63 (BBCU, HILC), 65 (except CHSW, ANPS dorsal), 67, 73 (DSTK, AMAV), 75 (AMGP, PAGP), 79 (LBCU), 107 (CORS), 111 (AWPE), 121 (MIKI), 123 (SSHA), 127 (RIHA), 129–35, 137 (except GCFL, STOF), 139 (HIKI), 141 (FBVI), 143 (PHVI, BWVI, YBCH), 145, 147, 153–7, 159 (PTWH), 161 (HICR, ANSI), 163 (except HOSP), 165 (except BFGR), 167–91, 193 (except BLGR).

Barry Kent MacKay: 99 (juv SOTE), 123 (SWHA), 125 (AMKE at rest), 127 (RTHA at rest), 137 (STOF), 141 (TBVI), 149 (GOSW), 161 (ANEU).

Tracy Pedersen: 41 (at rest), 43 (at rest, except GADW), 45 (at rest), 47 (at rest, except CANG), 49 (at rest, except GRSC), 53, 59 (NORP), 69, 71, 73 (LIMP, WOST), 75 (BBPL), 77, 97 (FRGU), 105, 107 (except CORS), 109 (MAFR), 111 (except AWPE), 113–19, 137 (GCFL), 139 (except HIKI), 141 (WEVI, YTVI), 143 (WAVI, REVI), 149 (except GOSW), 151, 159 (REAV, SBMU, TRMU).

Bart Rulon: 41 (in flight), 43 (in flight, except GADW), 45 (in flight), 47 (in flight, except CANG), 49 (in flight).

Kristin Williams: 47 (CANG), 55 (ROPI, WCPI), 57 (except EUCD), 63 (except BBCU, HILC), 65 (CHSW, ANPS dorsal), 91–5, 97 (except FRGU), 99 (except juv SOTE), 101, 103, 109 (except MAFR), 121 (except MIKI), 123 (OSPR), 125 (except AMKE at rest), 127 (BWHA; RTHA in flight), 159 (VIWE), 161 (CEDW), 163 (HOSP), 165 (BFGR), 193 (BLGR).

PHOTOGRAPHIC CREDITS

John Black: 24.
Sean Christensen: 33, 34 (top).
Brad Clements: 5.
Charles Gangas: *ix* (bottom).
James Goetz: 19.
Steven Latta: *ix* (top), 3, 7 (bottom), 8.
Danilo Mejía: 15.
Iván Mota: *xii* (bottom).
Luís Paulino: 38.
Christopher Rimmer: *ix* (middle).
Dax Román E.: 6, 7 (top), 9, 10, 22, 23, 25–31, 34 (bottom).
Brian Trevelline: *xii* (top).

Danilo Mejía, María M. Paulino, Steven Latta, and Julio Merced Medina put up a mist net in the Sierra de Bahoruco as part of one of the longest running avian monitoring programs in the Caribbean

Dominican field biologists Cristian Marte (left) and Misael Calcaño (right) examine a banded Red-legged Thrush during a bird monitoring workshop at Pueblo Viejo in the Sierra de Bahoruco, March 2010

INTRODUCTION

Our goal in writing the *Field Guide to the Birds of the Dominican Republic and Haiti* is to provide an updated and field-accessible guide to the birds of Hispaniola. This work rests on the success of the first comprehensive field guide devoted to birds of the island, *Birds of the Dominican Republic and Haiti* by Steven Latta, Chris Rimmer, Allan Keith, Jim Wiley, Herb Raffaele, Kent McFarland, and Eladio Fernandez, published in 2006 by Princeton University Press. That book was also translated into Spanish as *Aves de la República Dominicana y Haiti* for the Dominican market, and into French as *Les oiseaux d'Haïti et de la République Dominicaine* for the Haitian market. Those guides have contributed greatly to a strong growth in birdwatching, attention to conservation issues, and a boost in environmental education on the island.

That first complete field guide has since sold out in the English and Spanish editions. More than 20 new species have been reported for the island, names and taxonomies have changed, as has the conservation status of many species. We have also thought that a true field guide with a lighter, more compact format would be useful. Since much of the information on a given bird's ecology and natural history is already available in the earlier guide, here we elected to concentrate on identification of bird species through descriptions of body form, plumage, and behavior. Our overall goal remains unchanged, and that is to continue to help inspire a new generation of birdwatchers, ornithologists, and conservationists. With this guide in hand, we hope that many more Dominicans and Haitians will become as fascinated as we are by the diversity of Hispaniola's avifauna, and as committed to its conservation.

This *Field Guide to the Birds of the Dominican Republic and Haiti* draws on the second edition of *A Guide to the Birds of the West Indies* by Herb Raffaele et al. (2020), and incorporates detailed information on the status and range of species from the annotated checklist *The Birds of Hispaniola: Haiti and the Dominican Republic* by Allan Keith et al. (2003). Thanks to the generosity of the publishers and artists of these two works, we have been able to use much of the information and many of their fine plates. But we have also included more than 150 new images of Hispaniolan species painted by Dana Gardner, as well as new, detailed range maps of unsurpassed accuracy and precision prepared by Kent McFarland.

We are confident that by dramatically expanding possibilities to appreciate birds in the Dominican Republic and Haiti, this guide will promote conservation of migratory and resident species and build support for environmental measures to conserve and protect their habitats. The guide is certain to be used in the many educational, outreach, and training activities by local environmental organizations. We sincerely hope that it will increase public awareness throughout Hispaniola, as well as internationally, for the island's unique avifauna, underscoring the need to protect these special species and their habitats for future generations to cherish.

MAP OF HISPANIOLA:
TOPOGRAPHY AND CITIES

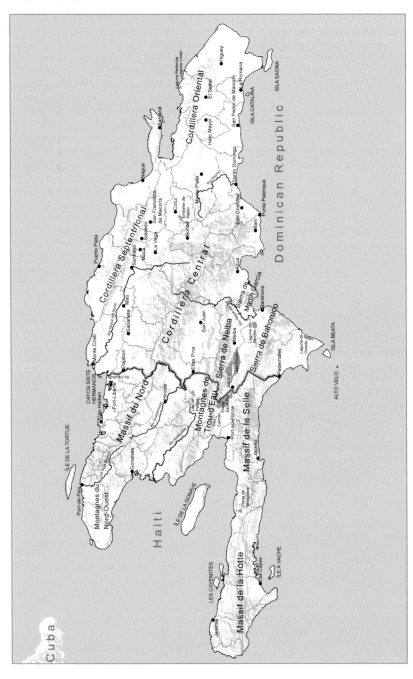

GEOGRAPHY

Hispaniola is a diverse island with many habitats and a highly diverse assemblage of birds, in part a result of its complex geological history. Although this history is not well understood, Hispaniola is thought to have formed by the merging of at least three land blocks, with two of these formerly attached to what are now Cuba and Puerto Rico. These three blocks probably came together about 9 million years ago, but change continued to take place. Global cycles of glacial and interglacial periods caused periodic rising and lowering of sea levels, and the alternation of dry and moist environments, resulting in drastic environmental changes and repeated isolation of higher elevation sites by the rising seas. Cyclic climatic changes contributed to the repeated separation of Hispaniola into two "paleo-islands" by a marine canal along the current Neiba Valley during much of the Pliocene and portions of the Pleistocene. These two paleo-islands are generally referred to as the North Island and the South Island of Hispaniola. In addition, the South Island was likely divided in pre-Pleistocene times by an intermittent sea passage across the peninsula at the Jacmel-Fauché depression. This would have effectively separated the Massif de la Hotte to the west from the Massif de la Selle and Sierra de Bahoruco to the east.

Cyclic climatic changes in the Pleistocene are likely to have contributed significantly to speciation and extinction events. Unique flora and fauna are thought to have existed on the two paleo-islands, as evidenced by several pairs of closely related bird species that are today found on the north and south paleo-islands. For example, the Eastern Chat-Tanager occurs in the Cordillera Central and the Sierra de Neiba, whereas the Western Chat-Tanager is found in the Sierra de Bahoruco and the southern peninsula of Haiti. Similar processes may have contributed

Kate Jordan Wallace, champion of environmental education and ecotourism in the Dominican Republic, holds a Broad-billed Tody mist netted during a monitoring program in the Sierra de Bahoruco

to speciation of the Gray-crowned and Black-crowned palm-tanagers, the two tody species, and two subspecies of La Selle Thrush.

Cyclic climatic changes also had dramatic impacts on the island's vegetation. It is clear that vegetation types such as conifers, now confined to higher elevations, occurred much lower during the cooler, drier periods, when glaciation occurred on Hispaniola down to 1,800 m above sea level. It was also during such periods that sea levels were significantly lower, allowing the appearance of a broad expanse of savanna and thorn scrub habitat in the Hispaniolan lowlands. During these periods of cold and aridity, the wet slopes of the Massif de la Hotte in particular likely served as a refugium for plants and animals adapted to mesic environments. The mountain range's geography with respect to winds and weather fronts positioned it to receive naturally high levels of rainfall. Today the Massif de la Hotte displays extraordinary levels of endemism in orchids, other plants, and amphibians.

The island is dominated by a series of roughly parallel mountain ranges and valleys that are aligned east to west. These ranges change names between Haiti and the Dominican Republic but effectively bridge both countries. The southern paleo-island features, from west to east, the Massif de la Hotte-Massif de la Selle-Sierra de Bahoruco range. High points in this range include Pic Macaya (2,347 m) in the Massif de la Hotte, Pic la Selle (2,574 m), and Loma de Toro (2,367 m) in the Sierra de Bahoruco. North of the Neiba Valley and the Cul de Sac Plain, on the northern paleo-island, lies the second major east–west range of mountains. These are the Montagnes de Trou-d'Eau in Haiti and the Sierra de Neiba in the Dominican Republic. At its summit, Monte Neiba reaches 2,279 m. Somewhat isolated to the east of the Sierra de Neiba, and southwest of Azua, is the Sierra de Martín García. Farther north, the Plateau Central and the Valle de San Juan separate this range from the next east–west range, the Cordillera Central, which extends into Haiti as the Massif du Nord. This is the island's largest mountain range, and it includes Pico Duarte, at 3,098 m the highest elevation in the Caribbean. North of the Cibao Valley lies the Cordillera Septentrional, which runs from Monte Cristi to Samaná Bay and rises to 1,250 m. Two additional, minor ranges include the Cordillera Oriental, southeast of Samaná Bay, and the Montagnes du Nord-Ouest in the northwestern peninsula of Haiti.

Hispaniola has several lakes and lagoons, many of which lie along the current Neiba Valley and Cul de Sac Plain. These include the hypersaline Lago Enriquillo (which can vary from 180 to 265 km^2) in the western Dominican Republic and, to its east, the largest freshwater lake on the island, Laguna de Rincón (30 km^2) at Cabral; and in Haiti, the slightly brackish Étang Saumâtre (113 km^2) and marshy freshwater Trou Caïman (7 km^2). Other large water bodies include Laguna de Oviedo (25 km^2) in the southeast of the Barahona Peninsula, Laguna Redonda (7 km^2) and Laguna Limón (5.1 km^2) on the northeastern coast, and Étang de Miragoâne, consisting of two freshwater lakes (combined 8 km^2) and adjacent marshes on the northern coast of the Tiburón Peninsula.

There are several significant river systems on the island, including the Río Yaque del Norte, Río Yaque del Sur, Río Ozama, and Río Dajabón in the Dominican Republic, and in Haiti the Guayamouc, Les Trois Rivières, and Artibonite. At 400 km, the latter is the longest river in the Caribbean.

Ten offshore islands contribute to Hispaniola's avifaunal diversity. These islands tend to be relatively low, small, and dry, but are often of high importance to birds. Many are crucial nesting sites for seabirds and other species, and some are home to endemic subspecies of land birds. Associated with the southern paleo-island are Isla Beata (47 km^2, 100 m elevation); Isla Alto Velo (1 km^2, 152 m elevation); Île Grande Cayemite and Île Petite Cayemite, with the larger being 45 km^2 and 152 m in elevation; and Île à Vache (52 km^2, 30 m elevation). Associated with the northern paleo-island are Isla Saona (111 km^2, 35 m elevation); Isla Catalina (18 km^2); the Cayos Siete Hermanos which are seven small, low, and sandy islands; Île de la Tortue (180 km^2, 325 m elevation); and Île de la Gonâve (658 km^2, 755 m elevation). Navassa Island (5 km^2, 77 m elevation), a U.S. possession 55 km due west of the westernmost point of Haiti, is included in this guide because of its zoogeographic association with Hispaniola. Birds recorded from these offshore islands are presented in Appendix 2.

HABITATS

Bisected by mountain ranges and rivers, and dotted with lakes and lagoons, Hispaniola contains a diversity of habitats. Most of the mountains are steep and rugged, and frequently cut by deep gorges or valleys. Mountain valleys tend to be cool and moist, supporting either pine or broadleaf forests, but lower elevations are dominated by dry forest and thorn scrub habitats. There are extensive areas of limestone karst in the southern paleo-island, including the Tiburón Peninsula, Barahona Peninsula, Sierra de Bahoruco, and Sierra de Neiba. In addition, much of the eastern Dominican Republic is limestone karst. Along the northern coast, limestone karst forms tower formations in Los Haitises National Park, on the Samaná Peninsula, and along the Cordillera Septentrional. Sand dunes are found in more than 20 coastal locations, and those near Baní on the southern coast are the largest in the Caribbean.

Mangroves. This habitat type is found at coastal sites around river mouths and lagoons where the soil is flooded most or all of the year, and also inland along the margins of both freshwater and saline lakes where the soil may only be flooded seasonally. In some places the mangrove forest reaches heights of 20 m and a density covering 70% to 85% of the ground surface. Dominant species are buttonwood mangrove (*Conocarpus erectus*), red mangrove (*Rhizophora mangle*), white mangrove (*Laguncularia racemosa*), and black mangrove (*Avicennia germinans*). In the Dominican Republic, mangroves cover less than 1% of the land area; in Haiti, mangroves cover about 0.5% of the land area.

Mangroves

Habitats

Freshwater swamps. This is an uncommon lowland habitat type on Hispaniola, usually occurring below 20 m elevation. It is sometimes forested, primarily with swamp bloodwood (*Pterocarpus officinalis*), or may occur in the form of marshlands characterized by dense growth of cattail (*Typha domingenis*). Some of the marshlands in this category may have significant moisture for only part of each year. On Hispaniola, freshwater swamps cover less than 0.5% of the land area.

Grasslands. This habitat type includes natural savannas at all elevations. They are mostly in the lowlands but are also found in several intermountain valleys. On Hispaniola, grasslands cover less than 1% of the land area.

Top: Freshwater swamps

Bottom: Grasslands

Agricultural lands

Agricultural lands. Included here are all lands cleared for agriculture, whether for large-scale farming enterprises such as sugarcane plantations and truck gardens or for subsistence agriculture, even at relatively high elevations in the foothills and mountains in many parts of the island, especially Haiti. Land cleared for pasture is also included here. In the Dominican Republic, agricultural lands and pastures cover about 55% of the land area; in Haiti, about 42% of the land is under cultivation, and another 19% is considered pasture.

Shrublands. This habitat type is typically dry and results from the recent removal of forest cover or because environmental or geological substratum conditions limit plant growth. It is now a

Shrublands

widespread habitat type in both countries from sea level to, at least locally, 500 m. Depending on the elevation and original forest type, typical shrub species may include mahogany (*Swietenia mahagoni*), botoncillo (*Ternstroemia peduncularis*), mastic (*Sideroxylon cubensis*), waltheria (*Waltheria indica*), escobón (*Eugenia maleolens*), logwood (*Haematoxylon campechianum*), cordia (*Cordia globosa*), and sensitive plant (*Mimosa pudica*). Especially typical of thorny shrublands are *Jacquinia berterii*, capertree (*Capparis ferruginea*), damiana (*Turnera diffusa*), and another sensitive plant species (*Mimosa azuensis*). In the Dominican Republic, shrublands cover about 6% of the land area; in Haiti, where the forest cover has been removed from more than 95% of the land area and 60% of the land is on mountainous slopes, shrublands and low dense vegetation cover about 35% of the land area.

Dry scrub. This forest type, also known as thorn scrub, now consists primarily of secondary growth of semideciduous trees growing at 40 to 500 m elevation in areas of 50 to 100 cm of rainfall annually. The canopy is largely open at a typical height of 10 m. Most of these forests are chronically disturbed because of cutting by humans. This vegetation type is widespread in lowlands of both the Dominican Republic and Haiti. Indicator species are gumbo limbo (*Bursera simaruba*), acacia (*Acacia sckeroxyla*), boxwood (*Phyllostylon brasiliensis*), tamarindo (*Acacia macracantha*), and white leadtree (*Leucaena leucocephala*). In the Dominican Republic, dry scrub covers about 8% of the land area; in Haiti, dry scrub is reduced to shrubland.

Dry forest. Typically found at elevations of 400 to 900 m on the coastal plain and in the foothills of mountains, this habitat type is often bordered by dry scrub at its lower edge and broadleaf forest at its upper edge. It occurs in areas with a distinct annual arid period and rainfall in the range of 100 to 180 cm. It is a common natural forest type over much of lower elevation Dominican Republic and Haiti but has been widely cut, especially in Haiti. In its undisturbed form it has a canopy density of 60% or greater; the canopy typically ranges from 3 to 10 m in height, less often to 20 m in wetter situations. Indicator species in drier areas are leadwood (*Krugiodendron*

Dry scrub

ferreum), mahogany (*Swietenia mahagoni*), seagrape (*Coccoloba diversifolia*), gumbo limbo (*Bursera simaruba*), lignumvitae (*Guaiacum sanctum*), poisontree (*Metopium brownei*), and crabwood (*Ateramnus lucidus*). Moister habitats usually contain oxhorn bucida (*Bucida buceras*), pond-apple (*Annona glabra*), and mara (*Calophyllum calabra*). In the Dominican Republic, dry forest covers about 8% of the land area; in Haiti, most dry forest has been converted to shrubland.

Broadleaf evergreen forest. Humid evergreen forest or rainforest is typically found below 500 m but locally up to elevations of 1,500 m. It is found in all Dominican Republic mountain ranges and very locally in Haiti, where extensive stands are now scarce. Typical canopy height is up to 25 m, and canopy density is 60% or greater. This forest type receives annual precipitation of 200 cm or more. Many humid evergreen forests are also mixed with pine or shade coffee. Indicator species

Dry forest

BELOW: Broadleaf evergreen forest

include wild mamee (*Clusia rosea*), myrtle laurelcherry (*Prunus myrtifolia*), lancewood (*Oxandra laurifolia*), manac palm (*Calyptronoma plumeriana*), tree-fern (*Cyathea arborea*), butterbough (*Exothea paniculata*), miconia (*Miconia dodecandra*), and coi (*Mora abbottii*).

At higher elevations up to 2,300 m, this habitat type is known as montane broadleaf forest or cloud forest. These humid forests are found in parts of the Cordillera Central, Cordillera Septentrional, Sierra de Neiba, and Sierra de Bahoruco; remnant stands in Haiti are found primarily in the Massif de la Hotte and Massif de la Selle. Canopy density is 80% or greater, and indicator canopy species include wind tree (*Didymopanax tremulus*), parrot-tree (*Brunellia comocladifolia*), bitter tree (*Garrya fadyenii*), tachvela (*Podocarpus aristulatus*), palms (*Coccothrinax* spp.), green ebony (*Magnolia pallescens* and *M. hamori*), rose-apple (*Clusia clusioides*), sierra palm (*Prestoea montana*), bone-tree (*Haenianthus salicifolius*), trumpet-tree (*Cecropia peltata*), swamp cyrilla (*Cyrilla racemiflora*), Florida trema (*Trema micrantha*), tabebuia (*Tabebuia berterii*), and laurel (*Ocotea* sp). In the Dominican Republic, broadleaf evergreen forest covers about 13% of the land area; in Haiti, broadleaf evergreen forests have probably been reduced to less than 1% of the land area.

Pine forest. Pine forest habitats include both pure pine stands and pine mixed with some broadleaf species. Pine forests can also be either closed pine forest, with a canopy density of 60% or greater, or open pine forest, with a canopy density between 40 and 60%. Virtually all closed pine habitat remaining in Hispaniola is in the Sierra de Bahoruco or above 2,000 m in the Cordillera Central of the Dominican Republic. Examples of open pine habitat are found in parts of the Cordillera Central, Sierra de Bahoruco, and Sierra de Neiba; small stands occur in the Macaya Biosphere Reserve and La Visite National Park, Haiti. Indicator species include Hispaniolan pine (*Pinus occidentalis*) in the canopy, and in the understory bitter tree (*Garrya fadyenii*), *Eupatorium illitium*, holly (*Ilex tuerckheimii*), and species of the genera *Fuchsia*, *Ambrosia*, and *Senecio*. In the Dominican Republic, pine forest covers about 6% of the land area; in Haiti the pine forests have been reduced to less than 1.5% of the land area.

Pine forest

ENDEMIC SPECIES OF HISPANIOLA

We recognize a total of 34 species endemic to Hispaniola and associated satellite islands. Those species include:

White-fronted Quail-Dove (*Geotrygon leucometopia*)
Bay-breasted Cuckoo (*Coccyzus rufigularis*)
Hispaniolan Lizard-Cuckoo (*Coccyzus longirostris*)
Least Pauraque (*Siphonorhis brewsteri*)
Hispaniolan Nightjar (*Antrostomus ekmani*)
Hispaniolan Emerald (*Riccordia swainsonii*)
Ridgway's Hawk (*Buteo ridgwayi*)
Ashy-faced Owl (*Tyto glaucops*)
Hispaniolan Trogon (*Priotelus roseigaster*)
Broad-billed Tody (*Todus subulatus*)
Narrow-billed Tody (*Todus angustirostris*)
Antillean Piculet (*Nesoctites micromegas*)
Hispaniolan Woodpecker (*Melanerpes striatus*)
Hispaniolan Parakeet (*Psittacara chloropterus*)
Hispaniolan Parrot (*Amazona ventralis*)
Hispaniolan Elaenia (*Elaenia cherriei*)
Hispaniolan Kingbird (*Tyrannus gabbii*)
Hispaniolan Pewee (*Contopus hispaniolensis*)
Flat-billed Vireo (*Vireo nanus*)
Hispaniolan Palm Crow (*Corvus palmarum*)
White-necked Crow (*Corvus leucognaphalus*)
Golden Swallow (*Tachycineta euchrysea*)
La Selle Thrush (*Turdus swalesi*)
Palmchat (*Dulus dominicus*)
Hispaniolan Crossbill (*Loxia megaplaga*)
Antillean Siskin (*Spinus dominicensis*)
Western Chat-Tanager (*Calyptophilus tertius*)
Eastern Chat-Tanager (*Calyptophilus frugivorus*)
Black-crowned Palm-Tanager (*Phaenicophilus palmarum*)
Gray-crowned Palm-Tanager (*Phaenicophilus poliocephalus*)
Hispaniolan Highland-Tanager (*Xenoligea montana*)
Green-tailed Ground-Tanager (*Microligea palustris*)
Hispaniolan Spindalis (*Spindalis dominicensis*)
Hispaniolan Oriole (*Icterus dominicensis*)

THREATENED AND ENDANGERED SPECIES

On Hispaniola, we consider 37 taxa to be threatened or endangered, or apparently extirpated from the island since 1968. We used a variety of published lists and assessments to determine each species' conservation status, including those from *Threatened Birds of the World* (BirdLife International 2000), *The Birds of Hispaniola: Haiti and the Dominican Republic* (Keith et al. 2003), *Birds of the Dominican Republic and Haiti* (Latta et al. 2006), the "Red List" of endangered species compiled by the Dominican Ministry of the Environment and Natural Resources (MIMARENA 2019), and two recent field guides to the birds of the West Indies by Kirwan et al. (2019) and Raffaele et al. (2020). We also solicited the expert input of a number of other birdwatchers and ornithologists, but ultimately the final list represents the opinion of the authors. Alarmingly, *half* (17 of 34) of the endemic species (names italicized below) are considered threatened with extinction.

Critically Endangered
Black-capped Petrel
Ridgway's Hawk

Endangered
Masked Duck
White-fronted Quail-Dove
Bay-breasted Cuckoo
Least Pauraque
Double-striped Thick-knee
Stygian Owl
Hispaniolan Parrot
Hispaniolan Kingbird
Golden Swallow
La Selle Thrush
Hispaniolan Crossbill
Western Chat-Tanager
Eastern Chat-Tanager
Hispaniolan Highland-Tanager

Threatened
West Indian Whistling-Duck
Scaly-naped Pigeon
White-crowned Pigeon
Plain Pigeon
Key West Quail-Dove
Northern Potoo
Black Swift
Spotted Rail
Black Rail
Piping Plover
Snowy Plover
Roseate Tern
Sharp-shinned Hawk
Short-eared Owl
Hispaniolan Trogon
Hispaniolan Parakeet
Hispaniolan Palm Crow
White-necked Crow
Bicknell's Thrush
Hispaniolan Oriole

Likely Extirpated
Wood Stork

AVIAN CONSERVATION ON HISPANIOLA

Hispaniola's contribution to global bird diversity is significant; some 318 bird species are now known to occur in Haiti and the Dominican Republic. More species are endemic to Hispaniola and its associated satellite islands than to any other Caribbean island, and Hispaniola provides important overwintering habitat for many Nearctic-Neotropical migrants. As a result, the island is highly ranked in biological importance in worldwide assessments of bird-protection priorities.

Today a growing number of species are listed under some level of threat on the Dominican Republic's National Red List. Threats to birds on Hispaniola are similar to those in other tropical regions, particularly due to habitat loss, forest degradation and fragmentation, overharvesting, and impacts of invasive species and climate change. Drivers of these threats, however, can vary widely across the island and among sites.

THREATS TO BIRDS

Habitat loss
The Dominican Republic has more extensive forest cover (41.0%) than Haiti (3.5%; FAO 2015). However, forest habitats supporting birds and other biodiversity have been (and continue to be) destroyed or degraded in both countries. For example, from 2001 to 2020, the Dominican Republic lost approximately 13% of its tree cover while Haiti lost 8.4%. In particular, high-elevation cloud forest and moist broadleaf forests are considered the most threatened; these broadleaf forest types have decreased from their original ~60% land cover and now occupy only ~15% of the island.

While causes of deforestation and forest degradation vary, the leading driver of forest loss appears to be farming. In the Dominican Republic, more than 60% of deforestation is attributed directly to the expansion of farming and cattle ranching. Farming in the Dominican Republic occurs even inside legally protected areas and can take the form of permanent plantations, seasonal crops at both industrial and small scales, or shifting agriculture. Of these, shifting agriculture drives most deforestation, often in combination with sharecropping arrangements on plots farmed every 2–3 years, such that land remains in a permanent cycle of slashing and burning. The main driver of forest degradation is selective logging, with timber removed for precious woods, fence posts, construction materials, charcoal production, and firewood.

Other habitats important to birds are also impacted by human activities. Because most human population centers are located in coastal lowlands, these areas are most heavily affected, with lowland forests, beaches, coastal swamps and lagoons, and mangroves all experiencing multiple threats. Both coastal and interior wetlands (including riparian habitats) are impacted by filling, drainage, and conversion to agriculture or cattle pastures, as well as by development for tourism (particularly in the Dominican Republic), mining, and urban sprawl. In addition, disruptions to water levels at key wetlands have resulted from the construction of canals, dams, roads, and other infrastructure, and from excessive water extraction for farming; these disruptions have been exacerbated in recent years by a pattern of more severe droughts.

Overharvesting
Overharvesting of species can take the form of hunting (for sport or control of perceived pests), subsistence harvesting, and capture for the pet trade. Hunting regulations in Haiti were recently established; hunting of most species in the Dominican Republic is currently illegal, but this can vary periodically. In the Dominican Republic, shooting at White-crowned Pigeon breeding aggregations is particularly popular, but other pigeons are also frequently hunted. Intentional killing of birds considered "pests" is common in farmlands, including the shooting of Hispaniolan Woodpeckers in cacao plantations, and the poisoning of migrant waterfowl in rice fields. Diurnal

and nocturnal raptors (including endemic Ashy-faced Owl and Ridgway's Hawk) have been historically targeted due to local myths and negative attitudes toward birds of prey.

Overharvesting of birds associated with subsistence hunting is not common. But harvesting of White-crowned Pigeon nestlings and of seabird eggs has been documented in coastal regions, wetlands, and cays. Occasional subsistence killing of wild birds for food by locals is also known, with pigeons, ducks, and gallinules the most frequent targets.

Finally, collection of birds for the pet trade has long been a serious threat to parrots and parakeets, but many other avian species are found in illegal zoos, private collections, and as displays at hotels and resorts. Known captive species include American Flamingo, Little Blue Heron, Hispaniolan Palm Crow, White-necked Crow, Hispaniolan Lizard-Cuckoo, Greater Antillean Bullfinch, and Village Weaver. Hispaniolan Parrots are, unfortunately, a very popular cage bird across the island, particularly in the Dominican Republic, where fledglings taken from nests in the wild are sold in urban centers. Nest cavities are often destroyed in the process, preventing their reuse and reducing future nesting opportunities. Hispaniolan Parakeets have also suffered from humans' appetite for pet birds, as naive buyers are often tricked into buying them in lieu of a parrot. Bird keeping has also been widely documented in Haiti, including the sale of birds captured in the Dominican Republic.

Invasive species

Invasive, exotic mammals, including dogs, cats, pigs, rats, and mongoose, adversely impact many native bird species, especially those nesting low to the ground or in cavities. For example, introduced mammals have led to reduced nesting success of Black-capped Petrel, Hispaniolan Parakeet, and Golden Swallow. Exotic plants are also rapidly changing some habitats, directly or indirectly affecting the species that rely on them. For instance, many frugivorous birds, including Palmchat and Hispaniolan Parrot, have been observed feeding on invasive plants in both cities and forested areas; direct impacts of this behavior are unknown, but it is certain to propagate these exotic species.

Climate change

According to several models of climate change, Hispaniola will experience rising temperatures, decreases in rainfall, and shifts in rainfall seasonality in the coming decades. This predicted transition to a drier, warmer climate will increase vulnerability of threatened and endangered bird species and exacerbate existing environmental pressures around protected areas. Eleven of 30 assessed endemic birds are considered highly vulnerable to climate change. Wetland bird assemblages will also be adversely affected by seasonal changes in water levels; these likely include the large flocks of migratory waterfowl and shorebirds that use wetlands as stopover or overwintering sites.

HOPEFUL SIGNS

Formal recognition of the importance of the environment in governmental decision-making has been achieved in both Haiti and the Dominican Republic. In 1994, Haiti created the Ministry of the Environment (MED) to "promote sustainable development while facilitating environmental conservation." Following suit, the Dominican Republic established the Ministry of the Environment and Natural Resources (MIMARENA) in 2000, uniting scattered government offices and professionals concerned with environmental issues. This includes the National Museum of Natural History, National Aquarium, National Zoological Park (ZOODOM), and National Botanical Garden. These institutions serve as important repositories of biodiversity collections and knowledge, and participate in nature conservation and research programs. The Dominican Republic also created within the National Attorney's Office the Specialized Attorneys for the Environment and Natural Resources. With 11 regional branches and staff, the goal of this unit is to prosecute environmental crimes.

The Paulino family searching for overwintering Louisiana Waterthrush to color band near La Loma de La Joya de San Francisco

During the past decade, local governments have also shown a commitment to nature conservation or enhancement. As an example, the City Mayor's office of the National District (which includes Santo Domingo) has collaborated with the National Botanical Garden to draft regulations on tree plantings in the urban environment. They are now embarked on an ambitious urban plan to promote the use of native, endemic, and biodiversity-friendly trees in the National District.

Nonprofit and other civil society organizations have a strong presence in the island's conservation community, especially in the Dominican Republic. Dominican groups such as Grupo Jaragua, Fundación Moscoso Puello, Grupo Acción Ecológica, Fondo Peregrino RD, Centro para el Ecodesarrollo de Samaná y su Entorno, ANA Ambiental, Acción Verde, SOS Ambiente RD, Sociedad Ecológica del Cibao, Sociedad Ecológica de Barahona, and Sociedad Ornitológica de Hispaniola, as well as Haitian groups such as Société Audubon Haiti and Fondation Seguin, have been very active in a variety of conservation efforts. These groups have worked diligently to foster an entirely new perspective of natural resource protection to conserve the island's national heritage. Some of these organizations work cooperatively for conservation and protected area advocacy, such as under the Consorcio Ambiental Dominicano and the Alianza para la Defensa de las Áreas Protegidas. In the Dominican Republic, academia-linked groups, such as the Comisión Ambiental de la Universidad Autónoma de Santo Domingo, the Academia de Ciencias de la República Dominicana, and Instituto Tecnológico de Santo Domingo, have also been strong advocates for protected areas and environmental health.

Private companies, especially in the Dominican Republic, have begun investing in conservation. For example, Fundación Propagas, established by a leading propane gas distributor, and the Sustainability Center of Grupo Punta Cana, a leading tourism group, have contributed significantly to conservation programs. Other companies have collaborated with local nonprofits to carry out conservation actions. For example, the cement company Cemex Dominicana collaborated with the nonprofit Grupo Jaragua in an innovative Biodiversity Action Plan.

It is noteworthy that both government and civil society actors have benefited from contributions from the international conservation community. This has included efforts to strengthen and increase technical capacity by the National Aviary, Vermont Center for Ecostudies, BirdLife International, Environmental Protection in the Caribbean (EPIC), American Bird Conservancy, BirdsCaribbean, and Caribaea Initiative. The contribution of foreign government agencies, such as the U.S. Fish and Wildlife Service, the U.S. Forest Service International Programs, and the Ministry of the Environment and Climate Change Canada (through the Nature Canada program), has been noteworthy. The Ministry of the Environment in partnership with the United Nations Development Program has also carried out a number of multi-million-dollar environment-related projects funded by the Global Environmental Facility.

CONSERVATION ACTIONS

Area-based conservation

Both the Dominican Republic and Haiti can boast of national protected area systems that protect important natural habitat for birds. In the Dominican Republic, the National System of Protected Areas has grown from 9 areas protecting 4.2% of the country's land area in 1980 to 123 areas covering 25% of Dominican territory (~12,000 km^2) in 2017. In Haiti, 20 protected areas cover ~7% of the country's land base. These include areas designated as national parks, managed natural resource protected areas, biological diversity areas, and exceptional natural elements. In 2015, Haiti's first protected area management plan was developed for Macaya National Park.

In the Dominican Republic, after a series of legislative attempts to eviscerate the national park system through the sale of protected lands for tourism and development, the conservation community attained inclusion of the Dominican Republic's protected areas under its constitution. In the 2015 constitution, protected areas are recognized as "an inalienable, non-sequestrable national heritage, not subject to statutory limitations." Additionally, the constitution explicitly bans protected area size reductions without favorable votes of two-thirds of both houses of Congress, making it much more difficult to modify existing protected areas.

Although the Ministry of the Environment is ultimately responsible for management of the Dominican Republic's protected areas, some civil society groups collaborate under formal co-management arrangements. These include Fundación Progressio with Ébano Verde Scientific Reserve, Grupo Jaragua with Jaragua and Sierra de Bahoruco National Parks, Fundación Moscoso Puello and Fundación Propagas with Valle Nuevo, Asociación Comunitaria de Ecoturismo del Salto del Limón with Salto del Limón Natural Monument, and Río Damajagua Guides Association with Salto de Damajagua Natural Monument. In recent years, a private reserve, Reserva Privada Zorzal, has also been added to the National Protected Area System.

At the international level, Hispaniolan sites have received recognition for hosting exceptional biodiversity, helping to prioritize conservation actions and funding streams. These include BirdLife International's Important Bird and Biodiversity Areas (IBAs), with 21 IBAs in the Dominican Republic and 10 in Haiti. All of these IBAs have also been designated as Key Biodiversity Areas (KBAs), a standard proposed by Conservation International and now recognized by the International Union for the Conservation of Nature. A third international coalition, the Alliance for Zero Extinction, has recognized a site in the Dominican Republic (Los Haitises) on behalf of its importance for Ridgway's Hawk.

Finally, Dominican and Haitian protected areas have also been included in international environmental conventions. Three sites are recognized under the Ramsar Convention for wetlands of international importance, including Lago Enriquillo, Laguna de Cabral, and Jaragua. These sites are also recognized under the Specially Protected Areas of the Wider Caribbean (SPAW) Protocol of the United Nations Environmental Program's Cartagena Convention. Another UN organization, UNESCO, has further recognized two International Biosphere Reserves on Hispaniola: the Jaragua-Bahoruco-Enriquillo Biosphere Reserve and the La Selle Biosphere Reserve.

Species-based conservation

Few Hispaniolan bird species have received focused conservation attention. One of the earliest species-specific programs targeted Ridgway's Hawk, a Critically Endangered endemic with fewer than 500 individuals remaining. Since 2000, breeding pairs and their nests have been monitored yearly by Fondo Peregrino RD. Related conservation actions have included securing unstable nests, protecting fledglings from botfly larvae infestations, and establishing new breeding populations via a translocation program. Since 2009, the private sector (Fundación Propagas and Grupo Punta Cana), in collaboration with ZOODOM, has joined this effort, successfully translocating hawks to Punta Cana, where wild breeding first occurred in 2013.

The Critically Endangered Black-capped Petrel has been another focus of monitoring and conservation efforts in the Dominican Republic and Haiti. Teams led and trained by Grupo

Jaragua, in collaboration with Environmental Protection in the Caribbean (EPIC) and the International Black-capped Petrel Working Group, have identified and monitored nesting sites in the Sierra de Bahoruco–Massif de la Selle range, and at Valle Nuevo National Park in the Cordillera Central. Unfortunately, dogs, mongoose, and forest fires take an annual toll on nest success. Related efforts for the petrel led by EPIC in Haiti focus on community-based habitat restoration, sustainable farming, and economic improvement programs near breeding sites.

The Endangered endemic Golden Swallow has been managed through the establishment of artificial nesting boxes in Valle Nuevo National Park. Beginning in 1998, boxes were built and monitored in the Sierra de Bahoruco by local birdwatchers with direction from Steven Latta and the Cornell Lab of Ornithology. More intensive research and critical monitoring efforts were pursued by Cornell University students at Valle Nuevo National Park, and that program has since been maintained with support and staff from Fundación Propagas.

Finally, two species of migratory birds overwintering on Hispaniola have received focused conservation attention. Steven Latta has collaborated with Grupo Acción Ecológica in long-term studies of the riparian-obligate Louisiana Waterthrush. These studies are contributing to development of full annual cycle models to identify what factors affect population sizes of migratory birds. Chris Rimmer of the Vermont Center for Ecostudies (VCE) has led a 25-year effort to monitor and investigate Bicknell's Thrush, a globally Vulnerable overwintering migrant. This program has built capacity by supporting local research and habitat restoration efforts. Partners were also instrumental in achieving a critically important land purchase for Reserva Privada Zorzal in the Cordillera Septentrional, now managed by Consorcio Ambiental Dominicano. VCE's work has also led to local reforestation efforts in Sierra de Bahoruco and a forest recovery program in Haiti that has been led by Cornell University's James Goetz at key Bicknell's Thrush sites.

Environmental education

Environmental education around birds of Hispaniola took shape in the 1960s, when naturalists Donald Dod and his wife, Anabelle Stockton de Dod, led bird-oriented education initiatives that included talks, walks, stakeholder workshops, and public forums on avian conservation. Their influence in the development of governmental organizations, including the National Museum of Natural History, and of grassroots groups led to the emergence of the first birdwatching clubs in the Dominican Republic. In addition, Mrs. Stockton de Dod contributed greatly to the production of education materials through the publication of bird books and illustrated pamphlets, and she compiled natural history and anecdotal information. Since then, avian education initiatives have increased slowly yet steadily across the island.

The 1998 National Planning Workshop for Avian Conservation in the Dominican Republic identified the need to create a national culture for environmental protection through the training of educators and the design of an environmental curriculum, in addition to strengthening stakeholder capacity for community organizing and advocacy. Although a national educational curriculum specific to avian conservation has not yet been established in either country, the Dominican Republic recently passed a new law regarding the implementation of environmental education and communication in public education and outreach. In addition, thanks to efforts led by BirdsCaribbean, educators from several Dominican organizations have adopted the BirdSleuth Caribbean curriculum developed by the Cornell Lab of Ornithology. In general, educators face many operational and capacity-related challenges, particularly in Haiti, given the limited number of didactic tools and materials translated to Kreyòl. Regardless, many conservation groups, including governmental agencies, actively participate in global and regional education schemes, such as World Migratory Bird Day, World Shorebirds Day, and the Caribbean Endemic Bird Festival.

Although early environmental education efforts were scattered and small-scale, by 2015 improved communication outlets through social media, as well as access to online and digital resources, allowed the development of medium- and large-scale initiatives to reach more diverse audiences. For instance, a concerted education campaign for parrot conservation reached more than 150,000 people in Santo Domingo during 2015–2016. In addition, bird-oriented summer camps and festivals have been held in several locations; these include migratory bird-themed camps led by Grupo Acción Ecológica, parrot-themed camps led by Grupo Jaragua, and Black-capped Petrel festivals led by EPIC. Since 2017, an annual festival has celebrated Ridgway's Hawk. Other novel approaches to community outreach and education include door-to-door efforts and a community theater program to deter persecution of Ridgway's Hawk; specialized training of farmers to promote tree diversification in cacao farmlands; linking birds to sports programs, such as a Black-capped Petrel soccer team; and the training of ZOODOM educators by the National Aviary in the use of "bird shows" to increase public awareness regarding birds of prey.

Ecotourism

The establishment of ecotourism programs has been linked to the success of local conservation efforts. During the last two decades, numerous newly created ecotourism activities have promoted both sustainable livelihoods and bird conservation programs. These include flamingo-watching tours in Oviedo Lagoon, agritourism in Reserva Privada Zorzal, and kayaking tours in Monte Cristi, Dominican Republic. These initiatives also contribute to pride-building, site recognition, and increased local awareness regarding the importance of birds and other biodiversity.

Despite the lack of an established birding culture in the Dominican Republic, the 2012 publication of the first bird-finding guide, *Ruta Barrancoli: A Bird-finding Guide to the Dominican Republic* by Steven Latta and Kate Wallace, has led to the emergence of regional and local collaborations aimed at strengthening guided interpretation, infrastructure, and marketing platforms for birdwatching tourism. Although birding tourism is still developing on the island, international and locally based tour operators have established a variety of high-potential ecotourism products.

CHALLENGES REMAIN

Most Hispaniolan protected areas face multiple threats to the effective conservation of their biodiversity. In Haiti, these weaknesses have more serious consequences, as the landscape is severely deforested. The country's high population density, chronic poverty, and political instability have prevented sustained conservation efforts. Despite the Dominican Republic's greater political and economic stability, and its ambitious protected area system, repeated evaluations of management effectiveness across 35 areas have yielded disappointing results. Site weaknesses include insufficient budgets, limited staff capacity, poor availability of proper equipment, and lack of infrastructure and visitor facilities. Other notable constraints include the lack or near-lack of patrolling systems, management plans (or their implementation), and local community involvement. Together, these contribute to very poor legal enforcement of protected areas, and the labeling of many protected areas as "paper parks."

In the Dominican Republic, some protected areas, especially those linked to international tourism, receive considerable revenue via entrance fees; however, there is no clear policy for the management of these funds. In 2006, a presidential order established that fees generated by protected areas should not be diverted to the general government account, but would remain within MIMARENA to improve protected area management. However, even with the public-private partnership Fondo MIMARENA, established as a trust to finance protected area management and infrastructure improvements, in 2009 one-third of all revenues were diverted to other uses.

Protected areas also suffer from uncertainties about land ownership. In the Dominican Republic, a double land tenure regime is in place, causing considerable confusion. Land titles include a formal title registered in a central government office, and a traditional title based on notarized sales contracts in the local mayor's office. Under the traditional system, which prevails in rural areas where most protected areas occur, tenure claims can be based on sustained, uninterrupted, and peaceful occupation, with rights increasing over time. The formal designation of protected areas has often clashed with land occupants and owners under both systems, since

Haitian field apprentices Françoise Benjamin (left) and Jean-François Orélien Beauduy (right) banding a Red-legged Thrush with Chris Rimmer during a training workshop in La Visite National Park, February 2014

compensation has been rare and the legitimacy of titles questioned. Due to the lack of legal enforcement of protected areas, most occupants continue farming inside parks as they had in the past, thereby locking habitats into a suboptimal state. These tenure issues are compounded by a lack of visibly marked boundaries for most protected areas, facilitating protected area violations, even by other government agencies.

Periodic reforestation programs have been executed by both government agencies and private sector organizations. In the Dominican Republic, these have been implemented mainly by a government program, Quisqueya Verde, which is financed by MARENA revenues. However, few statistics are available on these plantings, and little follow-up monitoring has been conducted; efforts have often been misguided by planting exotic tree species, including Caribbean pine, Australian grevillea, and Mediterranean cypress. Reforestation programs have been further hampered by the dominant use of only two native tree species for all sites (West Indian mahogany and Hispaniolan pine), both of which have commercial timber value.

There are two overarching challenges impeding further, effective conservation in Hispaniola. One, which derives from the underlying political culture in both countries, is a lack of institutional and staff stability, resulting in a shifting policy focus. This extends to the appointment of party members to key government positions, even when appointees lack the most basic aptitude for environmental management; this issue affects conservation all the way up to the Minister level. The second broad challenge hindering conservation across the island is poverty. Many rural communities surrounding protected areas lack opportunities for sustainable livelihoods, forcing people to violate environmental laws to survive. Even as many communities in the Dominican Republic have improved their living standards in recent years, local residents routinely hire low-wage Haitian workers to carry out their farming practices, especially those involving shifting agriculture inside protected areas, thus perpetuating the deforestation cycle.

Despite these challenges, both Haiti and the Dominican Republic have taken key steps to institutionalize and professionalize environmental conservation. Concurrently, the Dominican Republic's civil society has given rise to many strong and effective environmental advocates, educators, and conservationists, who work both independently and closely with the government. Similarly, emerging civil society groups in Haiti, working across the country via governmental and regional cooperative initiatives, provide a favorable scenario to strengthen avian conservation efforts. Finally, the use of social media and the increasing tendency of conventional media to highlight conservation issues and successes give us hope for the future.

MAP OF HISPANIOLA:
BIRDWATCHING SITES

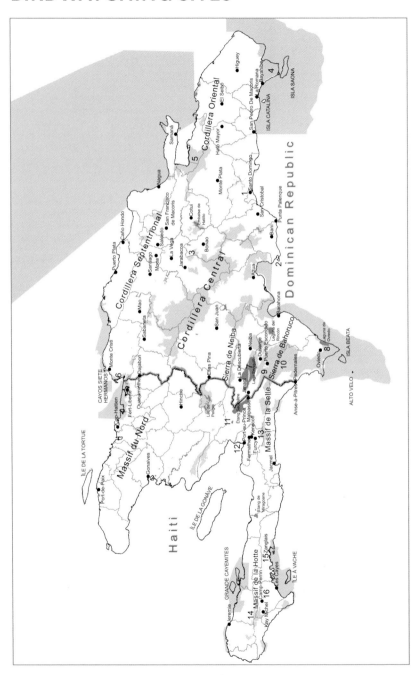

BIRDWATCHING ON HISPANIOLA

Comprising a small island with 34 endemic species, and many more regional endemics, the Dominican Republic and Haiti are growing in popularity for the birdwatcher. Here we outline a few of our favorite sites for sampling the island's diverse birdlife; these include sites suitable for day trips from Santo Domingo or Port-au-Prince, and sites that may require more extended travel.

While we provide information on a diverse array of birdwatching sites, please note that access to remote areas of the island can be difficult for those unaccustomed to rural travel. We recommend that for the sake of convenience, safety, and the best birding, everyone *please contact a local guide*. There are many well-trained and friendly birdwatching guides on the island who would love to help you discover Hispaniola's avifauna and tell you more about the island's habitats, plants, animals, history, culture, and conservation efforts! We particularly recommend Manny Jimenes at Explora EcoTour (https://exploraecotour.com/), Miguel A. Landestoy, Independent Guide (mango_land@yahoo.com), and Kate Wallace at Tody Tours (https://www.todytours.com/).

BIRDING SITES IN THE DOMINICAN REPUBLIC

These sites are a selection from a complete list of birdwatching sites contained in the book, *Ruta Barrancolí: A Bird-finding Guide to the Dominican Republic* by Steven Latta and Kate Wallace (National Aviary, 2012). The Ruta Barrancolí covers 44 sites dispersed across the Dominican Republic and represents the first national birding trail in Latin America and the Caribbean. Sites from the Ruta Barrancolí are also posted on BirdsCaribbean's Caribbean Birding Trail (https://www.caribbeanbirdingtrail.org/sites/dominican-republic/), where additional information can be found, including driving directions, access and trail maps, and bird lists.

1. Jardín Botánico Nacional

The Jardín Botánico Nacional Dr. Rafael Moscoso, or National Botanical Garden, is located in the northern part of Santo Domingo and is a fine place to encounter the country's common birds. An early morning walk of about two hours, encompassing wooded areas, a stream, and open palm savannas, will offer opportunities to see many species. The national bird, Palmchat, will be readily observed, and the endemic Hispaniolan Parakeet is likely to be found even though it is often hard to locate elsewhere on the island. The stream is home to Limpkins and Least Grebes, both of which are typically elusive elsewhere. Other more common birds to be found in the gardens include Black-crowned Palm-Tanager, Hispaniolan Woodpecker, Hispaniolan Lizard-Cuckoo, Mangrove Cuckoo, Antillean Palm-Swift, Gray Kingbird, Vervain Hummingbird, and Antillean Mango. Black-whiskered Vireos may be heard singing even if they are not easily seen. Many migratory warblers may also be seen in the Botanical Gardens during the nonbreeding season.

OPPOSITE PAGE: Numbered birding sites and nationally protected areas (shaded gray) as shown at www.protectedplanet.net, including marine and terrestrial national parks, biological reserves, natural monuments, and wildlife refuges.

1. Jardin Botánico Nacional
2. Salinas de Baní
3. Reserva Científica del Ebano Verde
4. Parque Nacional Cotubanamá
5. Parque Nacional Los Haitises
6. Monte Cristi
7. Lago Enriquillo
8. Laguna de Oviedo
9. Sierra de Bahoruco—North Slope
10. Sierra de Bahoruco—South Slope
11. Trou Caïman
12. Port-au-Prince
13. Parc National La Visite
14. Macaya Biosphere Reserve
15. Zanglais
16. Lakes between Cayes and Camp Perrin

American Redstart may be seen in the Jardín Botánico Nacional

2. Salinas de Baní

Salinas de Baní is located some 60 km west of Santo Domingo, or about an hour-and-a-half drive, making it an ideal destination for a day trip from the city. The Salinas de Baní area is characterized by extensive sand dunes, inter-dunal swales, thickets, mangroves, salt-drying pans, lagoons, mudflats, and both sandy and rocky beaches. Many of these are not common habitats on Hispaniola, and the site therefore provides extremely important habitat for both migratory and nesting shorebird species. All egret and heron species present on the island may be seen here, as well as Clapper Rails and Whimbrels. Shorebirds are plentiful in the mudflats, coastal areas, and especially the saltpans. Nesting species at Salinas de Baní include Snowy Plover, Wilson's Plover, Least Tern, and Willet. Many warblers frequent the mangroves and thickets along the lagoons, and the bay often hosts boobies and other seabirds. Many Hispaniolan rarities have first appeared here, including Black-legged Kittiwake, Great Black-backed Gull, Lesser Black-backed Gull, American Golden-Plover, Wilson's Phalarope, and Red-necked Phalarope. A spotting scope is recommended.

Salinas de Baní

3. Reserva Científica del Ebano Verde

Reserva Científica del Ebano Verde is located 1.5 hours from Santo Domingo on the easternmost slopes of the Cordillera Central. The best trail for birding is the Arroyazo Sendero de Nubes trail, which starts at the visitor center and ends at the top of Casabito. This trail extends 6 km through pine forest and second-growth areas which were formerly populated but are now recovering. Halfway up the trail, one starts walking beside El Arroyazo, where the vegetation changes to riparian forest characterized by the manacla palm (*Prestoea acuminata*), which typically grows in humid soil. The upper part of the trail passes through dense, undisturbed cloud forest that is very much worth seeing. For most of its length, the trail involves a relatively easy walk, although the final ascent to the top of Casabito Mountain is fairly steep. Along the trail it is common to encounter Stolid Flycatcher, Hispaniolan Elaenia, Hispaniolan Pewee, Hispaniolan Trogon, Narrow-billed Tody, Hispaniolan Woodpecker, Caribbean Martin, Vervain Hummingbird, Hispaniolan Emerald, Antillean Siskin, Rufous-collared Sparrow, Hispaniolan Spindalis, Black-crowned Palm Tanager, Rufous-throated Solitaire, Yellow-faced Grassquit, and Black-faced Grassquit. In the upper cloud forest, one has a chance at briefly sighting, or at least hearing, the elusive Eastern Chat-Tanager as well.

4. Parque Nacional Cotubanamá (del Este) and Isla Saona

Parque Nacional Cotubanamá (del Este) is located on the extreme eastern end of Hispaniola, close to some of the island's most popular resort areas. The national park contains an extensive area of dry forest where you are likely to find White-crowned Pigeon, Hispaniolan Parrot, Mangrove

Eastern Chat-Tanager occurs at the Reserva Científica del Ebano Verde

BELOW: Parque Nacional Cotubanamá (del Este)

Cuckoo, Hispaniolan Lizard-Cuckoo, Broad-billed Tody, Antillean Piculet, Hispaniolan Woodpecker, Stolid Flycatcher, Flat-billed Vireo, Black-whiskered Vireo, Greater Antillean Bullfinch, and other dry forest inhabitants. White-necked Crows may also be seen near Guaraguao. A productive walk is a 3 km trail from the Guaraguao Park Entrance near the village of Bayahibe that parallels the beach. It is at first sandy, and then passes over rough limestone with a slight rise in elevation, indicating a former marine shoreline accompanied by a slight change in habitat type. At the El Puente Cave, look for the Taino petroglyphs as well as an Ashy-faced Owl that sometimes roosts inside. Arrive early and carry plenty of water.

The main tourist attraction at Cotubanamá (del Este) is the trip to Isla Saona, also part of the parks system, although this is primarily a beach excursion. In order to visit the extensive Magnificent Frigatebird colony at Las Calderas on the way, it is advisable to contact the park office in the village of Bayahibe.

5. Parque Nacional Los Haitises

Los Haitises National Park is the stronghold of the endemic and Critically Endangered Ridgway's Hawk. The park consists primarily of dense lowland broadleaf forest covering very hilly karst limestone formations called mogotes. Although much of the area has been previously deforested, the extremely steep mogotes were often left untouched, forming small islands of intact habitat. Today, with protection afforded by the park, areas between the mogotes are regenerating with thick vegetation. Typical forest birds include White-crowned Pigeon, Plain Pigeon, White-necked Crow, Broad-billed Tody, Hispaniolan Pewee, Stolid Flycatcher, Black-crowned Palm-Tanager, Hispaniolan Parrot, and Hispaniolan Oriole. Off the coast, mogotes form islands in the bay and are nesting sites for egrets, pelicans, frigatebirds, and Brown Boobies.

One popular and pleasant route to visit Los Haitises is by hiring a boat and guide from Caño Hondo, proceeding down a river through mangroves to the Bahía de Samaná, and then stopping at various points to explore trails on the margins of the park that pass through lowland broadleaf forest. Otherwise access to Los Haitises is quite difficult. The best way to visit interior areas is to contact the park office where you can hire a guide who is familiar with the park. Please note that the trails in Los Haitises are not well maintained and can be lined with nettle and other irritant plants. Trails are often rocky and slippery due to the geological characteristics of the area and frequent afternoon rains. Humidity levels can reach 95% in the forest. Arrive early and carry plenty of water.

Parque Nacional Los Haitises

Monte Cristi

6. Monte Cristi

The town of Monte Cristi, and the Parque Nacional Monte Cristi, are located in the northwest corner of the country and best known for the massive El Morro headland, seen and named by Christopher Columbus (known in Spanish as Cristóbal Colón). The main birding attractions here are the extensive mangroves (which can be explored by boat), lagoons full of flamingos hidden in cactus forests (for which a local guide is essential), and the offshore islands of the Cayos Siete Hermanos. During the months of May through August, these islands are home to nesting seabirds, including large numbers of Brown Noddy, Sooty Tern, and Bridled Tern. Besides flamingos, the mangroves host many herons, egrets, spoonbills, ibis, and other large waders, as well as shorebirds and waterfowl, including some hard-to-find species such as Ring-billed Gull and Gull-billed Tern. Although numbers of wintering ducks are reduced from historic highs, Monte Cristi is still one of Hispaniola's better places to find wintering and resident waterfowl.

7. Lago Enriquillo

This large, hypersaline lake lies a remarkable 44 meters *below* sea level. It is a remnant of the open marine channel that during much of the Pliocene and Pleistocene separated the southern paleo-island of Sierra de Bahoruco, Massif de la Selle, and Massif de la Hotte from the rest of what is now Hispaniola. Lago Enriquillo is a surreal landscape and home to hundreds of egrets, terns, herons, and flamingos, as well as crocodiles and iguanas. The mud-sand flats fringing the lake's shore can provide good shore-birding. White-necked Crows may be seen around the town of La Descubierta, and Palm Crows are found on Isla Cabritos, a large island in the lake's middle. Access to the national park is a few kilometers east of La Descubierta on Lago Enriquillo's north shore. From here, one can arrange boat trips, which proceed along the shore to observe birds and crocodiles, stopping on Isla Cabritos to view the iguanas. Birdwatching from the northern shore is also possible in the Los Borbullones area near the village of Bartolomé, and on the south shore from the Duvergé–Jimaní road west of the town of Baitoa.

8. Laguna de Oviedo

To experience a close look at American Flamingo, Roseate Spoonbill, White Ibis, as well as other waders, shorebirds, gulls, terns, and pelicans, a boat trip on Laguna de Oviedo is recommended. This brackish lagoon is in southwestern Dominican Republic, halfway between Barahona and Pedernales. It is so shallow that after crossing the width of the lagoon to the mangrove edge, the boatman must get out and wade, pushing the boat by hand. By cutting the motor, it is usually possible to approach birds very closely. A longer trip down the length of the lagoon passes an island where White Ibis nest and may also include a stop at another island to see the two local iguana species, one of which is endemic to Hispaniola. Purchase tickets and inquire about tours in the Oviedo park office. Be sure to arrive at Laguna de Oviedo early in the morning, because winds typically pick up in late morning and can make for a wet, though not dangerous, trip.

Reddish Egret occurs at Lago Enriquillo

BELOW: American Flamingos at Laguna de Oviedo

9. Sierra de Bahoruco—North Slope; Puerto Escondido, Rabo de Gato, La Placa, and Zapotén

The Parque Nacional Sierra de Bahoruco is Hispaniola's premier birding area. Although some areas of the park are remote and difficult to reach, requiring a 4x4 vehicle, other areas are more easily accessed. Of the 34 Hispaniolan endemics, only Ridgway's Hawk and Eastern Chat-Tanager are not found in the region; in addition, the Grey-crowned Palm-Tanager, endemic to Haiti, rarely crosses into the Sierra de Bahoruco mountain range. The outstanding feature of the Bahoruco's north slope is its montane broadleaf evergreen forest, or Dominican cloud forest, marked by large tree ferns above Zapotén at about 1,200 m elevation. This is the best site for high-elevation endemics such as Scaly-naped Pigeon, White-fronted Quail-Dove, Hispaniolan Emerald, Hispaniolan Trogon, Narrow-billed Tody, Rufous-throated Solitaire, La Selle Thrush, Green-tailed Ground-Tanager, Hispaniolan Highland-Tanager, Western Chat-Tanager, Hispaniolan Spindalis, Antillean Euphonia, and Antillean Siskin.

North slope birding sites are accessed above the village of Puerto Escondido south of Duvergé. Just outside the town of Puerto Escondido, the area known as Rabo de Gato is an interesting narrow strip of riparian habitat with a surprising mix of birds. Both Broad-billed and Narrow-billed tody occur here, as well as Hispaniolan Lizard-Cuckoo, Antillean Piculet, Hispaniolan Trogon, Flat-billed Vireo, White-necked Crow, Hispaniolan Oriole, and Antillean Euphonia, and on occasion the Bay-breasted Cuckoo. Simple accommodations are available at Rabo de Gato and represent the best opportunity for early arrival at the higher elevation birding sites mentioned below. For accommodations at Rabo de Gato, contact Kate Wallace at Tody Tours (https://www.todytours.com/) or Manny Jimenes at Explora EcoTour (https://exploraecotour.com/).

From Rabo de Gato, one can follow the single road along the international border, but extreme caution is advised as the road is not well maintained and a 4x4 vehicle is essential. About 10 km beyond Rabo de Gato, and ascending in elevation, La Placa is a reliable spot for Bay-breasted Cuckoo and Flat-billed Vireo. At dawn and dusk, this is also one of the best places to see or hear Least Pauraque and Hispaniolan Nightjar. Continuing up the road for another 3–5 km, the area known as Los Naranjos has traditionally provided the most dependable sightings of Bay-breasted Cuckoo. About 3 km further on, the road enters a (normally) dry riverbed full of loose stone, and

Sierra de Bahoruco—North Slope

ascends into the moist broadleaf zone. About 5 km past the military guard post at Aguacate, the road enters a brief stretch of pine forest. The cloud forest zone begins just short of 2 km further on. Stop at a wide curve and park well off the road. The best birding strategy here is to walk up and down the road. Be advised, however, that in order to maximize the chance of seeing La Selle Thrush, you should arrive before dawn, after which you might find birds foraging in the road. Beyond Zapotén the road continues to ascend, crossing Loma del Toro and patches of excellent cloud forest, before descending through pine forest and the agricultural areas of Los Arrollos to the border town of Pedernales. This road is frequently impassable, even with a 4x4 vehicle, so *always* check local conditions before proceeding. From Pedernales, the south slope of the Sierra de Bahoruco is accessible via Aceitillar just east of town (see below).

10. Sierra de Bahoruco—South Slope; Cabo Rojo, Aceitillar

Cabo Rojo and the Aceitillar sector of the Parque Nacional Sierra de Bahoruco lie just east of the border town of Pedernales, and are about half an hour west of Oviedo, with a good paved road all the way. Cabo Rojo and the Aceitillar sector are linked by the Alcoa Road, a paved road that remains from the bauxite mining operations of Alcoa. At sea level, and the southern terminus of the Alcoa Road, Cabo Rojo contains a small wetland across from the mine shipping port. This wetland attracts a fair number of waterfowl and shorebirds of all kinds, including the regional endemic White-cheeked Pintail, White Ibis, occasional Roseate Spoonbill, and wintering ducks and shorebirds. The mangroves here harbor good numbers of Yellow Warblers, an endemic subspecies, and many other nonbreeding warblers. North from Cabo Rojo, the road climbs steadily through desert thorn scrub to dry forest and broadleaf forest until reaching pine forest

Sierra de Bahoruco—South Slope

at about 1,100 m elevation. This portion of the park is known as Aceitillar, taking its name from a local grass. Just after entering the pine forests, look for a national park sign for La Charca, which is a small catch basin for water runoff. When water is present, this is a great spot to look for Hispaniolan Emerald, Antillean Piculet, Caribbean Martin, and especially Golden Swallow and Hispaniolan Crossbill, as well as several species of warblers in season. The Hispaniolan Parrot, Hispaniolan Parakeet, Olive-throated Parakeet, and Plain Pigeon are also commonly seen here. Make frequent stops on the way down to find the piculet and other broadleaf specialists.

BIRDING SITES IN HAITI

Although the Dominican Republic's birding infrastructure is currently better developed than Haiti's, Haiti still offers remarkable opportunities to encounter many Hispaniolan and Greater Antillean endemics. Haiti supports all populations of the Gray-crowned Palm-Tanager, and finding this rare species is virtually guaranteed in proper habitat. In addition, other Haitian sites can provide excellent views of rare endemic birds such as La Selle Thrush, Western Chat-Tanager, and Hispaniolan Highland-Tanager.

Many of Haiti's premier birding sites are in remote and difficult-to-access locations, thus tending to appeal to more adventurous and hardy birders. Political stability in Haiti ebbs and flows, with direct effects on safety for travelers, so it is very important to check conditions in the country before making travel plans. The U.S. State Department assesses safety concerns in all countries, and these reports and recommendations can be found online at https://travel.state.gov/content/travel/en/traveladvisories/traveladvisories/haiti-travel-advisory.html. Often the situation described in the international media is bleaker than reality on the ground, so we also encourage you to seek local advice, such as that of guides listed here, whenever considering a trip to Haiti. Frequently the greatest security risks are in the capital of Port-au-Prince and surrounding areas, with more outlying departments in the south and the north being quite safe. As such, conditions may sometimes warrant passing in a 4x4 vehicle from Pedernales, Dominican Republic (see suggestions for birding in Pedernales, above), to Anse-à-Pitres (or Ansapit), Haiti, to access the departments of the south without passing through Port-au-Prince. Similarly, in the north, by passing from Monte Cristi, Dominican Republic (see suggestions for birding in Monte Cristi, above), to the border towns of Dajabon and Ouanaminthe (or Wanament), it may be possible to access the northern departments and their many waterbirds, waders, and other birdlife. Regardless, the rewards of birding in Haiti are great, and the country's rich cultural heritage and the friendliness of its people will be an unquestionable highlight of your visit. Since Haiti is not currently included in the Caribbean Birding Trail, here we provide more detailed information on driving directions and access for a number of sites.

11. Trou Caïman

Trou Caïman (or Dlo Gaye) is a shallow, freshwater lake approximately 25 km northeast of Port-au-Prince. As part of the lowland Cul-de-Sac / Neiba corridor, Trou Caïman attracts a wide variety of birds, particularly migrants. In recent years, more than 100 species have been recorded at this site, including rare vagrants like Neotropic Cormorant, American Golden Plover, Buff-breasted Sandpiper, Black Skimmer, American Pipit, and Bay-breasted Warbler. At least 30 species can be found at Trou Caïman on any given morning of the year.

Access to Trou Caïman is a relatively easy 45-min trip by vehicle from Port-au-Prince. Begin by taking the road to Croix-des-Bouquet. This is the same road that leads to the Haiti–Dominican Republic border at Malpasse and Jimaní. At the roundabout intersection in Croix-des-Bouquet, take the road north that leads to Mirebalais (Central Plateau). Eventually the houses become scarce, more scrub land is evident, and the pavement abruptly ends just before a lone gasoline station. Continue on for less than 1 km and veer right onto a rough dirt road leading toward Thomazeau. After a few minutes of driving, Trou Caïman will appear in the distance below. Eventually the road passes very close to the lake itself at a left-hand bend in the road just before

Northern Jacana occurs at Trou Caïman

the tiny village of Trou Caïman. At this point, look for a small entry in the brush barely wide enough to accommodate a vehicle. Beware of thorns when entering, and also soft ground under the grassy area next to the shoreline. From this point, one can view a portion of the cattail habitat and a large portion of the lake.

The wide, flat, grass-fringed western edge of the lake is the best area for birdwatching since it is relatively clear of trees and scrub. This habitat is especially attractive to ducks, herons, egrets, plovers, sandpipers, gulls, and terns. Pied-billed Grebe, Common Gallinule, and American Coot are often seen or heard. American Wigeon, Northern Shoveler, Lesser Scaup, and Ruddy Duck may be seen on the lake during the winter months. Walk south along the western edge for better viewing of the southwest corner, where bird activity is usually high. Make sure to check the scrubby areas for migrating and wintering warblers, as well as for local birds like Smooth-billed Ani, Broad-billed Tody, Hispaniolan Woodpecker, Hispaniolan Palm Crow, White-necked Crow, Gray Kingbird, and Village Weaver. This is one of the most consistent locations in Haiti to see American Flamingo; they are usually near the far eastern shore, so a spotting scope is highly recommended. From August to October, keep watch overhead for migrating Osprey. During winter months, Peregrine Falcon and Merlin can be observed hunting or resting. Large swaths of reeds dominate the northern part of the lake, where one can find wintering waterfowl, Fulvous Whistling-Duck, and Least Bittern. Local fishermen will take birders there in a small skiff for a negotiable fee. There are no amenities in this area, so be prepared with water and food. Sun and mosquito protection, plus sturdy, waterproof footwear, are strongly advised. Best viewing is in the early morning, as an easterly wind usually picks up later in the day, making it difficult to hear and occasionally to hold steady binoculars and spotting scopes.

12. Near Port-au-Prince: Fermathe, Kenscoff, Furcy

Approximately 20 km south of Port-au-Prince, this area offers an opportunity to see some of Haiti's high-elevation specialties like Hispaniolan Emerald, Narrow-billed Tody, Hispaniolan Elaenia, Hispaniolan Pewee, Golden Swallow, Rufous-throated Solitaire, Red-legged Thrush, Hispaniolan Spindalis, and Antillean Siskin. To reach the Fermathe, Kenscoff, and Furcy area, take the Route de Kenscoff out of the Port-au-Prince suburb of Petionville. This road is paved, but traffic can be heavy on the twisting road to Fermathe, so caution and patience are advised.

About 11 km from Petionville, stop at a small woodlot at the Baptist Haiti Mission in Fermathe, where one can find a variety of birds, especially during winter months. Park your vehicle next to the souvenir shop and restaurant. At the rear of the parking lot, pass through a gate on the right side of the church. Walk down the paved drive and look for a grassy playground lot on the left. At the rear of the grassy area is an opening to a terraced woodlot which is perched on the edge of a steep slope. There is an easily negotiated path across the top of the lot, but the more adventurous will want to find paths to the lower terrace levels that are vegetated with trees and dense shrubs. Green-tailed Ground-Tanager inhabits this area, as well as all three resident hummingbirds. Red-legged Thrush, Palmchat, Bananaquit, Black-crowned Palm-Tanager, Greater Antillean Bullfinch, and grassquits are commonly observed or heard. Listen for Black-whiskered Vireo during the spring and summer months. Regularly found nonbreeding residents include Black-throated Blue Warbler, Cape May Warbler, Black-and-white Warbler, American Redstart, Ovenbird, and Louisiana Waterthrush. More unusual species that have been observed in the woodlot include Yellow-bellied Sapsucker, Rose-breasted Grosbeak, Baltimore Oriole, and even Gray Catbird.

Take a right out of the parking lot and follow the paved road a few kilometers to the village of Kenscoff. Pine trees line some sections of the road, so listen for singing Pine Warblers. At the police station in Kenscoff, stay on the paved road that veers left. At the next major fork in the road, stay right and continue up the mountain toward Furcy. The road conditions are more rugged from this point on, the amount of pine cover increases, and houses become fewer. Finally, the road levels off briefly at the Sainte Helene (Sent Elèn) orphanage. The main unpaved road continues down to the tiny village of Furcy and enters more mixed pine woodland habitat. A narrow paved road veering right at Sainte Helene's leads to the very top of the area's highest point where dozens of communication towers are situated. Golden Swallow can be seen anywhere in this habitat, Rufous-throated Solitaire can be heard singing early and late in the day, and Antillean Siskins congregate on the power line along the roadway.

Red-legged Thrush may be seen near Port-au-Prince

Hispaniolan Trogon can be found in Parc National La Visite

13. Parc National La Visite

Parc National La Visite is located southeast of Port-au-Prince. Currently the best route is to drive west from Port-au-Prince and then south to Jacmel. Once in Jacmel, follow the road east of town, past Marigot, and then north up the mountain. You will need to ask farmers for directions in order to reach Fond Jean Noel and then Seguin. Past Seguin you will see Auberge La Visite on the left-hand side of the main road. Total driving time should be about 5 hours. Another popular route passes south of Port-au Prince through Petionville and on to the town of Kenscoff. Beyond Kenscoff the road is in rough, typically impassable, condition, so visitors should plan to make a 4–5-hour hike in the direction of the town of Seguin. Before reaching Seguin from this route, one must start asking for directions to Auberge La Visite, which is the only viable lodging facility in the area. Auberge La Visite can provide capable guides who know the La Visite area trails extremely well. Regardless of which route you elect, bear in mind that many rural roads in Haiti are in very rough condition, so 4x4 vehicles are essential.

Parc National La Visite has a system of unmarked trails, and birding in this area will require quite a bit of hiking. Keep your eyes open when you pass any ravines with broadleaf vegetation, as these are the best places to find Western Chat-Tanager and La Selle Thrush. Both species can often be seen foraging on the ground in open areas, especially after dawn. Stands of pines near Pic La Visite regularly support small flocks of Antillean Siskins and Hispaniolan Crossbills, and Golden Swallows may be seen over open habitats. Other Hispaniolan endemics of montane broadleaf forests, like Hispaniolan Trogon, Rufous-throated Solitaire, and Narrow-billed Tody, are restricted to the few remaining patches of this habitat type. Near some of the steep escarpments in La Visite are remnant breeding colonies of Black-capped Petrel, and the eerie nocturnal calls of these normally pelagic birds may be heard during winter months.

14. Macaya Biosphere Reserve

Macaya Biosphere Reserve, consisting of 5,500 hectares at the core of the Massif de la Hotte in extreme southwestern Haiti, supports a diversity of forest habitats, ranging from wet limestone forest at lower elevations to a complex mosaic of pine and cloud forest at upper elevations. The birdlife is correspondingly diverse, and many Hispaniolan endemics are found here. Reaching the reserve requires a serious commitment of time and effort, one that only the most hardy birders will likely be willing to make. Its distance from Port-au-Prince (6–7 hours' driving) and remoteness (4x4 vehicle and willingness to hike are a must) present daunting logistic challenges; however, the landscape is magnificent, the local people friendly and helpful, and the birding rewards superlative.

Gray-crowned Palm-Tanager is often seen at Macaya Biosphere Reserve

Birding in Macaya is best accomplished by coordinating with the Macaya Guide Association and using the tiny village of Kay Michel as a logistic base. A number of excellent and knowledgeable local guides are available. It is recommended that the Société Audubon Haïti be the point of contact for arranging a trip. Kay Michel is reached via a steep climb over a rough road that begins just west of the town of Les Cayes. From Kay Michel, a number of birding options exist. One can spend a full day or more in the nearby karst limestone forest, where Hispaniolan Trogon, Golden Swallow, Hispaniolan Highland-Tanager, Gray-crowned Palm-Tanager, and Western Chat-Tanager are virtually guaranteed. The more adventurous and physically fit can also ascend with camping gear (most of which can be carried by local guides for a reasonable fee) into the higher mountains, where the pine and dense broadleaf forests also harbor Gray-crowned Palm-Tanager and Western Chat-Tanager, as well as Hispaniolan Crossbill. For those able to travel in winter, the highest reaches of Pic Formon and Pic Macaya, with their magnificent mature pine forests, may yield nocturnal encounters with Black-capped Petrels, which breed on steep cliffs and are noisily active at night.

15. Zanglais d'Aquin

For a guaranteed Gray-crowned Palm-Tanager in an easily accessible location with lodging and food, an excellent option is the Reciprocal Ministries International (RMI) retreat center in Zanglais, just west of the city of Aquin along Haiti's southwest coast. RMI has trained guides, or you can explore on your own. The palm-tanager can be seen right on the grounds of the retreat center. Hiking up the mountain to the first "saddle" between mountain levels (330 m elevation) often produces Loggerhead Kingbird, Red-legged Thrush, Stolid Flycatcher, Hispaniolan Pewee, Hispaniolan Oriole, and all three hummingbird species. Hiking up another level (600 m elevation) to the valley between Morne Jaune and the third plateau can provide Hispaniolan Parrot, Black-faced Grassquit, Hispaniolan Spindalis, and Antillean Piculet. Occasionally Golden Swallows and White-collared Swifts zoom past or circle around the local summits. There is an artesian spring in the valley that is a source of potable water (although you should still treat or filter the water as a precaution), and a flat camping spot for the adventurer.

The Zanglais area also features the Cocoye Anglade Recreational Park, which is a small mangrove mudflat that often turns up surprising shorebirds and a variety of waders during winter and migratory periods. A small fee is charged to access the park. One can also rent a motorboat and captain in order to visit three islands in the bay. The largest, Grosse Caye, supports an abundance of Gray-crowned Palm-Tanagers, Greater Antillean Bullfinches, nesting Cave Swallows, and occasionally the White-tailed Tropicbird. Ocean birds regularly seen in the area include Magnificent Frigatebird, Brown Pelican, Gull-billed Tern, Least Tern, Sandwich Tern, Royal Tern, and Glossy Ibis.

Zanglais d'Aquin

For inquiries on the Zanglais Retreat Center contact: Dan Shoemaker of Reciprocal Ministries International at info@rmibridge.org or tel. 239-368-8390.

16. Lakes between Cayes and Camp Perrin

Another hotspot for birds on the southwestern peninsula consists of a series of lakes: Etang Lachaux, Etang Dwat, Etang Laborde, Etang Gentillotte, and Etang Flandiere. Farmland and small communities border the lakes, so having a bilingual guide is recommended. When birding, always be considerate of people's gardens. Do not take photos of people without their permission, and realize that most Haitians think binoculars are a camera, so it is often helpful to clarify what you are doing. These lakes support a variety of waterbirds, such as Northern Jacana, Purple Gallinule, Common Gallinule, Yellow-crowned Night-Heron, and other waders. During winter, expect Ruddy Duck, Pied-billed Grebe, plus unpredictable sightings of other duck species, including the West-Indian Whistling Duck. Special rarities in recent years have included a Eurasian Wigeon and Northern Pintail. More commonly seen are the White-cheeked Pintail, Ring-necked Duck, Lesser Scaup, Northern Shoveler, and Blue-winged Teal. Contact the Société Audubon Haïti or JACSEH (jacsehaiti@gmail.com) for local guides and more detailed information.

West Indian Whistling Duck may be found on lakes between Cayes and Camp Perrin

TIPS FOR FINDING BIRDS

Birdwatching in the Caribbean is not markedly different from birding in North America or elsewhere. For the greatest diversity of species you will want to visit the widest variety of habitats. Of course, some habitats are more productive than others, and some habitats will harbor more overwintering migrants or more endemics than other habitats. But in general, some of the most unusual species are found in the most difficult-to-reach habitats, particularly in the higher elevation moist broadleaf forest, and in the montane pine forest. Familiarity with calls and songs of the birds in advance will greatly increase your success, and this includes the challenging *chip* notes of the many migrant warblers you are likely to encounter; on Hispaniola these and other winter visitors seldom sing. This is especially important with the numerous skulkers that often inhabit the densest understory, but is also useful with some of the more ventriloquial species such as Hispaniolan Crossbill and Antillean Piculet. As in other bird communities, many species are more vocal and active early in the day, and some Hispaniolan species have unique dawn songs. By late morning, activity is often much reduced, providing the early riser with an opportunity for their own *siesta* (or butterfly watching), before returning to the field late in the day for a shorter period of activity. While flocking is characteristic of some Hispaniolan birds, mixed-species foraging flocks occur most conspicuously in pine forests. The Black crowned Palm-Tanager is frequently the most vocal and visible member of these flocks, which can include both permanent residents and overwintering migrants, but these congregations are seldom as large as those encountered in the continental tropics.

Perhaps the most noticeable difference between birding on Hispaniola and in North America may be simply the fact that in the Dominican Republic and Haiti birdwatchers are seldom encountered and so, especially in populated rural areas, you may attract a number of observers of your own. Children, being less inhibited, may be most likely to inquire as to what you are looking for, or be eager to follow along and even point out the birds that they know. Of course this is an excellent opportunity not only to make local friends, but also to form bridges of understanding on what we value and why. Local people are sometimes very aware of the birds in their area and so can be an excellent source of knowledge. Learning the often colorful, local names for birds can enhance interchange of knowledge, ideas, and mutual appreciation.

Finally, we also encourage independent birdwatchers to consider employing local guides whenever possible while visiting Hispaniola. A few excellent guides are available who know the birds, where to best find them, and their natural history and behavior. They are also familiar with travel logistics, as well as island cultures, food, and customs. Guides can make your birdwatching experience much more relaxing and rewarding. Employing these local entrepreneurs will also provide much-needed employment, help to develop an ecotourism economy, and aid in building a conservation ethic. If you are visiting as part of an organized birdwatching tour, we hope that you will encourage your tour company to hire a local guide as well!

REPORTING BIRD SIGHTINGS

We strongly encourage birdwatchers to report their sightings, both routine and rare, to eBird Caribbean (ebird.org/caribbean/home), a web-based system to report, store, archive, and analyze bird checklists. eBird data document bird distribution, abundance, habitat use, and trends through checklist data collected within a simple, scientific framework. Birders enter when, where, and how they went birding, and then fill out a checklist of all the birds seen and heard during the outing. Please help add to our knowledge of Hispaniola's avifauna, thereby contributing to science-based conservation!

PLAN OF THE GUIDE

Each species account follows a similar format. Headers include the species names (English and scientific) and status. Following an estimation of abundance, we describe the species' habitat and size, provide a detailed description, contrast similar species, describe vocalizations, and highlight any notable behaviors that may aid in identification. In the few cases where alternative names or taxonomies are available, these are mentioned at the end of the species accounts. Below we provide further explanation of these focal sections:

Names. In the species accounts, scientific and English names, and the sequence of species, follow those of the *Check-list of North American Birds*, seventh edition (American Ornithologists' Union [AOU] 1998) and all supplements through #62 (2021). Where subspecies are mentioned, names are those given in Keith et al. (2003). We use two common names that are not formally recognized; the genera *Microligea* and *Xenoligea* are now understood to not be wood-warblers in the family Parulidae, but closely aligned with the genus *Phaenicophilus*. As such, we follow Latta et al. (2006) and recognize the Green-tailed Warbler (also known as the Green-tailed Ground-Warbler) as the Green-tailed Ground-Tanager, and we recognize the White-winged Warbler as the Hispaniolan Highland-Tanager. We also recognize proposed splits of several species. We split the Hispaniolan Nightjar from the Cuban Nightjar (formerly united as the Greater Antillean Nightjar), based on distinct vocalizations and other characteristics as noted by Hardy et al. (1988), Garrido and Reynard (1993), and the AOU (1998). We follow Tang et al. (2018) and Raffaele et al. (2020) and recognize the Hispaniolan Elaenia *Elaenia cherriei*, sometimes considered part of the Greater Antillean Elaenia *E. martinica*. We follow Garrido et al. (2009) and Raffaele et al. (2020) and recognize the Hispaniolan Kingbird *Tyrannus gabbii*, sometimes considered a subspecies of Loggerhead Kingbird *T. caudifasciatus*. Finally, we follow Garrido et al. (1997) and Raffaele et al. (2020) in recognizing Hispaniolan Palm Crow as an endemic species, distinct from the Cuban Palm Crow.

Status. Immediately following the species name, we highlight whether that species is endemic to Hispaniola and associated islands, its threatened or endangered status (if any), and its relative abundance. Species threatened with extinction are listed as Threatened, Endangered, or Critically Endangered. Determination of such status is based on a variety of published accounts, including BirdLife International (2000), Latta and Lorenzo (2000), Keith et al. (2003), Latta et al. (2006), Kirwan et al. (2019), the Ministry of the Environment and Natural Resources of the Dominican Republic (MIMARENA 2019), Raffaele et al. (2020), and the authors' personal experience.

Abundance. In addition to a species' threatened status, we use the following status or abundance terms:

Introduced: A species that is not native to Hispaniola, but occurs via a population of escaped or intentionally released birds.

Breeding resident: A species known to breed on Hispaniola and that remains on the island year-round.

Breeding visitor: A species known to breed on Hispaniola but that generally migrates off-island during its nonbreeding period.

Nonbreeding visitor: A species that breeds elsewhere but is resident on Hispaniola during its nonbreeding season, generally from September to April.

Passage migrant: A species that migrates through Hispaniola on a seasonal basis but does not generally reside on the island for extended periods of time. Sometimes referred to as "transient"; this category also includes wanderers that may move throughout the West Indies or beyond at irregular intervals.

Vagrant: A species known to have occurred on Hispaniola fewer than five times or likely to occur less frequently than once every five years.

In some cases a species may be represented by more than a single distinct population. For example, a breeding resident population may be joined in the nonbreeding season by a migratory population from the north. In such cases, both populations are described, with the more common situation given first.

For each species we also characterize population status as abundant, common, uncommon, regular, or rare on Hispaniola. All abundance categories refer to a birdwatcher's chance of observing the species in its preferred habitat. Abundance categories are defined as follows:

Abundant: species is consistently encountered without much effort in large numbers.
Common: species is invariably encountered singly or in small numbers.
Uncommon: species is occasionally encountered but not to be expected on each trip.
Regular: species is regularly reported in small numbers, but is not likely to occur more than once or twice a year.
Rare: species has 10 or fewer records from Hispaniola.

In addition, these general categories may be qualified as, for example, "very" common, "fairly" common, or "moderately" common. Similarly, the use of "locally common" indicates a patchiness in site occupancy or the possibility that a species inhabits only a few favored sites.

Habitat. Here we describe the types of habitats on Hispaniola in which the species is likely to be encountered. Distributions of all but the rarest or most locally distributed species are also illustrated in range maps that depict where on Hispaniola the species might be expected in appropriate habitat.

Size. We provide size measurements for all species, including length (from bill tip to tail tip) and mass. Where size varies between sexes, or for example with the presence of tail plumes, more than one measurement is provided. The mass presented for each species is an average and is taken from Dunning (1993, 2007), Birds of the World accounts (Billerman et al. 2020), or the authors' own data.

Description. Descriptions of all commonly encountered plumages focus on key characteristics that enable field identification. In general, the most commonly encountered plumages are described first. For example, nonbreeding visitors are described in their nonbreeding plumage first; breeding residents are described in their breeding plumage first. Other plumages, including juvenal and immature, are subsequently described. Key field marks that are most helpful in definitively identifying a species are in ***bold italics***.

Age terminology of avian plumages can be confusing, as birders use several different systems. In this book we distinguish primarily between immatures and adults when plumages of the two differ markedly. We further discriminate between juveniles and immatures for those species that have a distinct juvenal plumage (the first true, nondowny plumage) that is likely to be seen by birders on Hispaniola. Many species retain their juvenal plumage for only a short period after leaving the nest and are seldom encountered by birders in this plumage; we do not describe these short-lived plumages. Other species (e.g., grebes, shorebirds, gulls, terns, and some passerines) retain their juvenal plumage for several months before molting into a subsequent plumage, which may or may not be distinguishable from the definitive adult plumage. We recognize those prolonged juvenal plumages in the species accounts. For those species that retain a juvenal plumage during their entire first year (e.g., some herons and hawks), we simply use the term "immature." We also use "immature" to describe the distinct plumages of many first-year birds (e.g., many passerines) between their juvenal and adult plumages. Thus, for simplicity, we recognize three typical age-related plumages in this book: juvenal, immature, and adult.

Frisel Francisco instructing students from the Colegio Doulos in Jarabacoa on how to describe the location of a bird by referring to the time on a clock

Similar species. Here we highlight differences among the species being described and any others occurring on Hispaniola with which a species might be confused.

Vocalizations. Each species' calls, songs, and other sounds as known on Hispaniola are described. In the case of winter visitors that rarely vocalize while on the island, their songs and calls are also described but noted as rare.

Behavior. We describe the behavior of a species when it may aid in field identification. Comments may include, for example, information on foraging, social behavior, or courtship. Because little is known about the ecology of many Hispaniolan species, these comments often incorporate the authors' own data and personal observations.

Distribution maps. Distribution maps are provided for nearly all species except vagrants, with gray shading indicating geographic areas where birds are more likely to occur in appropriate habitat. Distributions were determined by analysis of previously published data, Caribbean eBird records, expert opinions, and personal knowledge. Vegetation and topographic maps of Hispaniola were also utilized in determining potential distributions of bird species when habitat requirements and known elevation range could be incorporated.

DESCRIPTIVE PARTS OF A BIRD

Body Topography

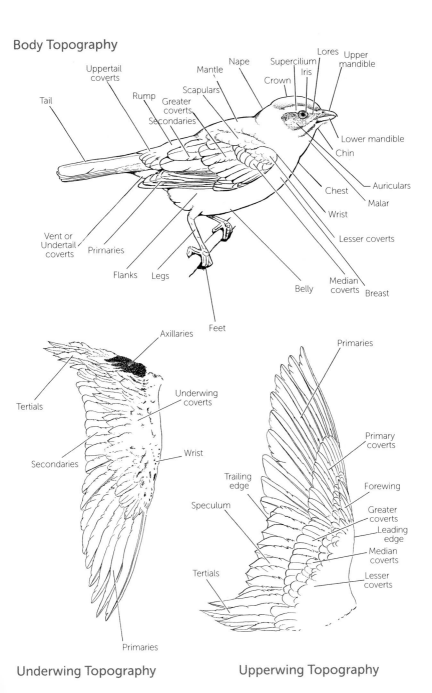

Underwing Topography

Upperwing Topography

White-faced Whistling-Duck *Dendrocygna viduata*
Vagrant
Possible in open water in fresh or brackish wetlands. A *long-legged duck* (44 cm; 690 g) with distinctive *white face*, with *black nape, neck*, and tail; otherwise mostly brown above. Maroon chest and black belly; *flanks barred black and white*. Immature paler with beige face. In flight, wings are dark above and below; no white markings except on the head. As in other whistling-ducks, flight is heavy with *feet extending beyond the tail*. Similar in profile to Fulvous, Black-bellied, and West Indian whistling-ducks, but all others lack white on the head. Voice a high-pitched 3-note whistle.

Black-bellied Whistling-Duck *Dendrocygna autumnalis*
Vagrant
Occurs in freshwater marshes and brackish lagoons. A gooselike, *long-legged duck* (50 cm; 830 g); note the dark body and gray face with whitish eye-ring in all plumages. In adults, the large *white wing patch, black belly, reddish bill*, and *pink legs* are distinctive field marks. Immature much duller than adult, primarily grayish brown above, blackish below, with gray bill and legs. In flight, underwing all blackish, but *upperwing has broad, bold white stripe*; head and feet droop, with feet trailing beyond the tail. Voice a characteristic shrill, chattering whistle, often heard in flight. Frequently perches in trees.

West Indian Whistling-Duck *Dendrocygna arborea*
Threatened Breeding Resident

Locally occurring at favored lowland sites, including mangroves, palm savannas, wooded swamps, and lagoons. A gooselike duck with *long legs and neck*, erect stance (52 cm; 1,150 g). Distinguished by deep brown coloration, *white lower belly and flanks with irregular black spots and splotches.* Immature less distinctly patterned with black on lower belly appearing as streaks rather than splotches. In flight, very dark overall; head and feet droop, feet extend beyond tail; look for *mottled belly* and *gray upperwing coverts*. Similar Fulvous Whistling-Duck has white uppertail coverts and white stripe along side. Feeds actively at night in stands of royal palm, rice-growing areas, and agricultural fields; roosts in deep vegetation during the day. Voice a shrill, whistled *chiriria*.

Fulvous Whistling-Duck *Dendrocygna bicolor*
Breeding Resident

Uncommon, but to be looked for on freshwater bodies with abundant water plants, especially rice fields. Gooselike with *long legs, long neck*, and erect stance (48 cm; 710 g). Blackish brown above, uniform *pale yellowish brown below, thin white stripe along sides*; white uppertail coverts. In flight, note *white uppertail coverts* and *stripe at wing base*. Upperwing blackish with reddish-brown coverts; underwing blackish. Head and feet droop when flying, feet trail beyond tail. West Indian Whistling-Duck is deeper brown and has dark uppertail coverts, black and white markings on sides and lower belly. Colonized Hispaniola in mid-1970s. Typically flocks and often wanders widely. Active during daytime but difficult to observe because of tendency to frequent dense vegetation. Voice a squealing whistle, *puteow*.

White-faced Whistling-Duck

Black-bellied Whistling-Duck

West Indian Whistling-Duck

Fulvous Whistling-Duck

Gadwall *Mareca strepera*
Vagrant

Almost strictly inhabits freshwater; typically found on reservoirs, small ponds, and coastal marshes during nonbreeding season. Medium-sized, nondescript dabbling duck, with slender bill and steep forehead (46–58 cm; male 850 g, female 700 g). Male has grayish-brown head; gray mantle, back and flanks vermiculated black and white. ***Undertail coverts and rump black; speculum white bordered by black in front, contrasting with chestnut wing coverts. Bill slate gray.*** Female similar to other female dabbling ducks with overall buffy tan coloration; mottled plumage shows little contrast between head/neck, body, and undertail coverts. Speculum white with reduced chestnut on median and lesser coverts; ***bill dusky with muted orange or yellow sides***. Typically silent.

Eurasian Wigeon *Mareca penelope*
Vagrant

Possible in freshwater ponds and lagoons during nonbreeding season. Moderate-sized duck (47 cm; 770 g) with relatively short bill. Male's dark reddish-brown head with golden ***cream-colored forecrown*** distinguishes it from all other red-headed ducks. Breast pinkish, rest of body mostly gray. Golden forecrown much reduced in nonbreeding male, which is more rufous overall. Females occur in two color phases: gray-phase is brownish overall with gray head and light blue bill; red-phase is similar but with reddish tint to head and neck. In flight, note large white patch on forewing (male), green speculum, white belly, and ***blackish flecks on grayish underwing coverts***. See similar American Wigeon with which they often co-occur. Generally silent during nonbreeding season.

American Wigeon *Mareca americana*
Nonbreeding Visitor

Uncommon to moderately common at low elevations islandwide, primarily in freshwater bodies, also saltwater ponds. Moderate-sized duck (52 cm; 755 g) with relatively short bill. Male generally pinkish brown overall with ***white crown***, buffy-white cheeks and neck, light blue bill, and green eye patch. Female brownish with gray head and light blue bill. In flight, note ***white patch on upper forewing***, green speculum, white belly, and prominent ***white patch on underwing***. See similar Eurasian Wigeon. Will graze on land, and picks food items off water surface. Generally silent during nonbreeding season.

White-cheeked Pintail *Anas bahamensis*
Breeding Resident

Uncommon at favored lowland localities, usually on freshwater but regular also on brackish ponds, mangrove marshes, and saltwater lagoons. Moderate-sized duck (44 cm; 535 g) with decidedly ***pointed*** buffy tail. Warm brown overall with prominent ***white cheek*** and ***red mark at base of bill***. Speculum green with buff-colored borders. Similar Ruddy Duck also has prominent white cheek, but is smaller, has blue bill, and short tail often cocked upright. Male pintail gives a squeaky call; female's call is a *quack*.

Gadwall

Eurasian Wigeon

American Wigeon

White-cheeked Pintail

Wood Duck *Aix sponsa*
Vagrant

Possible along canals, lagoons, and impoundments during nonbreeding season. Unmistakable. Small duck (51 cm; 650 g) with **crested head**. Male's **distinctive facial pattern** of green, purple, and white with red eye and burgundy breast is unique. Female brownish gray overall, identified by crest and large, **white, asymmetrical eye-ring**. In flight, note **long, squared tail** and large head with bill tilted down. Males, when alarmed, emit 3–4 thin, squeaky *jeeb* calls. Females issue peculiar wavering note, *oo-eek, oo-eek*, especially when taking flight. Often perches in trees. Largely nonvocal during nonbreeding period.

Blue-winged Teal *Spatula discors*
Nonbreeding Visitor

Fairly common on lakes, ponds, and coastal lagoons, but primarily freshwater. Small, brownish long-billed duck (39 cm; 385 g); female and nonbreeding male mottled brown with a **light spot at base of bill.** Breeding male mottled brown with grayish head, distinct **white crescent on face**, and **white patch on rear flank**. In flight, **pale bluish forewing** and green speculum are conspicuous. See similar female and nonbreeding male Green-winged Teal. The most common migratory duck on Hispaniola. Largely nonvocal during nonbreeding period.

Northern Shoveler *Spatula clypeata*
Nonbreeding Visitor

Uncommon and local at fresh and brackish water bodies; rarely saline lagoons. Medium-sized dabbling duck (48 cm; 615 g) with unusually **large bill**, **widened and spoonlike** toward tip. Male has green head, white breast, and **reddish-brown sides and belly**. Female mottled brown overall. In flight, note powdery-blue forewing and green speculum. Similar male Mallard also has green head, but breast maroon and bill smaller and yellow. See Blue-winged Teal. Generally silent during nonbreeding season.

Mallard *Anas platyrhynchos*
Vagrant

Possible on bodies of calm, shallow water during nonbreeding season. Large dabbling duck (58 cm; 1,082 g) with **bright blue speculum bordered by white**. Adult female mottled brown overall; bill orange with black markings; **tail whitish**. Nonbreeding male and immature similar to adult female but bill olive-colored. Breeding male has distinctive **rounded green head** bordered below by **white neck ring**, maroon breast, pale gray back and flanks, black tail-curl, and yellow bill. Similar male Northern Shoveler has green head but a white breast, reddish-brown sides, and noticeably larger bill. Among the most vocal ducks. Female gives loud, descending quacking calls, sometimes singly; male's call is a short, raspy quack, *quehp* or *rab*.

Green-winged Teal *Anas crecca*
Vagrant

Possible in shallow freshwater bodies during nonbreeding season. Small duck (36 cm; 340 g) with **bright green speculum**; no blue in forewing. Female and nonbreeding male mottled brown with dark lores, **pale undertail coverts**, whitish belly. Breeding males have reddish-brown head, large green eye patch, and **vertical white bar** in front of wing. In flight, note green speculum edged with white or buff in all plumages. Female and nonbreeding male Green-winged and Blue-winged teal very similar, but Green-winged lack distinctive whitish spot on lores and have smaller bill, whitish belly, and pale patch beneath tail. In flight, Green-winged lack the blue forewing of Blue-winged Teal. Generally silent during nonbreeding season.

Wood Duck

♀

♂

Blue-winged Teal

♀ & non-br ♂

br ♂

♀

♂

Northern Shoveler

♀

br ♂

♀

♂

non-br ♂

Mallard

♀

br ♂

♀

♂

♀ & non-br ♂

br ♂

♀

♂

Green-winged Teal

Canada Goose *Branta canadensis*
Vagrant

Possible during nonbreeding season at borders of wetlands, from saltwater lagoons to freshwater swamps, including flooded uplands; also grasslands adjacent to water. Unmistakable. Large, heavyset goose (90 cm; 2,500 g). Mostly grayish brown with a ***black head and neck***; distinctive ***white band forming a "chinstrap"*** on cheeks and throat; white lower belly, uppertail coverts, and undertail coverts; black tail. In flight, note dark wings with a white band across uppertail coverts. Voice a loud, resonant, honking, *h-ronk* and *h-lenk*.

Northern Pintail *Anas acuta*
Nonbreeding Visitor

Rare in freshwater bodies at low elevations, but also on salt ponds. Slender, elegant duck with long neck and small, rounded head (58 cm; male 950 g, female 805 g). Female and nonbreeding male mottled brown; ***bill gray***. Unmistakable breeding male has brown head, ***white breast and neck stripe***, and ***long, pointed tail***. Bill narrow and gray. In flight, female and nonbreeding male show brown speculum bordered by white trailing edge. Gray underwing contrasts with white belly. Breeding male has greenish speculum with buff inner border and white trailing edge. Female similar to Fulvous Whistling-Duck, but pintail lacks thin white stripe along side and shows white trailing edge to speculum. West Indian Whistling-Duck has darker wings and less pointed tail. Generally silent during nonbreeding season.

Canvasback *Aythya valisineria*
Vagrant

Frequents large, relatively deep lagoons and canals with well-vegetated edges. Large diving duck (50 cm; 1,220 g) with distinctive ***long, sloping forecrown*** in profile. Male has rich reddish-brown head and neck, black chest, whitish back and flanks, and brownish-black rump. Female and immature pale overall with light brown head, neck, and chest; throat buffy brown, back and flanks light gray, rump is brownish. Sloping ***bill is black*** in all plumages. In flight, long head and neck impart an elongated appearance; wings show extensive white above and below. Dark breast and undertail coverts contrast with very light belly. Similarly patterned Redhead lacks sloping forecrown of Canvasback; wings grayer above. Generally nonvocal during nonbreeding period.

Redhead *Aythya americana*
Vagrant

Possible at ponds and lagoons during nonbreeding season. Medium-large diving duck (45 cm; 1,045 g) with ***rounded head and steep forecrown***. Male has pale gray back and black breast contrasting with bright rufous head and neck; rump and tail coverts black; bill blue gray with black tip. Female uniformly dull brownish overall with whitish chin and eye-ring. In flight, all birds show pale gray secondaries contrasting with darker gray upperwing coverts. Similar Canvasback also has reddish head and neck, but has a distinctly sloping forecrown and white (versus gray) secondaries. Female Redhead similar to female Lesser Scaup and Ring-necked Duck, but both have different head shape, white belly, and white patch at base of bill. Generally silent during nonbreeding season.

Canada Goose

Northern Pintail

♀

♂

♀ & non-br ♂

br ♂

Canvasback

♀

♂

♀

♂

Redhead

♀

♂

♀

♂

Ring-necked Duck *Aythya collaris*
Nonbreeding Visitor

Rarely occurring on lowland freshwater lakes and ponds. Medium-sized diving duck (43 cm; 705 g) with **ringed bill** and short crest resulting in angular, peaked profile. Male has white bill-ring; black head, chest, back, and tail; gray sides; and **white vertical bar** in front of wing. Female uniformly dark grayish brown overall with light bill-ring and **whitish eye-ring**, sometimes with trailing white streak between auricular and crown. In flight, dark upperwing coverts contrast with pale gray secondaries in both sexes. Male distinguished from Greater and Lesser scaup by black back, white bill-ring, and white vertical bar on side of breast. Female distinguished by wide gray, rather than white, wing stripe. Generally nonvocal during nonbreeding period

Greater Scaup *Aythya marila*
Vagrant

Typically inhabits coastal areas during nonbreeding season, especially brackish lagoons, estuaries, sheltered bays and shallow marine waters. Moderately large diving duck (46 cm; 1,100 g). Male has head and neck black glossed green or purple; **breast, rump and tail coverts black**; lower mantle and scapulars grayish; **sides and belly white**. Female dull brownish overall with **white patch around base of bill**. Both sexes have **broad white band across secondaries and most of primaries**; bill lead gray. See similar Lesser Scaup. Largely nonvocal during nonbreeding period.

Lesser Scaup *Aythya affinis*
Nonbreeding Visitor

Uncommon, principally on freshwater ponds and lakes. Medium-sized diving duck (42 cm; 820 g). Male has black, **peaked head** (**glossed purple** in good light), black breast and tail, white flanks and belly, and whitish back flecked gray. **Bill blue.** Female brown with large **white mark around base of bill**. In flight, **secondaries white and primaries dark** in both sexes. Similar Greater Scaup has more rounded head with green gloss in good light; more extensive white band across wing. Male Ring-necked Duck has black back, white bill-ring, and white vertical bar on side of breast. Female Lesser Scaup distinguished from female Ring-necked Duck by bold white stripe on secondaries, and broad white patch at base of bill. Largely nonvocal during nonbreeding period.

Hooded Merganser *Lophodytes cucullatus*
Vagrant

Frequents lowland freshwater ponds and lakes, and open water of bays. Identified as a smaller merganser (45 cm; 610 g) by crest and **slender, serrated bill, hooked at tip**. Male distinctive with black head and neck and a **large crest containing white, fan-shaped patch** when raised. Bill black, **sides buffy cinnamon**. Female generally dark plumage; **bushy crest grayish brown**, giving "hammer-headed" appearance. **Dark bill** dull orange near base. In flight, male dark above with small white patch on secondaries and pale grayish forewing; female brown above with small white patch on secondaries. Wingbeats very fast and shallow. Generally silent.

Red-breasted Merganser *Mergus serrator*
Vagrant

Occurs primarily in open water of bays, the ocean near shore, and inland lagoons during nonbreeding season. Large diving duck (57 cm; 1,020 g) with **shaggy crest** and **slender, hooked bill**. Nonbreeding male and female mostly grayish brown with reddish-brown **head blending into whitish chin, foreneck, and breast**. **Bill reddish**. Breeding male has green head, white collar, and **reddish-brown breast**. Back dark; sides and flanks grayish. White patches on sides of breast and on wings. In flight, male's secondaries and forewing white, crossed by two narrow, horizontal dark bars; female's secondaries white and crossed by one dark bar. Female differs from female Hooded Merganser by larger size, lighter face and back, and reddish bill. Generally silent.

Ring-necked Duck

Greater Scaup

Lesser Scaup

Hooded Merganser

Red-breasted Merganser

Masked Duck *Nomonyx dominicus*
Endangered Breeding Resident

Local and rare in lowland freshwater ponds and lakes with dense emergent vegetation. Small, chunky duck (33 cm; 365 g) with conspicuous *erect tail*. Nonbreeding male, female, and immature mottled buffy brown with two dark brown *facial stripes* and white wing patch. Breeding male reddish brown overall with blackish horizontal barring on back and sides, *black face*, blue bill with black tip. In flight, all plumages show long tail and conspicuous white patch on secondaries and part of forewing. Ruddy Duck also typically cocks tail. Female Ruddy Duck has only one dark facial stripe and lacks white wing patch. Generally silent, but displaying males give series of short clucking calls, *coo-coo-coo*. Retiring, skulking species, easily overlooked.

Ruddy Duck *Oxyura jamaicensis*
Breeding Resident

Uncommon and local, principally in lowland freshwater ponds and lakes. Small-bodied, compact, stiff-tailed duck (39 cm; 545 g). Breeding male reddish brown overall with black cap, contrasting *white cheek patch*, and *blue bill*. Nonbreeding male similar to female but with white cheeks. Females and immatures grayish brown with *whitish cheeks cut by single brown stripe* below eye. In flight, appears chunky with relatively long tail and dark upperwings. Similar female Masked Duck has two dark facial stripes rather than one. Silent most of year, but males give muffled staccato clucking calls during courtship displays.

Least Grebe *Tachybaptus dominicus*
Breeding Resident

Uncommon and local in lowland, freshwater cattail swamps and small ponds with water plants for cover. Small diving bird (25 cm; 122 g), sooty blackish overall; *thin bill* and *yellow-orange iris* diagnostic. Breeding birds have black throat; nonbreeding adults and immatures have white throat. Unique *white wing patch* not always visible. Similar Pied-billed Grebe is larger, bulkier, with stouter bill, dark eye, and all-dark wing. Voice a descending chatter, *te-te-te-te-te-te*; also a rising, reedlike *week* or *beep*. Generally solitary, shy and difficult to observe; often stays among aquatic vegetation. When alarmed, dives rapidly and emerges only under cover of dense vegetation.

Pied-billed Grebe *Podilymbus podiceps*
Breeding Resident

Common on lowland lakes, ponds, and slow-moving rivers; prefers freshwater but will also inhabit brackish and hypersaline lagoons. Small, stocky, ducklike (34 cm; 442 g) with brown back, buffy gray sides of neck and flanks, and *short, conical bill*. Breeding adult has *black throat; bill has black band*. Nonbreeding adult has whitish throat; bill lacks black band. Head of juvenile distinguished by mottled brown and buffy white markings. Similar Least Grebe smaller and has thin, straight bill; yellowish eye. Voice a harsh cackle breaking into a distinctive *kowp, kowp, kowp*, slowing at the end. Usually solitary or in small family groups. Often frequents open water. If alarmed, dives instantly and swims to protection of dense aquatic vegetation.

Masked Duck

♀ & non-br ♂

♂

Ruddy Duck

♂

non-br ♂

♀ & imm

Least Grebe

non-br

br

Pied-billed Grebe

non-br

br

Helmeted Guineafowl *Numida meleagris*
Breeding Resident

Introduced; uncommon and local in semiarid thorn scrub, dry forest, and savanna habitat. Unmistakable. Distinguished by unusual, **bulbous body shape** (53 cm; 1,300 g), dark gray feathering with **extensive white spotting**, and nearly naked head and neck. Ground-dwelling in small flocks; flushes with burst of whirring wings. Roosts in trees and bushes. Most birds receive handouts from local farmers and are semidomesticated, but truly wild populations also exist. Once very common nearly islandwide; now increasingly confined to sparsely populated regions, private property, or protected areas where hunting is controlled. Distinctive voice a rhythmic series of raucous, cackling calls.

Northern Bobwhite *Colinus virginianus*
Breeding Resident

Introduced; uncommon and increasingly local in scrubland and pasture with ample cover, and especially pine forest. Unmistakable. Chunky, small brown bird (25 cm; 178 g), finely barred tan and black above, barred white and black below; chestnut streaking on sides. Male has **white throat and supercilium**, and shaggy head crest. Female similar but with tan throat and supercilium. Resembles a small, rounded chicken quickly scampering in small groups about the underbrush. Voice a clear whistled rendition of its name, *bob-white* or *poor bob-white*. Often does not flush until nearly underfoot, then bursts from cover.

Ring-necked Pheasant *Phasianus colchicus*
Breeding Resident?

Introduced; very local in fields and at forest edges. Unmistakable. Large and chickenlike with a **very long tail** (male 65 cm, 1,317 g; female 55 cm, 953 g). Male spectacularly multicolored; note **red face**, yellow bill, glossy purple head and neck, white collar. Mantle and flanks golden brown spotted black, blending to gray on rump. Tail chestnut brown and buff, prominently barred black. Breast and belly dark brown. Female mottled pale brown throughout, with shorter, **pointed tail**. Voice a harsh, loud crowing *uurk-iik*, not unlike male Red Junglefowl, and various clucking sounds. Scattered reports suggest multiple introductions. Not known to breed, but likely to do so.

Red Junglefowl *Gallus gallus*
Breeding Resident

Introduced; occurs in a wide variety of rural habitats. Familiar and unmistakable. Extremely variable in size, mass, and plumage (male 71 cm, female 43 cm) including mix of black, brown, reddish brown, gray, and white. Male rooster resplendently plumaged with **red comb and wattle** on head; **long, bushy, decurved tail**. Female hen has smaller comb and wattle; tail much reduced. Voice of male a universally recognized *cock-a-doodle-doo* or *chi-qui-ri-qui*. Also variety of clucks and other notes. Chicks give soft, characteristic call note, *pee-o*. Found in a wild state only very locally; domesticated birds common on farms and villages throughout island, and commonly left running free.

Helmeted Guineafowl

Northern Bobwhite

♂
♀

Ring-necked Pheasant

♂

♀

Red Junglefowl

♂

♀

Rock Pigeon *Columba livia*
Breeding Resident

Introduced; abundant in and near most major towns and cities. Medium-sized (33 cm; 355 g), stocky, short-necked pigeon with highly variable plumage. Most birds feature combination of black, gray, and white, including **dark tail band**, white underwings with dark border, **two dark wingbars**, and conspicuous **white rump**. Generally unmistakable, but in flight large body size and sharply pointed wings appear almost falconlike; distinguished by stockier build, short tail, white rump. Similar White-crowned Pigeon is dark gray with white cap; Scaly-naped Pigeon is also dark gray but sides of neck suffused with iridescence. Voice a varied assortment of low, gentle cooing notes. Rarely occurs in forests or more remote habitats occupied by other large pigeons.

Scaly-naped Pigeon *Patagioenas squamosa*
Threatened Breeding Resident

Found in remote moist broadleaf forests of interior hills and mountains. Large pigeon (38 cm; 250 g) **entirely slate gray at a distance**; at close range, note **purplish red tint to head, neck, and breast**. Bare skin around eye yellow to reddish orange. Immature has more reddish-brown head and neck. Larger and darker than any doves. See somewhat similar White-crowned and Plain pigeons. Distinctive call an emphatic, mournful *cruu … cruu-cru-CRUUU*; very soft first syllable separated by pause. Last 3 syllables sound like *Who are YOU*. Primarily arboreal; feeds opportunistically on ground. Most frequently observed flying over forest canopy.

White-crowned Pigeon *Patagioenas leucocephala*
Threatened Breeding Resident

Uncommon; roosts and nests colonially in coastal mangroves, but feeds on fruit in interior broadleaf forest during day. Large pigeon (33 cm; 245 g) appears entirely slate gray except **white crown**; clear white on males, grayish white on females; reduced on immatures. **Bill red** with pale tip; iris white. Scaly-naped Pigeon paler overall, with white band and reddish-brown patch on wing. Voice high-pitched *cruu, cru, cu-cruuu*, sounds like *Who took two*; second syllable rises; faster and less deliberate than Scaly-naped Pigeon. Powerful flier; may commute >45 km between roosting and feeding grounds. Breeding colonies may have hundreds to thousands of birds.

Plain Pigeon *Patagioenas inornata*
Threatened Breeding Resident

Uncommon and declining; mostly restricted to less populated areas, especially in pine zones. Large pigeon (39 cm; 250 g), paler than other arboreal species. **Head, neck, and underparts pinkish tan**; reddish brown on wings, with thin white edges to upperwing coverts. Iris white; eye-ring red. Immature birds darker and browner. Distinguished from Scaly-naped and White-crowned pigeons by Plain Pigeon's uniformly lighter coloration. Similar White-winged and Zenaida doves are smaller, browner, with bolder white wing markings. Voice a deep, deliberate *whoo, wo-oo*, or *who, oo-oo*, emphasis on first syllable. May be more frequently heard than seen. Arboreal, typically in flocks. Can be surprisingly tame.

Rock Pigeon

Scaly-naped Pigeon

imm

♂

White-crowned Pigeon

Plain Pigeon

Eurasian Collared-Dove *Streptopelia decaocto*
Breeding Resident

Introduced; increasingly common and widespread dove, occurring in urban areas, villages, pastures, and other open habitats
at low to mid-elevations. Medium-sized, long-tailed dove (30 cm;
male 205 g, female 155 g). Adults mostly uniform buffy gray
with lighter gray crown and forecrown, and pinkish-gray neck and breast. Distinctive **black
band bordered with white on hindneck**. **Undertail coverts gray**. In flight, **dark primaries**; buffy-
gray tail, with all but central rectrices bearing broad, pale tips. Immatures lack black band on
hindneck. Similar Mourning Dove lacks black band on hindneck and has long, pointed tail. Three-
syllabled song, with distinct pauses, *kuk … kooooooo … kook*; also a nasal *whew*.

Common Ground Dove *Columbina passerina*
Breeding Resident

Common to abundant in lowland pastures, fields, and clearings;
also at higher-elevation sites with patches of open ground.
Unmistakable. **Tiny, stocky dove** (16 cm; 30 g). Sandy brown
overall with rufous primaries; dark tail with white-tipped corners.
Male has bluish-gray crown and nape; pinkish tint on underparts. Female has sandy-gray crown.
In flight, stubby wings flash **rufous primaries and underwings** in quick, shallow wingbeats. Voice
a monotonous call of single or double notes, *coo, coo, coo, coo…*or *co-coo, co-coo, co-coo…*or a
staccato *hoop, hoop, hoop*.

White-winged Dove *Zenaida asiatica*
Breeding Resident

Moderately common, but especially numerous in lowland dry
woods and mesquite scrub. Medium-sized (29 cm; 150 g), heavy-
bodied, grayish-brown dove with **large, white, central wing patch**,
visible in flight or along edge of folded wing. Small black crescent
below auricular. **Tail rounded, broadly tipped white**. Similar Zenaida Dove has white band on wing
restricted to trailing edge of secondaries. Mourning Dove has no white in wing and long, pointed
tail. Voice a rhythmic *coo-co, co-coo* or *coo-co, co-co-coo* on a single pitch; sounds like *who cooks
for you*. Also distinctive yodel-like cooing modulating between two notes. Usually flocks.

Zenaida Dove *Zenaida aurita*
Breeding Resident

Common in open country lowlands, second growth, and scrub;
occasionally in gardens and cultivated areas. Medium-sized
(27 cm; 159 g), warm brown dove, paler below, with **white
trailing edge to dark secondaries**. Tail rounded with black
subterminal band; broad white tips. Violet sheen on neck visible in good light. Similar Mourning
Dove has no white in wing and longer, pointed tail. White-winged Dove has large, white central
wing patch. Voice a gentle, mournful cooing, almost identical to Mourning Dove, *coo-oo, coo,
coo, coo*, the second syllable rising sharply.

Mourning Dove *Zenaida macroura*
Breeding Resident

Common islandwide, particularly in disturbed lowlands. Medium-
sized (29 cm; 120 g), slender, with small head and **long, tapered
tail tipped with white**. Upperparts grayish blue to grayish brown;
underparts buffy. Upperwing coverts contain black spots, but **lacks
white in wing**. Male has purplish sheen on neck; bluish crown. Female has reduced iridescence on
neck; brownish crown. Immatures browner than adults, heavily spotted with black, lack iridescence.
Similar Zenaida and White-winged doves have white wing markings and rounded tails. Mournful
cooing almost identical to Zenaida Dove, *coo-oo, coo, coo, coo*, the second syllable rising sharply.

Eurasian Collared-Dove

Common Ground Dove

White-winged Dove

Zenaida Dove

Greater Antilles
race

Mourning Dove

Ruddy Quail-Dove *Geotrygon montana*
Breeding Resident

Moderately common in mid-elevation dense humid forest, coffee and cacao plantations; local on coast. Medium-sized (24 cm; 110 g), plump, short-tailed dove. Male **rufous brown above**, glossed violet; buffy brown below. Conspicuous **light buffy auriculars** cut by rufous-brown stripe beneath eye. Female **brownish olive**; less conspicuous facial stripe. Immatures resemble females but paler; back feathers edged cinnamon. Similar Key West Quail-Dove has more pronounced white stripe beneath eye. Ventriloquial voice a mournful *hoooooo*, gradually fading in strength and sometimes in pitch. Distinguished only with extreme caution from call of Key West Quail-Dove that fades more rapidly. Ground-dwelling, much more often heard than seen.

White-fronted Quail-Dove *Geotrygon leucometopia*
Endangered Endemic Breeding Resident

Uncommon in remote humid mountain forests. Medium-sized (28 cm; 171 g), ground-dwelling pigeon. Crown, nape, and sides of head **slate gray**; sides of neck suffused with reddish purple or violet, sometimes extending onto breast. Back slightly darker with metallic purplish-blue sheen. **Underparts gray**, becoming rufous on lower belly and undertail coverts. Striking **forecrown white**; eye red. Bill reddish, paler toward tip. Legs reddish. Immatures similar but browner, lacking metallic sheen on mantle and neck. Only quail-dove **lacking facial stripes**. Typically calls with continuous *uup-uup-uup-uup* without pauses, then changing to prolonged *coo-o-o*. Forages on ground alone or in pairs. Displays peculiar balance of neck and tail while walking or perching.

Key West Quail-Dove *Geotrygon chrysia*
Threatened Breeding Resident

Moderately common in lowland dry forests. Strikingly beautiful, medium-sized (29 cm; 170 g), ground-dwelling pigeon. Upperparts reddish brown suffused with violet, blue, and green iridescence on nape, mantle, and sides of breast; underparts tawny. **Bold white line under eye**. Legs and feet red. Females duller with less iridescence. Immature more uniformly brown and buff, but bold facial stripe and pinkish legs still present. Similar Ruddy Quail-Dove has more reddish-brown underparts and duller buff streak below eye. Ventriloquial call a low moan on one pitch, *ooo-wooo*, gradually increasing in volume and then fading rapidly. Secretive ground dweller of dense woods and scrubby thickets; more often heard than seen.

Northern Potoo *Nyctibius jamaicensis*
Threatened Breeding Resident

Local, uncommon to rare resident of edges of arid and humid forests; also scrublands, palm groves, pastures. Large (44 cm; 280 g), nocturnal bird with cryptic plumage. **Perches upright** atop snag or pole. Upperparts mottled brown, gray, and black; underparts grayish brown to pale grayish cinnamon with dark streaking. Yellow iris appears reddish in beam of light. Juvenile paler than adult. Distinguished from nightjars and poor-wills by **longer tail**, **more rounded wings**, and larger size. Voice deep and guttural *kwaaaaaah*, *waugh*, *waugh*, *waugh*, *kwaah*. Also a hoarse, emphatic *waark*. Often allows close approach. Sallies for insects from favorite tree perch.

Ruddy Quail-Dove

White-fronted Quail-Dove

Key West Quail-Dove

Northern Potoo

Common Nighthawk *Chordeiles minor*
Passage Migrant
Regularly occurring, but distribution and abundance poorly documented. Medium-sized (23 cm; 61 g), cryptically plumaged nightjar with large, flattened head, large eyes, small bill, enormous mouth. Wings project beyond tail tip at rest. In flight, wings slender, pointed, with conspicuous **white bar across primaries**. Flight graceful but erratic, almost batlike, with sporadic flaps interspersed with gliding. Virtually identical Antillean Nighthawk about 10% smaller; flight tends to be more "fluttery" with shorter wings; wing tips appear more rounded and blunt; white wing band typically more mottled. Identified with certainty only by voice; Common Nighthawk has single-noted, very nasal *neet* or *peent*, but unknown how much vocalization occurs outside of breeding season.

Antillean Nighthawk *Chordeiles gundlachii*
Breeding Visitor

Common in open country, pastures, and coastal fringes. Medium-sized (21 cm; 50 g) nightjar, dark and hawklike; long, slender wings, medium-length notched tail. Erratic, graceful flight; note conspicuous **white band across dark primaries**. At rest, wings the same length as tail. Male has narrow white band near tail tip; white throat patch. Female lacks tail band; has buffy throat patch. Juvenile similar to female but lacks throat patch. See very similar Common Nighthawk; distinguished with certainty only by voice. Antillean Nighthawk has loud, raspy *quere-bebé*. Typically seen foraging for insects high over open areas at dawn or dusk. Occurs March to October; some breeding birds may remain through nonbreeding season, but poorly documented.

Least Pauraque *Siphonorhis brewsteri*
Endangered Endemic Breeding Resident

Scarce and local, primarily in lowland dry habitats and semiarid areas of cactus and thorn scrub, but extends into mid-elevation pine. Very small (19 cm; mass unavailable), darkly mottled nightjar. Adult has distinct **white throat band** and narrow **white terminal band** on tail. Juvenile more buffy than adult. Flight mothlike, erratic and floppy. Similar Greater Antillean Nightjar is larger and darker; Chuck-will's-widow much larger and more reddish brown. Both lack white terminal tail band. Voice a guttural *torico, torico*, heard at dawn and dusk; also a rising whistle. Entirely nocturnal, but most active just after sunset and just before sunrise.

Chuck-will's-widow *Antrostomus carolinensis*
Nonbreeding Visitor

Moderately common in lowland dry forest and transitional broadleaf forest. Large (30 cm; 120 g), cryptically patterned, mottled cinnamon brown overall. Throat collar whitish on male, pale buff on females and immatures. Males have **white on inner webs of three outer tail feathers**; females lack white in tail. Both sexes have buffy tips on these rectrices. Similar Hispaniolan Nightjar is smaller, darker, less reddish, has white breast spots. Least Pauraque much smaller, less reddish brown, has terminal white tail band. Voice distinctive, clear, whistled *chuck- will's-WID-ow* but seldom calls on Hispaniola.

Hispaniolan Nightjar *Antrostomus ekmani*
Endemic Breeding Resident

Fairly common at middle elevations in foothills and mountains of western Dominican Republic and Haiti; rare and local elsewhere. Large nightjar (28 cm; 64 g). Mottled dark grayish brown overall; narrow buffy band below blackish throat; breast and belly irregularly spotted white. **Outer tail feathers broadly tipped white in male; buff in female.** Smaller, darker, and less reddish brown than similar Chuck-will's-widow, which lacks white breast spots. Least Pauraque is smaller and paler. Voice a plaintive *pi-tan-guaaaa*. Nocturnal. Some authorities include *A. ekmani* as a subspecies of Greater Antillean Nightjar, *A. cubanensis*.

Common Nighthawk/
Antillean Nighthawk

Least Pauraque

Chuck-will's-widow

Hispaniolan Nightjar

Yellow-billed Cuckoo *Coccyzus americanus*
Passage Migrant; Breeding Resident

Common migrant and uncommon breeding resident in lowland scrub and dry forests islandwide, primarily below 700 m. Slender cuckoo (28 cm; 64 g); brownish olive above with **no black on auriculars** and **clean white underparts**. Tail long and graduated with broad white tips. Long, decurved **bicolored bill, yellow below with black tip**. **Reddish-brown wing patch** in flight. See similar Mangrove and Black-billed cuckoos. Voice a throaty *ka-ka-ka-ka-ka-kow-kow-kowlp-kowlp-kowlp-kowlp*. Volume increases initially, then remains constant; call slows during final syllables. Species absent from island late November until March.

Black-billed Cuckoo *Coccyzus erythropthalmus*
Passage Migrant

Regular but rare in scrublands, mangrove, and other lowland forests. Smaller, slender cuckoo (29 cm; 51 g); long tail dark below with distinct but small white tips; dull white underparts; slender, **dark, decurved bill**; **reddish or yellowish eye-ring**; and upperwing coverts entirely gray brown. Similar Yellow-billed Cuckoo lacks red eye-ring, has yellowish lower bill, prominent reddish brown primaries, and more conspicuous white markings under tail. Voice a series of 3–4 hollow notes, *cu-cu-cu-cu*.

Mangrove Cuckoo *Coccyzus minor*
Breeding Resident

Fairly common islandwide in mangroves, lowland thickets, dry scrub, and dry forest. Slender cuckoo (30 cm; 64 g); long tail blackish below with prominent white spots; long, decurved bill with yellow lower mandible. Note **black "mask" through eyes** and **buff-colored belly**. Flight direct with short glides; **wings lack reddish brown**. All other cuckoos lack black mask through eye. Call similar to Yellow-billed Cuckoo but slower, lower-pitched, more nasal.

Bay-breasted Cuckoo *Coccyzus rufigularis*
Endangered Endemic Breeding Resident

Rare and very local in narrow transition zone between dry and moist broadleaf forest; occasionally in mixed pine and broadleaf. A large, active cuckoo (47 cm; 128 g) distinguished by its dark **reddish-brown throat and breast** and heavy, somewhat **decurved** bill. Also has a reddish-brown wing patch and **very long, black tail with broad white tips**. Similar Hispaniolan Lizard-Cuckoo has pale gray breast. Voice a strong *cu-aa*, sometimes followed by guttural, accelerating *u-ak-u-ak-ak-ak-ak-ak-ak-ak-ak*. Found most often on northern slope of Sierra de Bahoruco, Río Libón valley, and Río Limpio-Carrizal area of northwestern Dominican Republic.

Hispaniolan Lizard-Cuckoo *Coccyzus longirostris*
Endemic Breeding Resident

Generally common and widely distributed in wooded areas, gardens, and shaded coffee. Large cuckoo (44 cm; 110 g) identified by size, **pale gray breast**, dull rufous-orange throat and lower belly, long tail with white tips, and **fairly straight and slender bill** prominently hooked at tip. Bare skin around eye red. Wing patch reddish brown. Voice a prolonged throaty *ka-ka-ka-ka-ka-ka-ka-ka-kau-kau-ko-ko* in descending tones. Also a guttural *tuc wuh-h-h* with the *tuc* being sharp and staccato.

Smooth-billed Ani *Crotophaga ani*
Breeding Resident

Common to abundant in open habitats with scattered trees or bushes, agricultural areas, scrub, gardens. Large (33 cm; 105 g), entirely black, with **heavy, parrotlike bill** and conspicuously **long, flat tail**. Flight straight and slow, with rapid, shallow wing flaps alternating with longer glides. Anis typically fly in single file in small, noisy flocks. Voice a loud slurred and whining whistled *ah-nee* or *a-leep*. Also a variety of short "growls," "coughs," and "barks."

Yellow-billed Cuckoo

Black-billed Cuckoo

Mangrove Cuckoo

Bay-breasted Cuckoo

Hispaniolan Lizard-Cuckoo

Smooth-billed Ani

Black Swift *Cypseloides niger*
Threatened Breeding Visitor

Locally common in flocks; most often in mountains, less frequently in lowlands. Medium-sized (17 cm; 46 g), blackish swift with long, pointed wings; ***slightly notched tail***. At close range, ***white forecrown*** and supercilium visible. Flight less erratic than other swifts; when gliding, wings held below horizontal. Similar White-collared Swift is larger, with pronounced white on neck. Chimney Swift and Antillean Palm-Swift markedly smaller, with short, squared tails, more darting flight, quicker wingbeats. Mostly silent, but occasionally gives a soft *tchip, tchip* when flying. Frequently descends into lowlands at leading edge of rainstorms. Migratory patterns not well known; part of population thought to remain through nonbreeding season.

White-collared Swift *Streptoprocne zonaris*
Breeding Resident

Moderately common, principally in foothills and mountains at middle and upper elevations. Large (21 cm; 98 g) black swift with prominent ***white collar*** and slightly forked tail. Immatures similar; collar narrower and paler. Flight rapid and powerful, with deep, slow wingbeats, spectacular swoops and aerobatics; often soars without flapping. Unmistakable; all other regularly occurring swifts are smaller and lack white collar. Voice a high-pitched, screeching *screee-screee* or rapid, chattering *chip-chip-chip-chip*. Typically in small flocks, but sometimes up to 200 birds. Strong-flying, wide-ranging; could appear virtually anywhere.

Chimney Swift *Chaetura pelagica*
Passage Migrant

Rare in spring; very rare in fall, foraging for flying insects above cities, towns, woodlands, and open fields. Medium-sized (13 cm; 24 g), dark, ***uniformly colored swift***, sooty olive or brown above, plain grayish brown below; noticeably paler on throat, chin, and auriculars. Plumage slightly glossy, especially on wings. ***Very short, rounded tail*** barely visible in flight. Black Swift is larger, with a longer, slightly notched tail. Voice a loud, rapid, high-pitched twittering in flight, seldom heard during migration. May occur more often in western Hispaniola than farther east; migration may be concentrated at high elevations and thus go largely undetected.

Antillean Palm-Swift *Tachornis phoenicobia*
Breeding Resident

Locally common at lower elevations islandwide; reported in moist and dry habitats, over forest, scrub, cultivated areas, seashores, towns, and cities. ***Very small swift*** (10 cm; 9 g); dark brown above, conspicuous ***white rump***. Adults have narrow blackish breast band. Males dark with white throat; females paler below with grayish white throat. Immatures similar to females but darker; more buffy below. Flight erratic and darting. No other swift is as small and boldly patterned. Constantly emits faint, high-pitched twittering. Forages in flocks for flying insects with rapid, erratic, batlike flight; glides between spurts of flapping. Usually forages relatively low to ground; no higher than 20 m.

Black Swift

White-collared Swift

Chimney Swift

Antillean Palm-Swift

Antillean Mango *Anthracothorax dominicus*
Breeding Resident

Common from coasts well into mountains islandwide. Most abundant hummingbird in dry forest and desert habitats; common in broadleaf forests, but unusual in pine forest. *Large hummingbird* (12 cm; 5.4 g) with pale, yellowish-green upperparts; *long, black, slightly decurved bill*. Adult males primarily black below with green throat. Tail *maroon with dark tips*. Females whitish below; whitish tips to *reddish-brown tail*. Immature males similar to females, but with black stripe down center of whitish underparts. Similar female Hispaniolan Emerald is smaller, with straighter and shorter bill. Voice rather loud, unmusical, thin trill; also sharp, chipping notes. Some authorities split this species into an endemic Hispaniolan Mango (*A. dominicus*) and the Puerto Rican Mango (*A. aurulentus*).

Ruby-throated Hummingbird *Archilochus colubris*
Vagrant

Possible at flowers in large gardens, woodland edges, and clusters of trees during nonbreeding season. Small hummingbird (8 cm; 3.2 g) with metallic bronze-green upperparts. Male has *brilliant red throat*, moderately forked tail, whitish underparts with dull greenish sides. Female's throat whitish; rest of underparts dull grayish white, with some *buff coloration on sides*. Tail *rounded* and broadly tipped white. Both sexes have small white spot behind eye. Bill of adults is *dark*. Female Ruby-throated Hummingbird similar to Hispaniolan Emerald, which has paler bill, more conspicuous white stripe behind eye, greenish sides. Voice high, squeaky, rapid series of chips, *tchi-tchi-tchi-chit*.

Hispaniolan Emerald *Riccordia swainsonii*
Endemic Breeding Resident

Generally common in moist forest, clearings of interior mountains and foothills, limestone karst, and pine forests. Small (10 cm; 4.9 g), *straight-billed* hummingbird. Male green overall; dull *black breast patch*, deeply forked tail, lower mandible *mostly pinkish*. Female green above, dull grayish below, *metallic green sides*, and whitish outer tail tips. Similar female Antillean Mango is larger, has reddish-brown outer tail feathers, darker bill. Vervain Hummingbird much smaller. Voice a series of sharp, metallic chips, *tic-tic-tic*.

Vervain Hummingbird *Mellisuga minima*
Breeding Resident

Widespread but locally common in all habitat types except dense, moist forest. *Tiny hummingbird* (6 cm; 2.4 g); green above, whitish below with *straight black bill*. Chin and throat sometimes flecked greenish; sides and flanks dull green. Adult male has deeply notched tail; adult female has rounded tail tipped white. Immature male similar to adult female except chin and throat flecked gray; softer white tips on outer tail feathers. Similar female Hispaniolan Emerald much larger, with longer, paler bill. Voice a loud, rhythmic song of high-pitched, metallic squeaks; also extended throaty buzz. Often hovers with tail cocked up; more often heard than seen. The world's second-smallest bird.

Antillean Mango

Ruby-throated Hummingbird

Hispaniolan Emerald

Vervain Hummingbird

Spotted Rail *Pardirallus maculatus*
Threatened Breeding Resident

Uncommon local inhabitant of freshwater swamps with dense emergent vegetation, but breeding not yet proven. Medium-sized (25 cm; 171 g), strikingly plumaged rail with long, pinkish-red legs. Bill long, greenish yellow, slightly decurved; red at base. Adult slate black, head and upperparts *heavily spotted white*; underparts *boldly barred white*; undertail coverts white. Iris red. Immature browner with fewer and duller spots, bill and legs duller, iris brownish. *In all plumages spotting unmistakable*. Voice a peculiar high, guttural screech; may be preceded by short grunt. Also an accelerating *tuk-tuk-tuk-tuk* or *wuh-wuh-wuh*. Generally solitary and very secretive. Much more often heard than seen.

Clapper Rail *Rallus crepitans*
Breeding Resident

Moderately common rail inhabiting largely undisturbed salt marshes and mangroves. *Large rail* (37 cm; male 323 g, female 271 g), relatively long-necked with *long bill*. Upperparts olive brown to gray brown mottled black; *auriculars gray*. Underparts grayish, with cinnamon buff on throat and belly; flanks faintly barred whitish. Similar Common Gallinule has much shorter bill. Call a grating series of rising and falling *kek* notes, slowing at end. Cackle of one rail often sets off chorus of others. Difficult to observe; may be seen stalking among mangrove roots, but far more often heard than seen; most active at dawn and dusk.

Sora *Porzana carolina*
Passage Migrant; Nonbreeding Visitor

Regularly occurring in rice fields, mangroves, and freshwater marshes in lowlands and middle elevations. Relatively *small rail* (23 cm; 75 g), brownish gray with *black mask* and *stubby yellow bill*. Breeding adult has *blackish face*, throat, and chest; belly barred black and white. In nonbreeding plumage, throat and chest mostly gray. Black absent in immatures, which have buffy-brown face, throat, and chest. See similar, but much smaller, juvenile Yellow-breasted Crake. Voice a clear, descending whinny, *ko-WEEee-ee-ee-ee-ee-ee*, and plaintive, rising whistle, *koo-wee*. Secretive; seldom reported but surely overlooked.

Yellow-breasted Crake *Hapalocrex flaviventer*
Breeding Resident

Rare and local resident of freshwater marshes, swamps, and canals with borders of short grass or other water plants. *Tiny rail* (14 cm; 25 g) distinguished by its size, rich *buffy sides of neck and breast*, and *bold black-and-white barring on flanks*. At close range, note blackish crown, white supercilium, black eye-line, and small, dark bill. When flushed, flies weakly a short distance, the feet dangling and head drooping. Similar Sora is much larger with stouter, paler bill. Voice a low, rough, rolled or churring *k'kuk kuh-kurr* and a high-pitched, plaintive *peep*. Like many other rails, very secretive behavior; seldom observed. Status poorly known.

Black Rail *Laterallus jamaicensis*
Threatened Nonbreeding Visitor? Breeding Resident?

Rare and local, possible in saline or fresh grassy marsh edges. *Tiny* (12 cm; 34 g), *slaty gray* rail with scattered *white spots on back and wings*; dark reddish-brown nape. Underparts dark gray with white barring on flanks. *Bill short and black*. Other rails considerably larger; downy young of gallinules, coots, and other rails very similar but are uniformly black. Male territorial call a rich, nasal *keeic-keeic-kueerr* or *kic-kic-kic-kurr*, the first 2–3 syllables high-pitched whistles, followed by distinctly lower note. Females give low, cooing *croocroocroo*. Defense call an emphatic and irregularly pulsing cackle. Rarely vocalizes during day; shy and usually active only after dark. Rarely leaves cover of marsh grasses. Status not well documented.

Spotted Rail

Clapper Rail

imm

Sora

Yellow-breasted Crake

Black Rail

Common Gallinule *Gallinula galeata*
Breeding Resident; Nonbreeding Visitor

Common in lowland freshwater marshes, less often brackish water and coastal lagoons bordered by mangroves. Adult (33 cm; 305 g) slaty gray overall; brownish gray on upper back, flanks, and sides; prominent *white stripe along upper flanks*. Undertail coverts white with dark central stripe. Red bill tipped yellow; *red frontal shield*. Immature gray and brown; flank stripe white; bill dusky. Similar Clapper Rail has much longer bill; immature Purple Gallinule lacks flank stripe; immature American Coot has whitish bill. Voice a variety of clucks, cackles, and grunts; most commonly a piercing series of clucks slowing to long, whining notes, *ki-ki-ki-ki-ka, kaa, kaaa*. Not particularly shy. Swims with characteristic bobbing motion of head.

American Coot *Fulica americana*
Breeding Resident; Nonbreeding Visitor

Fairly common to common in freshwater ponds, lakes, and river courses with submerged vegetation; occasionally in slightly brackish coastal sloughs. Stocky, *slaty gray to black* marsh bird (39 cm; 650 g); head and neck black in adults, contrasting sharply with *white undertail coverts*. *Bill white*; variable *frontal shield white* (sometimes tinged yellow) with maroon base (may be lacking). White tips on secondaries visible in flight. Immature paler than adult. See similar immature Purple Gallinule and Common Gallinule. Voice a variety of short clucks, croaks, and cackles, usually lower-pitched than Common Gallinule. Often flocks. Swims with bobbing motion of head. Dives proficiently. This species now includes the former "Caribbean Coot."

Purple Gallinule *Porphyrio martinicus*
Breeding Resident

Moderately common but local in relatively undisturbed freshwater marshes and rivers islandwide. Adult (32 cm; 235 g) *bluish purple overall*; iridescent olive green back and wings; white undertail coverts. Red bill tipped yellow; topped by *pale blue frontal shield*. Legs bright yellow. Immature pale buffy brown, with olive green sheen on wings and back. Bill duller with smaller, grayish frontal shield. Immature similar to Common Gallinule and immature American Coot. Varied vocalizations include high-pitched, melodious *klee-klee* and many cackling and guttural notes.

Northern Jacana *Jacana spinosa*
Breeding Resident

Locally common in lowlands, principally at freshwater and saline ponds in interior; sparingly in marshes associated with rivers and streams. Unmistakable wading bird (23 cm; male 82 g, female 135 g) with *large yellow wing patches*, and *extremely long, slender, greenish toes*. Adult deep reddish brown, with blackish head and neck. *Bill and forehead shield yellow*. Immature whitish below, olive brown above, with whitish supercilium and face; brown eye-line, crown, and nape. Sexes similar. Flight characteristically low over water with shallow wingbeats and dangling legs. Often raises wings after landing, exposing yellow flight feathers. Voice a loud, sharp cackle *scraa scraa scraa*. Also rasping, chattering, and clacking notes. Very active and noisy; jacanas walk slowly over floating plants.

Common Gallinule

American Coot

N American race

imm

Caribbean race

Purple Gallinule

imm

Northern Jacana

imm

Limpkin *Aramus guarauna*

Breeding Resident

Increasingly local and scarce resident in grassy freshwater swamps, wooded floodplains, upland dry and humid forest, cacao plantations, and savannas. Large, long-legged, and long-necked (69 cm; 1,080 g) wading bird; entirely **brown with white streaking and triangular spotting**, especially on neck, mantle, and wings. Long, slightly **decurved bill**. Limpkin possibly confused with young night-herons but distinguished by larger size and longer, decurved bill. Immature ibises have more slender and strongly decurved bills. Voice a loud, rolling, piercing scream, *carrao*. Secretive; reluctant to fly; often located by call.

Double-striped Thick-knee *Burhinus bistriatus*

Endangered Breeding Resident

Uncommon and local in grasslands, savannas, arid lowland scrub, and some agricultural areas. Unmistakable. Large, ploverlike shorebird (41 cm; 787 g) with **long, sturdy legs**; short, heavy bill; **large yellow eye**. Mostly brown, streaked tawny and white. Face, neck, and chest grayish buff with dark streaking; **broad white supercilium** bordered by black above; throat and belly white. In flight, shows conspicuous white wing patches. Immature duller and grayer. Voice a loud rattling *ca-ca-ca-ca-ca-ca-ca-ca!* accelerating and rising in volume, then descending in pitch and fading away. Usually calls at dusk, dawn, and night. Secretive. Primarily nocturnal and ground-dwelling. Generally found in pairs or family groups.

Black-necked Stilt *Himantopus mexicanus*

Breeding Resident

Generally common and widespread at coastal lagoons and marshes; less often at interior freshwater and saline lakes in lowlands. Unmistakable. A slender, striking shorebird (37 cm; 166 g), black above, white below, with **extremely long red or pink legs**. Black bill very fine and straight. In flight, wings black above and below; underparts and tail white, extending as a **white chevron onto lower back**. Female has browner back than male; immature resembles female with pale edgings to back feathers, and paler legs. Voice a loud, barking series of short notes, *wit wit wit wit*; often described as "yapping." Frequently seen foraging in large flocks, wading with an almost exaggerated grace. When disturbed, calls loudly and frequently.

American Avocet *Recurvirostra americana*

Vagrant

Vagrant during nonbreeding season to areas of fine sediments and mud, such as intertidal mudflats and brackish impoundments. Large, long-legged shorebird (45 cm; 210 g). Plumage and morphology distinctive. Strikingly contrasting **black-and-white uppers** with white underparts; **long, thin, upturned bill**; **long, grayish-blue legs**. Nonbreeding avocet have pale gray head and neck (rusty when breeding). In flight, black-and-white uppers form a **bold chevron pattern**. Easily distinguished from Black-necked Stilt by upturned bill, contrasting pattern of uppers, and leg color. Less vocal than stilts; calls lower-pitched and include single high, sharp *kweep*, lower *pwik*, or sharp *pleek*.

Wood Stork *Mycteria americana*

Extirpated? Breeding Resident

Formerly locally common but presence not documented since 1968. Inhabited mangroves, coastal mudflats, swamps, rice fields, and inland water bodies. Distinctive, large (100 cm; male 2,600 g, female 2,100 g), long-legged, mostly white bird with dark, naked, scaly head and upper neck; large, **heavy bill, decurved at tip**. Blackish, iridescent primaries, secondaries, and tail feathers. Adult distinguished by **unfeathered, blackish head and upper neck**, and black bill; legs blackish to bluish gray, feet pink. Immature has feathered and paler, dusky gray head; yellowish bill. Frequently soars high on thermals with feet trailing beyond tail. Note **extensive black flight feathers contrasting with white coverts**. Usually silent.

Double-striped Thick-knee

Limpkin

Black-necked Stilt

imm

Wood Stork

American Avocet

non-br

American Oystercatcher *Haematopus palliatus*
Breeding Resident; Nonbreeding Visitor

Rare inhabitant of stony beaches and rocky headlands of coastal sites, offshore islands, and cays. Unmistakable. Large, pied shorebird (42 cm; 632 g) with black hood and back, white breast and flanks, and long, heavy bill. Adult has **orange-red bill** and pinkish legs. Immature has dark-tipped bill and gray legs. In flight, white uppertail coverts and broad white wing stripe distinctive. Voice a loud, emphatic, coarsely whistled *wheep* or *queet*, often running into a piping chatter. Restricted to relatively scarce habitat type seldom occupied by other bird species except perhaps Ruddy Turnstone.

Black-bellied Plover *Pluvialis squatarola*
Passage Migrant; Nonbreeding Visitor

Regularly occurring in variable but moderate numbers on mudflats around entire coast, and along inland saltwater and freshwater lakes. Large plover (30 cm; 220 g) with heavy body and thick, pigeon-like bill. Nonbreeding birds lightly mottled gray above, whitish below with light streaking on breast; belly white. Note **indistinct contrast between gray crown and whitish supercilium**. Breeding birds mottled white and black above, with solid black underparts from chin through belly; **undertail coverts white**. In flight, white uppertail coverts, white tail with dark bars, and distinct **white wing stripe**; conspicuous **black patch on axillaries**. See very similar American and Pacific golden-plovers. Voice a single, plaintive *klee* and a sweet, slurred whistle, *klee-a-lee* or *pee-u-wee*. Typically in loose flocks.

American Golden-Plover *Pluvialis dominica*
Passage Migrant

Rare visitor to grasslands, agricultural lands, and savannas. Fairly large and stocky plover (26 cm; 145 g) with short bill. In nonbreeding plumage, mottled gray with **distinct contrast between dark crown and whitish supercilium**. In breeding plumage, mottled black and golden-brown upperparts, underparts black, including **black undertail coverts**. Note **bold white stripe** from forecrown down sides of neck to upper breast. In flight, **underwings gray** with **no black in axillaries**, tail and **rump dark**, white wing stripe absent. See very similar Pacific Golden-Plover and Black-bellied Plover. Variety of calls, including a high, sharp *quit* and a soft, warbled whistle, *queedle*.

Pacific Golden-Plover *Pluvialis fulva*
Vagrant

Most likely in varied habitats during migratory periods, including cultivated fields, pastures, mudflats, beaches, grassy airport runways, athletics fields, parks, and golf courses. Medium-sized, stocky plover (25 cm; 135 g). Nonbreeding bird mottled grayish tan overall with **yellow-golden spotting on upperparts**. Supercilium whitish, breast yellowish buff grading to whitish on belly and vent. In breeding plumage, underparts black, separated from mottled black and brown uppers by bold white vertical stripe. May be impossible to reliably distinguish from similar American Golden-Plover, but averages brighter golden spotting above with yellow gold wash on face and neck. Separated from nonbreeding Black-bellied Plover by smaller size, darker upperparts, absence of white wing stripe, and black axillaries in flight. Alarm and flight calls a rising *chuEET*, sharply accented on second syllable.

American Oystercatcher

non-br

non-br

Black-bellied Plover

br

non-br

American Golden-Plover

br

non-br

br

non-br

Pacific Golden-Plover

Killdeer *Charadrius vociferus*
Breeding Resident; Nonbreeding Visitor

Locally common in relatively undisturbed meadows, fields, savannas, beaches, and edges of freshwater ponds; often, but not always, near bodies of water. Large, slender plover (24 cm; 95 g), with relatively long wings and tail. Upperparts grayish brown, underparts whitish; **two conspicuous black bands** across breast. In flight, bright **reddish-brown rump and uppertail coverts** are distinctive; broad white wing stripe. Bill relatively long; legs dusky pink. Voice a strident, high-pitched *kee* and *kill-deer* or *ti-íto*; also an agitated *teeee di di*.

Semipalmated Plover *Charadrius semipalmatus*
Passage Migrant; Nonbreeding Visitor

Regularly occurring on coastal mudflats, but also recorded inland at saline, and occasionally freshwater, lakes. Small (18 cm; 47 g), distinctive plover with **very short, dark bill**. **Upperparts brown**, underparts white. Nonbreeding adults and juveniles have grayish-brown crown and line through eyes, white forecrown and supercilium, and **single grayish-brown band across breast**. Legs yellowish orange. Breast band sometimes incomplete. Breeding birds have black replacing grayish brown on breast; black line through eyes extends onto crown. Bill often shows orange at base. Flight call, a plaintive *weet* or husky, whistled *chu-WEE*.

Piping Plover *Charadrius melodus*
Threatened Nonbreeding Visitor

Rare visitor to sandy water edges, fresh or saline. Small plover (17 cm; 55 g), distinguished by **pale sandy gray upperparts**, white underparts, **short stubby black bill**, and yellow-orange legs. Black breast band on nonbreeding birds may be partial or absent, re-placed by pale brownish-gray patches on sides of upper breast. Breeding birds have single, narrow black breast band, usually broken; narrow black band across head bordered below by white forecrown; and orange bill with black tip. In flight, **white band across uppertail coverts** and **black spot** near tip of tail. Similar Snowy Plover smaller, with thinner, longer bill; grayish legs; Semipalmated Plover browner, with darker facial markings. Voice a clear, mellow whistled *peep* or *peep-lo*.

Wilson's Plover *Charadrius wilsonia*
Breeding Resident

Common along beaches, mudflats, and other coastal sites; especially along borders of salt ponds. Slightly larger than other banded plovers (18 cm; 55 g), with distinctive **heavy, black bill**. Breeding plumage grayish brown above, white below, with **single broad breast band**. Forecrown and supercilium white; legs dull pinkish. Breast band and forehead patch black in males, brown in females, nonbreeders, and immatures. Call an emphatic, raspy whistled *peet*, *quit*, or *wheet*. When flushed, high-pitched, hard *dik* or *kid* uttered. Gives grating or rattling notes, *jrrrrid-jrrrrid*, when agitated or during flight displays.

Snowy Plover *Charadrius nivosus*
Threatened Breeding Resident

Moderately common on beaches and lagoon borders with exten-sive saltflats. Very small (16 cm; 41 g), pale plover with **slender black bill**, dark neck marks do not meet to form collar. Legs black or dark grayish. Upperparts pale sandy gray, underparts white. In breeding plumage, note **black auricular patch** and black forehead bordered below by white forecrown and supercilium. Immatures lack black markings of adults. In flight, **tail and upper-tail coverts edged white**. See similar Piping, Semipalmated, and Wilson's plovers. Voice a weak, husky whistle, *ca-WEE*, and a low, slightly rough *quip* or *krut*. Breeding display song a repeated whistle, *tuEEoo*.

Killdeer

Semipalmated Plover

non-br

br

Piping Plover

non-br

br

♀

♂

Snowy Plover

Wilson's Plover

non-br

br

Whimbrel *Numenius phaeopus*
Passage Migrant; Nonbreeding Visitor

Uncommon spring and fall passage migrant and rare nonbreeding visitor in lowlands at ponds, swamps, and marshes, and along coastline. Unmistakable. Large, sturdy shorebird (42 cm; male 355 g, female 404 g) with *long, decurved bill*. Upperparts dark brown marked with pale buff; underparts pale buff, streaked dark brown on neck and breast; lower belly pale and mostly unmarked. Distinctly *dark crown has well-defined buff median stripe*. In flight, shows grayish brown and barred underwings. Flight call is a hard, rapid, tittering whistle, *pip-pip-pip-pip* or *kee-kee-kee-kee*.

Long-billed Curlew *Numenius americanus*
Vagrant

Typically occurs during nonbreeding season at tidal estuaries, wet pasture habitats, and sandy beaches. Large, long-legged shorebird (60 cm; 600 g) with *extremely long, decurved bill*. Body plumage rich buff throughout tinged with cinnamon; upperparts streaked and barred with dark brown. In flight, *underwing is contrasting cinnamon*; upper surface of flight feathers contrasting orange brown. *Large size, long, decurved bill, and buffy cinnamon color* distinguish this species from all other shorebirds on Hispaniola. Most common call is a clear whistled, rising *curluoo* or *coooLI,* given both in flight and on ground.

Hudsonian Godwit *Limosa haemastica*
Vagrant

Possible at grassy freshwater pond edges and mudflats during migratory periods. Large, dark-legged shorebird (39 cm; male 222 g, female 289 g), with long, *slightly upturned bill*, pinkish at base but dark at tip; *black underwing coverts*. Nonbreeders plain gray overall, paler below, with distinct white supercilium. Breeding birds have dark brown upperparts mottled with light spots, neck gray, underparts dark reddish brown with dark barring. Female paler below than male. Immatures resemble nonbreeding adults, but upperparts browner with scaly feather edgings. In flight, shows narrow white stripe on upperwing, white underwing stripe bordered by *blackish underwing coverts*; *tail black with white base*. See similar Marbled Godwit and Willet. Usually silent during migration, but may give high *god-wit* or *quik-quik*.

Marbled Godwit *Limosa fedoa*
Vagrant

Possible at mudflats and marshy areas during migratory periods. Large shorebird (45 cm; male 320 g, female 421 g) with long, bicolored, *slightly upturned bill*; long dark legs. Nonbreeding plumage tawny brown above, speckled and barred dark brown and black; underparts buffy and unmarked. Breeding plumage similar, except fine black breast streaks; barred underparts. In flight above, blackish primary wing coverts and plain rump; below, *cinnamon-colored underwing coverts* contrasting with paler flight feathers. Similar Hudsonian Godwit grayish overall with black-and-white tail; white wing stripe. Voice a nasal, laughing chatter, *ah-ha* or *ah-ahk* on nonbreeding grounds; a loud *god-wit* on breeding grounds.

Whimbrel

Long-billed Curlew

non-br

Hudsonian Godwit

non-br

br

non-br

Marbled Godwit

br

Red Knot *Calidris canutus*
Passage Migrant
Rare migrant in fall at sandy tidal flats; more common in spring. Stocky, medium-sized shorebird (24 cm; 135 g) with *short legs and neck*, and *medium-length straight bill*. Nonbreeding birds plain gray above, dingy white below, with indistinct dusky streaking on breast and flanks. Breeding birds dark gray above with buffy and rusty feather edgings and spots; *orangish-red face and underparts*. Immature resembles winter adult but note scaly pattern on back; buffy wash on breast. In all plumages, legs dull greenish. In flight shows pale gray underwing coverts; narrow, white wing stripe; *pale gray rump with fine barring*. Voice a soft, hoarse *chuh chuh*.

Buff-breasted Sandpiper *Calidris subruficollis*
Vagrant
Possible in fields, pastures, and areas with short grass during migratory periods. Medium-sized, ploverlike shorebird (18–20 cm; male 70 g, female 55 g) with slender build and *strong buff wash* on face and breast. Upperparts of adults have scaled appearance; underparts pale buffy with sides of neck and breast lightly spotted blackish. *Large, dark eye* stands out on clean buffy face; bill thin and black; *legs and feet yellow*; long wings extend beyond short tail at rest. In flight, shows *bright white underwing coverts*. Immatures similar to adults. Similar Baird's and Pectoral sandpipers have buffy breasts, but buff divided sharply from white belly. Legs black in Baird's Sandpiper. Call a quiet, trilled *preeet* or *greeet*; also short, soft *tick* and *chup* notes.

Short-billed Dowitcher *Limnodromus griseus*
Passage Migrant; Nonbreeding Visitor
Regularly occurring at coastal lagoons and mudflats, occasionally inland lake shores. Medium-sized (27 cm; 110 g), stocky shorebird with *long, straight bill*. Nonbreeding birds brownish gray above, paler below, with dark tail, white upper rump, and whitish supercilium.
In breeding plumage, upperparts reddish brown mottled black and buff; pale *reddish-brown head and breast blending to white belly*. Breast finely barred; flanks heavily barred. Immatures similar to breeding adults but more brownish; indistinctly marked below. In flight, all plumages show *white upper rump extending as V on back*. See very similar Long-billed Dowitcher. Best identified by flight call, a soft, rapid, whistled *tu-tu-tu*. Feeds in sediments with vertical thrusting of bill.

Long-billed Dowitcher *Limnodromus scolopaceus*
Vagrant
Possible primarily near shallow fresh and brackish water during migratory periods. Medium-sized (29 cm; 115 g), chunky shorebird with *long, straight bill*. Nonbreeding individuals dull gray above, paler below, with dark tail, white upper rump, whitish supercilium. In breeding plumage, reddish-brown upperparts mottled black and buff; *underparts uniformly reddish brown* with fine barring and spotting on breast; heavier barring on flanks. Immature resembles nonbreeding adult but darker on back. In flight, *white rump patch extends in V on back*. See very similar Short-billed Dowitcher. In nonbreeding Long-billed Dowitcher, face less streaked; gray breast tends to be darker, less streaked, and extends lower on belly. In breeding Long-billed Dowitcher, reddish underparts extend to lower belly. Flight call, a thin, high-pitched *keek* or *pweek*.

Wilson's Snipe *Gallinago delicata*
Passage Migrant; Nonbreeding Visitor
Regularly occurring in wet meadows, savannas, and water edges in coastal lowlands and the interior. Medium-sized (28 cm; 105 g), stocky sandpiper with an *extremely long, straight bill* and fairly short legs. Upperparts black and dark brown with *four bold, buffy*
stripes running down back. *Head also striped black and buff*. Underparts mostly white, with neck and breast streaked brown; flanks heavily barred. *Tail reddish brown*. Similar dowitchers are slimmer, lack striping on back, and have a distinct white V patch on rump and back. Voice a harsh, rasping *scaap* or *rrahk*, when flushed.

Red Knot

br

non-br

non-br

Buff-breasted Sandpiper

Short-billed Dowitcher

non-br

br

non-br

Long-billed Dowitcher

non-br

br

Wilson's Snipe

non-br

Lesser Yellowlegs *Tringa flavipes*
Passage Migrant; Nonbreeding Visitor

Regularly occurs at coastal lagoons and marshes, lowland lakes and ponds. Medium-sized (24 cm; 80 g), slender, long-necked, long-legged shorebird. Distinctive *orangish-yellow legs* and *thin, straight bill*. Winter plumage mottled gray brown above, white below; faint gray streaking on neck and breast. Breeding plumage darker, more heavily mottled above; heavy brownish streaking on throat and breast; flanks barred irregularly blackish. In flight, dark above with *white uppertail coverts*. Distinguished from similar Greater Yellowlegs by thinner, shorter bill (only slightly longer than head), and call. See also Solitary and Stilt sandpipers. Call single (usually) or double notes *tu* or *tu-tu*. Typically flocks; often seen with Greater Yellowlegs. Feeds actively, picking and jabbing; often runs through shallow water.

Willet *Tringa semipalmata*
Nonbreeding Visitor; Breeding Resident

Moderately common visitor along coast; regular but very local breeding resident. Large (37 cm; 265 g), stocky, light gray shorebird; *gray legs; long, thick bill*. Open wings display *bold black-and-white pattern*. Nonbreeding birds uniformly pale gray above, on throat and breast; belly and undertail coverts white. Breeding birds mottled grayish brown above, streaked and barred black on head, neck, and breast. In flight, *prominent white stripe on black flight feathers* and white rump are distinctive. Call a loud, ringing *kyaah yah* or *kyeh yeh-yeh*; also a persistent *keh-keh-keh*. Territorial song a clear, rolling *pill WILL WILLET*, given both on ground and in flight. The only nesting sandpiper on Hispaniola. Some authorities split Eastern Willet (*T. semipalmata*) and Western Willet (*T. inornata*), with the somewhat slimmer, browner, Eastern Willet appearing to have slightly shorter legs, neck and bill. Almost all Hispaniolan Willets appear to be *T. inornata*, but some passage migrants, and all breeding individuals, are thought to be *T. semipalmata*. Photodocumentation is needed to elucidate the status of these two subspecies on Hispaniola.

Greater Yellowlegs *Tringa melanoleuca*
Passage Migrant; Nonbreeding Visitor

Common migrant and regular visitor to coastal mudflats and lagoons; occasionally inland waters. Fairly large shorebird (31 cm; 171 g) with *long, slightly upturned bill*; *long orangish-yellow legs*. In nonbreeding plumage, gray to grayish-brown upperparts with pale spots; underparts pale with faint streaking on throat and chest. Breeding plumage darker above, more conspicuously spotted; underparts heavily streaked; dark bars on flanks. In flight, dark above, lacking wingbars, but *white uppertail coverts*. Similar to more common Lesser Yellowlegs; Greater Yellowlegs has relatively longer, thicker bill, appearing slightly upturned and two-toned, with paler base. Voice a loud, ringing whistle of 3–4 notes, *tew tew tew* or *klee-klee-cu*. Forages actively, often running after prey. Bobs head and body emphatically when alarmed.

Lesser Yellowlegs

Willet

non-br

br

Greater Yellowlegs

Stilt Sandpiper *Calidris himantopus*
Passage Migrant; Nonbreeding Visitor

Moderately common at coastal lagoons and mudflats, also interior ponds and rice-growing areas; less frequent in spring. Medium-sized sandpiper (22 cm; male 54 g, female 61 g) with relatively *long, greenish legs*; *long bill droops slightly at tip*. In all plumages, shows **whitish supercilium**. Nonbreeding birds pale brownish gray above, whitish below; light streaking on neck and upper breast. Breeding birds dark brown above, edged whitish to pale rusty; underparts whitish, heavily barred. **Auricular reddish brown**. Juvenile resembles breeding adult but unbarred below; lacks rusty auriculars. In flight, **white rump and whitish tail**. See similar Greater and Lesser yellowlegs, Solitary Sandpiper and dowitchers. Voice a low, muffled *jeew* or *toof*. Often forages in belly-deep water, rapidly probing with head submerged and **tail tilted up**.

Dunlin *Calidris alpina*
Vagrant

Possible at borders of still water, particularly mudflats along coast; most likely during migration. Medium-sized, stocky sandpiper (19 cm; 55 g) identified in all plumages by relatively long, heavy bill with **drooping tip**; short-necked, hunched appearance; black legs. Nonbreeding birds have dull brownish-gray back with **pale brownish wash on breast** and head; rest of underparts white. Breeding birds have **reddish-brown back** and cap; whitish underparts with fine streaking on breast; **black belly patch**. In flight, note white wing stripe; white rump divided by black bar. Similar Red Knot is larger with short, straight bill. Flight call a raspy, rolled *tzeep* or *jeeep*.

Pectoral Sandpiper *Calidris melanotos*
Passage Migrant

Uncommon; typically found on mudflats of fresh or brackish water bodies, in agricultural areas and savannas. Medium-sized sandpiper (22 cm; male 95 g, female 56 g) with yellowish-green legs and a **sharp demarcation** between heavily streaked, brownish breast and white belly. Nonbreeding birds have gray-brown upperparts, head, and breast. Breeding plumage more mottled brown above, with breast more heavily streaked with black. In flight, sharp breast demarcation is evident; also note fine white wing stripe, and white rump divided by black bar. Voice a low, reedy *trrip* or *brrrp*.

Spotted Sandpiper *Actitis macularius*
Passage Migrant; Nonbreeding Visitor

Common in coastal lowlands but also regularly at edges of water bodies of interior; not generally found on mudflats. Fairly small (18–20 cm; 40–50 g), short-necked sandpiper with near-constant, **exaggerated rocking motion**. Nonbreeding birds plain grayish brown above, white below, with gray extending from neck onto breast resulting in **white "finger" on shoulder**. Legs greenish; bill dusky to fleshy. Breeding birds have upperparts with indistinct black spotting and barring, white underparts with **bold black spotting**, and black-tipped orange bill. In flight, shows short, white wing stripe. Flies low over water with **shallow, stiff, rapid wingbeats**. Flight call a high, whistled *weet-weet* or descending *peet-weet-weet-weet*.

Solitary Sandpiper *Tringa solitaria*
Passage Migrant; Nonbreeding Visitor

Regularly occurring singly at freshwater lakes, ponds, and river-banks. Slender (19–23 cm; 48 g), dark sandpiper with conspicuous **white eye-ring**. Nonbreeding plumage olive brown above, finely **spotted with white**. Head, neck, and chest grayish, faintly streaked white; rest of underparts white. Breeding plumage darker above with pronounced white spotting; head, throat, and breast with heavy, dark streaking. **Legs olive green**; bill thin, straight, medium length. In flight, **entirely dark above**, **barred white outer tail feathers**. See similar Lesser Yellowlegs and Spotted Sandpiper. Voice a clear, rising series of whistles when alarmed, *peet-weet-weet*. Also soft *pip* or *weet* when undisturbed. Frequently bobs and teeters. Flicking, erratic wingbeats distinctive; when landing, often holds wings straight up, then slowly closes them.

Stilt Sandpiper

non-br

br

non-br

Dunlin

non-br

br

non-br

Pectoral Sandpiper

non-br

br

non-br

Spotted Sandpiper

non-br

br

non-br

non-br

br

Solitary Sandpiper

non-br

Baird's Sandpiper *Calidris bairdii*
Vagrant
Possible around dry, upper edges of inland wetland habitats during migratory periods. Broad-breasted, short-legged sandpiper (16 cm; 40 g) with short, straight, black bill; *very long wings* extend beyond tail at rest. In nonbreeding plumage, gray brown above, scaled with reddish-brown tints and pale feather edges. *Breast buffy, finely streaked brown*; belly white. Breeding birds and immatures similar but brighter. In flight, note long wings and indistinct white wing stripe. White rump divided by *dark central stripe*. Voice a hoarse, somewhat trilled *krreep*. Picks for its invertebrate food rather than probes.

Least Sandpiper *Calidris minutilla*
Passage Migrant; Nonbreeding Visitor

Common migrant regularly occurring at drier margins of mudflats, lagoons, ponds, and lakes. World's smallest shorebird (14 cm; 22 g); generally *dark brown upperparts*; *finely, but heavily, streaked breast*; *yellowish-green legs*; short, thin *bill droops slightly at tip*. Nonbreeding birds mottled grayish brown above and on breast; belly white. Breeding plumage is darker brown, more heavily mottled with reddish brown. In flight, dark above with faint wing stripe. See similar Western and Semipalmated sandpipers, which have blackish legs. Typical call a high, reedy trill, *brreep*; also thin, twittering in flocks.

White-rumped Sandpiper *Calidris fuscicollis*
Passage Migrant
Uncommon at mudflats and borders of still water, principally along coast. Medium-sized sandpiper (17 cm; 42 g) with *long wings* and *white rump*. Bill short and straight; pale, reddish base of lower mandible sometimes visible. Wing tips extend beyond tail at rest. In nonbreeding plumage, brownish gray above and on upper breast; underparts whitish. Breeding birds browner, with reddish-brown tints on crown, upper back, and auriculars; streaking heavier and more extensive on breast and sides. Immature resembles breeding adult. In all plumages, shows *whitish supercilium*, thickest behind eye. In flight, white rump distinctive. Voice a high, thin squeak, *peet* or *jeet*. Also gives high-pitched twitter in flocks.

Semipalmated Sandpiper *Calidris pusilla*
Passage Migrant; Nonbreeding Visitor

Abundant; found at coastal lagoons, mudflats, and beaches. In all plumages, identified by *small size* (14 cm; 31 g), *black legs*, and *straight black bill*. In nonbreeding plumage, grayish brown above, whitish below with diffuse streaking on chest; whitish supercilium. Breeding birds reddish brown above with buffy feather edgings; breast heavily streaked brown. Immature more scaled, less rusty above; dingy wash on breast. In flight, narrow white wing stripe; black center of rump and tail. See similar Western, White-rumped, and Least sandpipers. Voice a sharp, husky *chrit* or *chert*. Generally pecks faster than other sandpipers.

Western Sandpiper *Calidris mauri*
Passage Migrant; Nonbreeding Visitor

Uncommon but regular on coastal mudflats and beaches, occasionally at inland saline lakes. Small sandpiper (15 cm; 26 g). Bill black, relatively long and *heavy at base*; *narrower and drooping at tip*. Nonbreeding plumage brownish gray above, whitish below, with finely streaked breast band. Breeding plumage, brownish mottled black above; reddish-brown crown, auriculars, and upper scapulars; upper breast more heavily streaked. Immature similar to breeding adult, but chest finely streaked and washed buffy. In flight, shows narrow white wing stripe; rump and center of tail black; white outer tail feathers. Very similar to Semipalmated Sandpiper but note especially differences in bill. Call a high, thin *kreep* or *cheet*. Generally feeds in deeper water than Semipalmated Sandpiper; probes more methodically.

Baird's Sandpiper

br

Least Sandpiper

non-br

non-br

White-rumped Sandpiper

non-br

br

non-br

non-br

br

non-br

Semipalmated Sandpiper

br

non-br

Western Sandpiper

Ruddy Turnstone *Arenaria interpres*
Passage Migrant; Nonbreeding Visitor

Common migrant and nonbreeding visitor at coastal lagoons, mudflats, beaches. Unmistakable. Medium-sized (23 cm; 115 g), stocky shorebird with short, *orange legs* and short, wedge-shaped, *slightly upturned, black bill*. Nonbreeding adults mottled grayish brown and blackish above; head brownish with smudgy black-and-white markings; broad, brownish breast band; belly white. Breeding birds *reddish brown above* with blackish patches; striking *black-and-white facial markings*. Distinctive *white markings on upperwings, back, and tail in flight*. Flight call a low, guttural rattle, *ki-ti-tuk*, increasing in volume; also single, sharp *kek*. Typically forms looser flocks than other sandpipers. Uses bill to overturn small stones, shells, and piles of seaweed in search of invertebrate prey.

Sanderling *Calidris alba*
Passage Migrant; Nonbreeding Visitor

Moderately common at coastal lagoons, mudflats, beaches; rarely at inland saline lakes. Small, plump, active shorebird (19 cm; 57 g) with short, stout bill. *Very pale* nonbreeding plumage with light gray upperparts, *snow-white underparts*, white face. Often shows *black mark on bend of folded wing*. Bill, legs, and feet black. In breeding plumage, head, neck, and breast reddish brown; back brown mottled black and rufous; belly and undertail coverts white. Immature resembles winter adult, but upperparts blackish, spangled with white and buff. In flight, shows black leading edge of wing bordered by *bold white wing stripe above*; underwing white. Similar nonbreeding Red Knot is larger, stockier, darker, and lacks black shoulder patch. Voice a sharp *kwit* or *klip*. Often seen in small flocks running rapidly before advancing and retreating waves.

Wilson's Phalarope *Phalaropus tricolor*
Vagrant

Possible in shallow saline ponds and lagoons during nonbreeding season. Small, slender sandpiper (23 cm; male 52 g, female 68 g) with *needlelike bill*. Adult nonbreeding plumage pale gray above with *white rump*; thin gray mark through eye; white underparts. Breeding female blue-gray above with *two chestnut Vs on back*; brownish-gray wings. Black face blends to reddish-brown band along sides of neck; nape white. Underparts white; throat washed buffy chestnut. Breeding male similar but less contrasting. Immature resembles nonbreeding adult but browner above; buffy wash on breast. In flight, all birds show *white rump, gray wings*. See similar Red-necked Phalarope. Mostly silent. Like other phalaropes, spins in water, stirring up food.

Red-necked Phalarope *Phalaropus lobatus*
Vagrant

Possible in shallow saline ponds and lagoons during nonbreeding season. Small, delicate sandpiper (19 cm; 29 g) with *very thin, straight black bill*. Nonbreeding adults have gray upperparts streaked white on mantle, blackish cap above white forecrown, and *black patch through eye*. Breeding female brighter, with black cap, dark back with *two buffy white Vs*, *reddish-brown sides of neck and lower throat*, and white throat. Rest of underparts whitish with grayish breast. Male duller; immature duller still. In flight, shows *white wing stripe* and *whitish stripes on back*. See similar Wilson's Phalarope. Like other phalaropes, often seen spinning in water to stir up food.

Ruddy Turnstone

non-br

br

non-br

Sanderling

non-br

br

non-br

Wilson's Phalarope

non-br

br ♀

non-br

non-br

Red-necked Phalarope

br ♀

non-br

Pomarine Jaeger *Stercorarius pomarinus*
Passage Migrant; Nonbreeding Visitor

Regularly occurring, but often far offshore. The largest jaeger (49 cm; male 648 g, female 740 g), powerful and heavy-bodied, with *conspicuous white base to primaries*. Adults have *elongated, spoonlike, twisted central tail feathers*. Two variable color phases. Light-phase birds: blackish cap extending on face below bill, yellowish wash on nape and sides of neck, *broad, dark band across breast*. Dark-phase birds: less common; entirely dark. Subadult and juvenile plumages heavily barred below, especially along sides and under wings; central tail feathers not elongated. Similar Parasitic Jaeger smaller, lacks heavy barring on sides; flight more buoyant. Long-tailed Jaeger smallest, most slender; adults have very long, pointed tail feathers, no breast band. Generally silent. Occasionally seen close to land harassing gulls and terns in dramatic twisting, acrobatic pursuit.

Parasitic Jaeger *Stercorarius parasiticus*
Passage Migrant; Nonbreeding Visitor

Regularly occurring, but often far offshore. Medium-sized jaeger (56 cm; male 400 g, female 485 g) with elongated, *sharply pointed central tail feathers*; white patches at base of primaries in flight. Light-phase adults: dark brownish gray above with *grayish-brown cap*; white forecrown; yellowish wash on nape and sides of neck. Underparts whitish with *partial to complete pale brown band across upper breast*; lower belly gray. Dark-phase adults: dark brown overall, slightly paler below. Subadults and juveniles finely barred dusky below; central tail feathers may protrude slightly. See similar Pomarine and Long-tailed jaegers. Generally silent. Occasionally seen close to land harassing gulls and terns in prolonged, twisting pursuit.

Long-tailed Jaeger *Stercorarius longicaudus*
Vagrant

Rarely seen; more likely far offshore. Most delicate jaeger (54 cm; male 280 g, female 310 g). Adults have *very elongated, pointed central tail feathers*; white wing flash in flight less noticeable than other jaegers. Adults have *blackish cap*, white collar; most upperparts pale grayish brown contrasting with darker primaries; underparts white, unmarked, fading to gray on lower belly; underwings uniformly dark. Juveniles occur in light, intermediate, and dark phases. Light phase: finely barred below; fine white barring on back; sometimes with pale head and nape. Dark phase: grayish brown with darker cap; slightly paler below. See similar Parasitic and Pomarine jaegers. Juvenile and subadult Long-tailed Jaegers without long tail feathers cannot be distinguished reliably by any single trait. Generally silent.

light phase

dark phase

Pomarine Jaeger

Parasitic Jaeger

subadult & juv

light phase

dark phase

subadult & juv

subadult & juv

Long-tailed Jaeger

Ring-billed Gull *Larus delawarensis*
Nonbreeding Visitor

Uncommon but regular in harbors, lagoons, and fields. Medium-sized (49 cm; male 550 g, female 470 g). First-year birds: gray back, mottled grayish-brown wings, ***broad black subterminal band on tail***. Head streaked brownish. ***Bill pinkish with black tip***. Second-year birds: mantle and upperwing coverts mostly gray, black primaries tipped white. Tail mottled gray forming a partial band with white base. Head and nape flecked brown. Bill greenish with black band at tip. Nonbreeding adults: similar but ***yellowish bill with black band, yellowish-green legs***. Breeding adults: similar to nonbreeding adults, but white head and nape unspotted. Juveniles: brownish gray overall with black bill and pinkish legs. Compare with similar but larger and stockier Herring Gull. Numerous hoarse, wheezy calls, including a series of *kreeeee*, *kow*, or *kah* notes.

Herring Gull *Larus argentatus*
Nonbreeding Visitor

Uncommon in coastal areas, harbors, lagoons. Large (59 cm; male 1,200 g, female 1,000 g), variably plumaged gull with ***heavy bill***. First-year: back and wings mottled grayish brown; underparts lightly streaked pale brown; pinkish bill black at tip; tail with broad dark terminal band. Second-year: similar to first-year but variable amounts of gray on back and wings, outer primaries black, bill pinkish with pale gray band. Third-year: white tail with broad black band; yellowish bill with dark band. Nonbreeding adults: head and underparts white, head and nape flecked pale brown, mantle pale gray, ***outer primaries black with white spots***. ***Legs pink***. Bill yellow with red spot near tip of lower mandible. Breeding adult: similar to nonbreeding adult, but head and nape clean white. See similar Ring-billed Gull. Call a clear, flat bugling, often with paired syllables; also yelping *kyow* or *klaaw* notes.

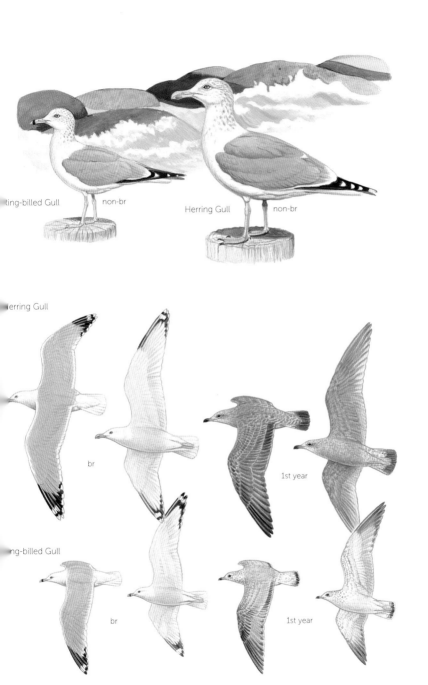

Ring-billed Gull   non-br

Herring Gull   non-br

Herring Gull

br

1st year

Ring-billed Gull

br

1st year

Great Black-backed Gull *Larus marinus*
Nonbreeding Visitor

Uncommon at coastal areas where other gulls congregate. Largest and heaviest gull (75 cm; male 1,800 g, female 1,490 g) on Hispaniola. Identified in all plumages by *large size* and *massive head and bill*. First-year: mottled grayish brown above and below; head white with pale flecks on nape; bill black; tail with broad dark terminal band; rump whitish. Second-year: pinkish bill with large black band near tip, white rump, grayish mantle with black blotches. Third-year: slaty mantle, paler upperwing coverts, yellowish bill with narrow black tip. Nonbreeding adults: *black mantle*, pale flecks on head, bright yellow bill with small red spot near tip of lower mandible, *pink legs*. Breeding adult: similar to nonbreeding adult, but head entirely white. See similar Herring and Lesser Black-backed gulls. Voice a deep, hoarse trumpeting, lower than Herring Gull.

Lesser Black-backed Gull *Larus fuscus*
Nonbreeding Visitor

Rare, but increasingly regular. Found at coastal areas where other gulls congregate. Large but slender gull (55 cm; 800 g) with *relatively long and narrow wings*. First-year: mottled brownish gray overall, with paler head, streaked underparts. Bill black. In flight, dark primaries, *broad tail band, pale rump*. Second-year: *dark gray (not black) back*, broad black tail band, white rump, and brownish-gray wings with no white spots at tips. Bill pinkish with large black band near tip. Third-year: *dark gray mantle* and upperwing coverts, yellowish bill with black band around tip. Nonbreeding adults: *dark grayish-black mantle*, *pale yellow legs*, mottled brown head and neck, yellow bill with red spot near tip. Breeding adult similar to nonbreeding adult, but head and neck mostly white. See similar Great Black-backed and Herring gulls. Calls variable; guttural; deeper and more nasal than Herring Gull.

Great Black-backed Gull

2nd year

Lesser Black-backed Gull

2nd year

non-br

non-br

Great Black-backed Gull

br

1st year

br

1st year

Lesser Black-backed Gull

Black-legged Kittiwake *Rissa tridactyla*
Vagrant

Rarely seen, but may be more common far offshore during nonbreeding season. Medium-sized gull (40 cm; 400 g) with *pearly gray mantle and wings* in all plumages. First-year birds: white head with black ear spot; *horizontal black bar forming collar at base of nape*; black bill; narrow black terminal tail band. In flight, gray upperparts with bold *dark M from wing tip to wing tip*. Nonbreeding adults: yellow bill, white head, dull black mark behind eye; nape washed gray. Mantle gray; *wings tipped black with no white*. Breeding adult similar to nonbreeding adult, but head entirely white. Similar immature Bonaparte's Gull lacks black half-collar of first-year birds. Generally silent away from breeding grounds.

Bonaparte's Gull *Chroicocephalus philadelphia*
Vagrant

Possible in coastal areas, harbors, lagoons, and at sea during nonbreeding season. Small (28 cm; 210 g), graceful gull with slender black bill; pink legs. First-year birds: mostly pale gray mantle and nape, *black terminal tail band*, white head and underparts. Note *black ear spot*, black primaries and *narrow, dark M across upperwings* in flight. Undersides of primaries whitish. Nonbreeding adults: similar to immatures, but mantle entirely pale gray; tail and outer primaries white. Breeding adult: similar to nonbreeding adult, but *head black*; *white crescents above and below eye*; legs orange red. Similar adult Laughing Gull has dark mantle and black primaries, whereas first-year birds have broader tail band and darker underwing coverts. See also Black-legged Kittiwake. Voice mostly buzzy, grating *keh* or *kaa-aa* notes, singly or in descending series.

Laughing Gull *Leucophaeus atricilla*
Breeding Resident; Nonbreeding Visitor

Most common gull on Hispaniola. Moderately common at calm bays; regular at interior lakes in coastal lowlands. Medium-sized (43 cm; male 325 g, female 290 g), black-hooded gull. Breeding adults: note *black head* with *narrow white eye-ring*,
white collar, *dark gray mantle blends into black wing tips*, bold white trailing edge to wing. Underparts and tail white; bill and legs reddish. Nonbreeding adults: mostly white head with *diffuse gray mark* around and behind eye; bill and legs black. First-year birds: gray mantle; upperwings mottled gray and brown. Sides gray. *Rump white*, contrasting with broad, black tail band. Partial hood and slaty mantle may show in some individuals. Juvenile: dull brown upperparts and white rump. See similar Bonaparte's Gull and Franklin's Gull. Voice a nasal, laughing *ka-ka-ka-ka-kaa-kaa-kaaa-kaaaa*.

Franklin's Gull *Leucophaeus pipixcan*
Vagrant

Possible at bays and estuaries during nonbreeding season. Small gull (34 cm; 280 g) with dark gray mantle and black hood in breeding plumage; wing tips with *black bar bordered by white on both sides*; bill and legs reddish. Nonbreeding plumage similar, but *black hood only partial* and forecrown whitish. First-year individuals show *incomplete black tail band*, white underparts, gray back (washed brown; extends onto nape in juveniles), *partial blackish hood with white nape*, and white forecrown. Similar to Laughing Gull in all plumages, but Franklin's Gull is smaller with a *shorter, slightly stouter bill*. Voice a nasal, laughing *kuk-kuk-kuk-kuk* or *kah* followed by long *keeaaahh*; also commonly gives short, hollow *keeah* or *kowii* notes.

Black-legged Kittiwake

non-br

br

1st year

Bonaparte's Gull

non-br

br

1st year

Laughing Gull

juv

br

1st year

non-br

Franklin's Gull

non-br

Brown Noddy *Anous stolidus*
Breeding Visitor

Common near coastline during breeding season; otherwise remains far offshore. Medium-sized (42 cm; 180 g) ternlike seabird. Adult entirely dark brown except **silvery-white forecrown and crown** fading to gray brown on nape. Tail dark brown and **wedge-shaped**, with shorter interior tail feathers giving a unique "**double-rounded**" appearance. Bill and legs black. Immature similar to adult, but only forecrown is white; upperwing coverts often paler. Stiff, strong wingbeats during flight. Voice a low, grating *brraak*.

Sooty Tern *Onychoprion fuscatus*
Breeding Visitor

Common near entire coastline; otherwise remains far offshore. Medium-sized (40 cm; 200 g), dark tern. Adult blackish above, white below, with **white forecrown extending just to eye**. In flight, underwing shows dark primaries contrasting with white coverts; **tail deeply forked** and mostly black with **narrow, white outer margins**. Immature dark brown overall with whitish spots on mantle and wings; tail less deeply forked than adult's; undertail coverts and underwing coverts whitish. Similar Bridled Tern grayer above; white on forecrown extends behind eye; white nape and more extensive white in outer tail. Call note a nasal, plaintive *wide-a-wake* or *wacky-wack*, often given at night. Highly aerial, rarely alighting on water. Captures prey primarily by dipping, and occasional shallow dives.

Bridled Tern *Onychoprion anaethetus*
Breeding Visitor

Easily seen at offshore breeding islets, otherwise uncommonly observed from boats at sea. Medium-sized (31 cm; 130 g), strictly marine tern. Breeding adults dark grayish brown above, white below; black cap; **white V-shaped patch across forecrown extends above and beyond eye; white collar on nape**. Tail deeply forked with **narrow gray median stripe**; **extensive white on outer feathers**. Bill and legs black. Nonbreeding adults similar but paler with black cap streaked white. Immature similar to nonbreeding adult, but upperparts scaled pale gray; head markings paler. Similar Sooty Tern blacker above, lacks white nape; white on forecrown does not extend behind eye. Voice a puppy-like barking *yep* or *wup*, a whining *yerk*, also a continuous *ah-ah-ah*. Typically feeds by hovering and picking from the ocean surface.

Black Tern *Chlidonias niger*
Passage Migrant

Uncommon; primarily frequents marine waters, lagoons, and lowland lakes. Unmistakable, small (25 cm; 65 g), dark tern. Nonbreeding adult gray above. Forecrown, nape, and underparts white except for smudgy dark patches at sides of breast; **prominent dark patch behind eye and on hindcrown**. Breeding adult has **black head, breast, and belly**; white vent and undertail coverts. In all plumages, underwings gray, bill black, **tail only slightly forked**. Immature similar to adult, but upperparts washed brownish; sides washed grayish. Flight buoyant and slightly erratic; bird darts, flits, dips, and hovers over water surface. Frequently forages in flocks. Voice a harsh, sharp *kip* or *kek*, higher than similar Black-necked Stilt.

Black Skimmer *Rynchops niger*
Vagrant

Possible in calm coastal waters, harbors, and lagoons. Unmistakable coastal waterbird (45 cm; male 355 g, female 260 g). Adult solid blackish above, white below, with unique **scissorlike black and orange bill**; lower mandible extends 2–3 cm beyond upper. Immatures similar but upperparts mottled blackish brown. Voice a soft, nasal, doglike barking, *yep, yep*, given singly or in series. Graceful, buoyant flier on long wings, with **head always held below the level of tail**. Skimmers forage with longer lower mandible slicing through water surface. Often forages at night.

Brown Noddy

imm

Sooty Tern

imm

juv Sooty Tern

Bridled Tern

imm

non-br

Black Tern

Black Skimmer

Caspian Tern *Hydroprogne caspia*
Passage Migrant; Nonbreeding Visitor

Uncommon but regularly occurring at coastal lagoons, and fresh and saline lakes in lowlands. Largest tern (50 cm; 655 g), heavy-bodied and gull-like. Mostly white with pale gray upperparts; black crest; ***massive, dark red bill with dusky tip***; ***dark gray undersides to outer primaries***. Tail only slightly forked; legs black. Breeding adult has ***entirely black crest***; nonbreeding adult has ***black crest flecked white***. Wingbeats stiff and shallow. Similar Royal Tern distinguished by smaller size, bright orange-red bill, pale underside to primaries, and in nonbreeding plumage, white forecrown. Call a hoarse, low bark, *rau* or *kraau*, and other rasping or grating notes.

Roseate Tern *Sterna dougallii*
Threatened Passage Migrant; Breeding Visitor

Uncommon but regular only along coast; breeds locally in small numbers. Medium-sized (37 cm; 110 g), pale tern with ***long, deeply forked tail*** projecting well beyond wing tips at rest. Mantle pale gray; cap black; primaries pale gray with underwings pure white and translucent. Breeding adult has ***thin, black bill*** with some red at base. Legs dark red. Pinkish flush on breast difficult to see. Nonbreeding adult has blackish bill; white forehead extends to above eye. Immature birds have dark forehead and crown, blackish bill and legs, mottled back, shoulders with indistinct markings. Similar adult Common Terns have darker gray mantle; primaries blackish on underside. Immature Common Tern has distinct black shoulder mark. Nonbreeding Forster's Tern has black patch behind eye. Voice a raspy, sharp, high-pitched *krek* and soft, two-syllabled *tu-ick* or *chi-vik*; alarm a high, clear *keer*.

Forster's Tern *Sterna forsteri*
Vagrant

Possible at coastal areas, harbors, and lagoons during migration and the nonbreeding season. Mostly ***immaculate white tern*** (34 cm; 160 g) with ***deeply forked tail***; broader wings and thicker bill than similar species. Flight less buoyant and graceful, with shallower, stronger wingbeats. Nonbreeding adult shows ***silvery-white primaries***; ***black mask*** through eye and across auriculars not extending to nape or hindcrown. Bill black. Breeding adult white with pale gray wings and mantle; cap black. White rump does not contrast sharply with gray of back. Bill orange with black tip. Immature similar to nonbreeding adult but tail shorter; generally darker primaries. Forster's Tern whiter than similar Common Tern, which also has broader dark wing tips. Roseate Tern has pure white underwings, more deeply forked tail. Voice similar to Common Tern, but a lower, more raspy, one-syllable descending *kerrr*.

Royal Tern *Thalasseus maximus*
Breeding Resident; Nonbreeding Visitor

Fairly common at coastal lagoons, beaches, and harbors; regular at lowland lakes; less common as a breeder. Large tern (48 cm; 400 g), pale gray above, white below, with a ***bright orange-red bill*** and a ***black cap across top and back of head*** with elongated feathers forming a shaggy crest. Legs black; tail moderately forked. Breeding adults have entirely black crown. Nonbreeding adults and immatures have black crown streaked with white, ***white forecrown and lores***, and paler bill. Similar Caspian Tern is slightly larger, has dark red bill with dusky tip, and more extensive blackish on underside of primaries. Voice a harsh, high-pitched *krit-krit* and throaty, rolling *keer-reet*.

Caspian Tern

non-br

Roseate Tern

non-br

imm

Forster's Tern

non-br

non-br

Royal Tern

non-br & imm

Least Tern *Sternula antillarum*
Passage Migrant; Breeding Visitor

Regularly present at favored coastal areas, harbors, and lagoons along the coast. Unmistakable due to *small size* (22 cm; 48 g). Breeding adult distinguished by light gray mantle with white underparts, black crown contrasting with V-shaped white forecrown, pale yellow bill with black tip, *yellow legs*. In flight, white wings contrast with *black outer two primaries forming a long wedge*; tail short and moderately forked. Nonbreeding adult shows less sharply defined head pattern; bill blackish. Immatures have black bill and eye-stripe; back and hindcrown whitish flecked grayish brown; dark outer primaries and bar on shoulder form distinctive M on upperwing. Voice a shrill, chattering *kip* or *ki-dik* and a high-pitched, rising *zreeep* alarm call.

Gull-billed Tern *Gelochelidon nilotica*
Passage Migrant; Breeding Visitor

Uncommon at coastal lagoons and beaches, and both fresh and saline lakes in lowlands. Stocky, gull-like tern (36 cm; 170 g) with *proportionately short and heavy black bill*, broader and longer wings than other terns, and *very shallow tail fork*. Legs relatively long and black. Breeding adult pale gray above with clean white body; black crown and nape. Nonbreeding adult has whitish crown with pale gray flecks; distinct gray smudge behind eye. Immature birds have back and scapulars mottled grayish brown; bill brownish. Stout black bill separates this tern from others except more lightly built Sandwich Tern, which also has longer, deeply forked tail. Voice a raspy 3-syllabled *za-za-za* or 2-syllabled, nasal *kay-wek, kay-wek*.

Common Tern *Sterna hirundo*
Passage Migrant; Nonbreeding Visitor

Regularly occurs along coast, in harbors and lagoons. Medium-sized (36 cm; 120 g), "typical" tern, light gray above, paler gray below. Breeding adult distinguished by black cap, orange-red bill with black tip, red legs. Leading and trailing edges of *outer primaries black, forming dark wedge* in flight. Tail moderately forked. Nonbreeding adult shows blackish bill, *shoulders with dark bars*, black hindcrown and nape, white forecrown. Immature birds have similar head pattern and bill; mantle, rump, and uppertail coverts gray mottled light brownish; primaries and shoulders dark. See similar immature Roseate Tern and nonbreeding Forster's Tern. Voice a harsh *kee-arr-r*, dropping in pitch. Also single, sharp *kip*.

Sandwich Tern *Thalasseus sandvicensis*
Breeding Resident; Nonbreeding Visitor

Uncommon breeding resident and regular nonbreeding visitor at coastal lagoons, beaches, and saline lakes. Relatively large, crested tern (37 cm; 200 g). Breeding adult has very pale gray upperparts, with *shaggy black crest*, and long, slender *black bill with yellow tip*. Tail moderately forked; does not extend beyond wings at rest. Legs black. Nonbreeding plumage similar to breeding plumage, but forecrown white to behind eye; cap often flecked white. Immature like adult, but back, rump, scapulars, and uppertail coverts pale gray mottled with brown or gray. See similar Gull-billed Tern. Cayenne Tern (*T. s. eurygnathus*), a subspecies sometimes considered a separate species, has dull yellow bill; occasionally recorded on Hispaniola. Voice a metallic, abrupt, grating *kirrik* or *kerr-ick*.

Least Tern

non-br

Gull-billed Tern

non-br

Common Tern

imm

non-br

Sandwich Tern

yellow-billed form

non-br

White-tailed Tropicbird *Phaethon lepturus*
Resident

Widespread, fairly common; observed along coastline and in offshore waters. Very local breeder at coastal cliffs. Medium-sized (70 cm; 365 g), ternlike, highly aerial seabird. Adult white with narrow black patch through eyes, ***long tail feathers***, ***heavy diagonal black bar on upperwing coverts***, and black on outermost primaries. Bill orange to red orange. Immature ***coarsely barred black and white above***, with short central tail feathers; bill yellowish, sometimes ringed black near tip. Immature differs from similar immature Red-billed Tropicbird in having coarser black barring on upperparts and lacking black band across nape. Voice a raspy *crik-et* or *clik-et*. Best observed flying near vertical sea cliffs used to breed. Landing on cliffs is often difficult, so several hovering passes sometimes required.

Red-billed Tropicbird *Phaethon aethereus*
Vagrant

Possible along coastline and in offshore waters. Large (98 cm; 750 g), striking, mostly white seabird. Adult white overall with ***fine black barring on back***, black eye-line, conspicuously black wing tips, ***long tail plumes***, and red bill. Immature lacks long tail plumes; bill yellowish ringed with black near tip; ***black band extends from eyes across nape***; back barred with black. Similar immature White-tailed Tropicbird more coarsely barred on back; black eye-line does not meet across nape. Voice a shrill, grating *keé-arrr*.

Black-capped Petrel *Pterodroma hasitata*
Critically Endangered Breeding Resident

Rare in offshore waters and near nesting colonies at remote inland cliffs. Large (38 cm; 280 g) petrel; upperparts black with variable ***white patches on rump, nape, and forecrown***. Underparts mostly white; leading and trailing edges of wings black; distinctive ***black bar on underwing***. In flight, ***tail pointed***; wings relatively long and pointed. Dark morph has less extensive white on crown, collar, uppertail coverts, and rump, and a more developed breast band. Distinguished from similar Great Shearwater by whiter upperparts, especially on forecrown and rump; blacker mantle heightens contrast with more extensive white markings. In flight, wrist more bent, flight more erratic with faster wingbeats and high, arching glides. Calls heard at night around nest include drawn-out, eerie, wailing *aaa-aw*, *eek*, and yelps. From October to June arrives in darkness at breeding cliffs in Massif de la Selle, Massif de la Hotte, western Sierra de Bahoruco, and at Valle Nuevo in the Cordillera Central.

Great Shearwater *Ardenna gravis*
Vagrant

Occurs most often far offshore. Large shearwater (48 cm; 840 g), grayish-brown upperparts, mostly light below, but underwings with considerable dark markings. Note distinctive ***black cap***, ***white collar***, and narrow ***white band on rump***. Generally similar to Black-capped Petrel but larger; white of upperparts much reduced on nape and rump and absent from forecrown. Black-capped Petrel's mantle is blacker, heightening the contrast with whiter upperparts. Great Shearwater's wingbeats much slower than those of Manx and Audubon's shearwaters or Black-capped Petrel. This shearwater nests in the southern Atlantic, November—April, then makes a circular migration of the Atlantic in the nonbreeding season. Usually silent at sea.

White-tailed Tropicbird

Red-billed Tropicbird

imm

Black-capped Petrel

typical above

darker, atypical

typical below

Great Shearwater

Wilson's Storm-Petrel *Oceanites oceanicus*
Nonbreeding Visitor

Generally a rare nonbreeding visitor to offshore waters. Small (18 cm; 34 g), dark brownish-black seabird with conspicuous **white rump merging with white patch of lower flanks**. **Tail short and squared**; legs long with **feet projecting beyond tail** in flight. Distinguished from similar Leach's Storm-Petrel by rump pattern; and by having blacker, shorter, broader, more rounded wings; less angled wrists; and more direct flight with briefer glides, reminiscent of a swallow. At close range, voice consists of soft peeping when birds are feeding.

Leach's Storm-Petrel *Hydrobates leucorhous*
Vagrant

Transient visitor to offshore waters. Small (20 cm; 35 g) brownish-black seabird with **notched tail** and **pale brown vertical bar on wings**. **White rump often bisected by dark median line**. Flight erratic, with sudden, sharp changes of direction and deep wingbeats. Distinguished from similar Wilson's Storm-Petrel by longer, narrower, more pointed wings with more sharply angled wrists; pale brown wing band; white rump patch appearing divided at close range; and forked tail. In flight, feet do not extend beyond tail. Voice includes a variety of purrs, trills, and chatter notes. Leach's Storm-Petrel does not follow boats as does Wilson's.

Cory's Shearwater *Calonectris diomedea*
Vagrant

Pelagic. Rarely observed from land; most likely at sea or around offshore islands. Large (47 cm; 650 g), bulky shearwater with broad, blunt-tipped wings and **heavy yellowish bill**. Pale grayish brown above, clean white below with broad, solid dark tip on underwing. Characteristic flight style, with **slow, deliberate wingbeats and prolonged glides**. Generally silent at sea, but may give nasal bleating calls while foraging.

Manx Shearwater *Puffinus puffinus*
Vagrant

Occurs most often far offshore. Intermediate-sized (34 cm; 400 g) shearwater with short tail. Blackish above and mostly white below. **Undertail white**. **Pale crescent behind dark auriculars**. Flight characterized by four or five distinctive snappy wingbeats and a rocking glide, especially in light winds or flat seas. Similar Audubon's Shearwater slightly smaller, with browner back and upperwings, longer tail, grayer underside of primaries, and undertail coverts usually dark. Great Shearwater is larger, has slower wingbeats, and white rump. Manx Shearwater has long-winged and short-tailed appearance, whereas Audubon's Shearwater appears short winged and long tailed. Generally silent at sea.

Audubon's Shearwater *Puffinus lherminieri*
Nonbreeding Visitor

The most common shearwater around Hispaniola, but still generally uncommon in nearshore waters. Relatively small (32 cm; 200 g), short-winged, and long-tailed shearwater. **Entirely dark, blackish brown above**; white below but with **dark undertail coverts**. Rounded tail and distinctive rapid wingbeats between glides distinguish this species from dark-backed pelagic terns. Has faster wingbeats than the larger Great Shearwater and lacks white nape and rump. Manx Shearwater has longer wings, shorter tail, and white undertail coverts. Suspected of breeding on offshore islets but never proven. Generally silent at sea, but may give high, nasal, whining calls, especially around nest site at night.

Wilson's Storm-Petrel

Leach's Storm-Petrel

Cory's Shearwater

Manx Shearwater

Audubon's Shearwater

Magnificent Frigatebird *Fregata magnificens*
Breeding Resident

Regular and moderately common along entire coast. Unmistakable. Large, dark bird (100 cm; male 1,100 g, female 1,600 g), frequently seen soaring and easily identified in silhouette by **long, forked tail**, and long, slender, pointed **wings sharply bent at wrist**. Adult males appear entirely black, but during courtship develop bright red inflatable throat pouch. Adult females blackish overall with white breast. Immature dark brownish black with white head and breast. Silent except for guttural noises during courtship. May occur singly or in flocks. Frigatebirds rarely, if ever, rest on water, but roost among mangroves or on offshore islets. Notorious for stealing fish from other seabirds.

Anhinga *Anhinga anhinga*
Vagrant

Possible in shallow, calm water bodies, either fresh, brackish, or saline. Distinctive large, dark, **long-necked bird** (85 cm; 1,200 g) with long, white-tipped tail; **long, pointed bill**, and silvery to white streaks and spots on upperwing and back. Adult male mostly glossy black. Adult female's head, neck, and breast pale brown. Immature similar to female but more buffy brown on head and neck; reduced white markings above. Resembles cormorant, but neck more snakelike, tail longer, and bill longer and pointed, not hooked. Sometimes vocal when perched, producing guttural croaking and clicking sounds. Often soars with neck extended. Like cormorants, swims with only slender neck and head above surface; perches with wings spread to dry feathers.

Double-crested Cormorant *Nannopterum auritum*
Nonbreeding Visitor

Uncommon, large, dark waterbird (80 cm; 1,700 g) with **long neck** and **hooked bill**; often seen perched on rocks, pilings, or trees near water bodies. Breeding adult appears totally black except for bright **orange-yellow skin** on face and throat. Small ear tufts sometimes visible. Nonbreeding adults similar but lack ear tufts. Immature similar to adults but browner above, much paler below. Similar Neotropic Cormorant is smaller bodied, has longer tail, especially noticeable in flight, and smaller, more yellowish throat patch. Generally silent, but emits deep guttural grunts. Often occurs in flocks. Cormorants often seen in open, deeper water with body submerged and only head above surface. Perching birds often hold wings spread.

Neotropic Cormorant *Nannopterum brasilianum*
Vagrant

Dark waterbird with **long neck** and **hooked bill** (66 cm; 1,200 g); may perch on rocks, pilings, or trees near coast. Breeding adult appears totally black except **small, yellowish patch of skin edged with white** on face and throat. Nonbreeding adults similar, but white edging of throat patch reduced or absent. Immature similar to adults but browner and much paler. Similar Double-crested Cormorant considerably larger and has heavier bill, shorter tail, and larger, brighter yellow throat patch. Also look for feathering on head continuing in front of eye, and sharper angle to skin patch at base of bill on Neotropic Cormorant. Generally silent, but emits a guttural grunt. Like other cormorants, perches in sun with wings spread to dry feathers.

Magnificent Frigatebird

imm

♀

Anhinga

♂

♀

Double-crested Cormorant

br

non-br

imm

Neotropic Cormorant

non-br

br

imm

Brown Booby *Sula leucogaster*
Breeding Resident

Uncommon but occurring regularly around most of Dominican coast. Dark brown (75 cm; 1,200 g) with whitish or dull brown belly. Adult shows brown head and upperparts **sharply demarcated** across breast from white belly; **underwing coverts white**. Feet bright yellow, bill dull yellowish. Immature dull brown above and on upper breast, sharply demarcated from mottled light brown and white belly; feet drab yellowish. Voice a hoarse, grunting *kak*. Most common booby of Hispaniola. Often flies low over sea. Plunge-dives like other boobies, but often at lower angles and with fanned tail.

Masked Booby *Sula dactylatra*
Nonbreeding Visitor

Very rare and local nonbreeding visitor to near-shore and offshore waters, especially along eastern coast. Largest booby (80 cm; male 1,700 g, female 1,900 g); adult primarily bright white with **brownish-black tail**; primaries and secondaries also black, forming **wide black trailing edge** of white wing. Bill yellow. Subadult similar to adult, but upperparts show brown on head and rump; brown flecks on upperwing coverts. Immature has dark brown head and upperparts and **white collar**; underparts primarily white except for brownish throat, undertail, and flight feathers. Adult distinguished from similar white-phase Red-footed Booby by dark tail. Generally silent.

Red-footed Booby *Sula sula*
Breeding Resident

Uncommon but widespread, most often near scattered, remote, roosting and nesting islands. Smallest booby (74 cm; 1,000 g), with slender bill; long, pointed, **white tail**. In all adults, **feet orangish red to red**, bill grayish, bare face patch pinkish. Two color phases, brown and white. Brown-phase adults pale buffy brown head and underparts; pale brown back and upperwing coverts; contrasting white tail, rump, and undertail coverts. White-phase adults entirely white with black primaries and secondaries. Immatures of both phases sooty brown, including all-dark underwings; paler below, sometimes with slightly darker band across breast; feet gray or dull reddish. Distinguished from Masked and Brown boobies by white tail. Voice a guttural *ga-ga-ga-ga*; also rattling squawk. Flight buoyant with deeper wingbeats than other boobies.

American White Pelican *Pelecanus erythrorhyncos*
Vagrant

Nonbreeding birds favor shallow coastal bays, inlets, and estuaries. Unmistakable. **Very large white bird** (150 cm, 7,500 g) with **black flight feathers** and **enormous pinkish or yellow-orange bill** with distensible throat pouch. Legs and webbed feet orange. Similar Brown Pelican is smaller with generally darker body plumage and often forages by plunge-diving; American White Pelican feeds by bill-dipping. Generally silent. Growing North American breeding population appears to be expanding its nonbreeding distribution in the Caribbean.

Brown Pelican *Pelecanus occidentalis*
Breeding Resident

Common along all coastlines, often near bays, docks, and wharfs. Large, dark seabird (120 cm; male 3,300 g, female 2,800 g) with **unmistakable large bill with distensible throat pouch**. Breeding adult has whitish head and neck with yellowish wash on crown; reddish-brown nape and back of head. Upperparts and wings silvery gray, underparts darker, flight feathers blackish. Nonbreeding adult has white nape and back of head. Immature grayish brown overall, paler below. Adults generally silent. Typically seen in small flocks, flying low over wave crests in tight formation, often gliding. Makes spectacular aerial dives for fish; body disappears beneath surface.

Brown Booby

Masked Booby

brown phase

white phase

Red-footed Booby

American White Pelican

non-br

non-br

br

imm

Brown Pelican

American Bittern *Botaurus lentiginosus*
Vagrant

Possible in thick, emergent vegetation of freshwater swamps during nonbreeding season. Stocky, cryptically plumaged heron (75 cm; 750 g) with short neck and *long, yellowish bill*. Brown above flecked finely with black, coarsely streaked brown and white below, with *black stripe along side of neck*. Immatures lack black neck mark. In flight, *blackish primaries and secondaries* contrast strongly with lighter brown underwings and body. Similar immature night-herons more grayish brown, show less contrast between flight feathers and body, lack black on neck, and have shorter bills. Immature Green Heron smaller, darker, and lacks black neck mark. Emits a loud, hoarse, grunting *wok* or *coc* when flushed. Typically "freezes" with bill pointing upward when disturbed.

Least Bittern *Ixobrychus exilis*
Breeding Resident

Fairly common and widely distributed along rivers, lake shores, and lagoons in lowlands where rushes, cattails, or mangroves occur. *Smallest heron* (32 cm; 80 g), with distinctive *buffy coloration overall*. Upperparts greenish black; neck and underparts pale buff; belly and undertail coverts white; wings chestnut with large, *cream-colored patch on upperwing*. Bill thin and yellow; legs yellowish. Adult male has black crown and back; adult female has dark brown crown and back. Immature resembles female but paler brown above and heavily streaked on back and breast. Breeding "song" a series of low, descending cooing notes, *koo-koo-koo-koo*, accelerating slightly. Gives loud, harsh *kak* or *kak-kak-kak* when flushed.

Green Heron *Butorides virescens*
Breeding Resident, Nonbreeding Visitor

Common islandwide; commonest in coastal lowlands, but found at interior sites with water. *Small, dark, compact heron* (44 cm; 240 g). Adult blue gray with glossy greenish-black cap and back. Neck dark chestnut with narrow white stripe from throat down foreneck. Wings blackish; coverts edged buff. Belly gray. *Legs greenish yellow to orangish*; bright orange when breeding. Immatures have duller, brownish back; heavily streaked below. When flushed, calls a sharp, piercing *skeow*. When undisturbed, issues low clucking notes, *kek kek kek, kuk kuk kuk*.

Black-crowned Night-Heron *Nycticorax nycticorax*
Breeding Resident; Nonbreeding Visitor

Uncommon; occurs primarily at lowland freshwater swamps. Medium-sized, stocky, black, white, and gray heron (62 cm; 875 g) with *large head and short neck*. Adult identified by *black crown and back*; gray wings, rump, and tail; white face, underparts, and head plumes. Eyes red; bill black. Immature brown with white flecks on upperparts, largest on wing coverts; underparts have broad, blurry, pale brown streaks. *Bill dusky yellow with greenish base*. Legs greenish yellow on all birds. In flight, only feet extend beyond tail. Immature distinguished from similar immature Yellow-crowned Night-Heron by browner appearance, larger white flecks on wings and upperparts, more blurred streaks on underparts, thinner and paler bill. Voice a flat, barking *quok* or *quark*.

Yellow-crowned Night-Heron *Nyctanassa violacea*
Breeding Resident

Commonly occurs in mangroves, also edges of lakes and ponds; occasionally away from water in dry thickets. Medium-sized, stout-billed heron with stocky appearance (62 cm; 725 g). Adult mostly blue gray; back feathers edged light gray. Head boldly patterned; *black-and-white striped crown, white auriculars*. Immature grayish brown with fine white to buff spotting above; underparts narrowly streaked brown and white. In all plumages, *bill blackish*, leg yellow, eyes red. Voice a squawking *quok* or *quark*, higher than Black-crowned Night-Heron.

American Bittern

Least Bittern

imm

Green Heron

imm

imm

imm

Black-crowned Night-Heron

imm

Yellow-crowned Night-Heron

imm

imm

Great Blue Heron *Ardea herodias*
Breeding Resident; Nonbreeding Visitor

Fairly common islandwide in both saltwater and freshwater ponds and lagoons, primarily in lowlands. Largest (120 cm; 2,300 g) regularly occurring heron. Two color phases occur. Much more common dark phase **primarily bluish gray** with large, heavy, yellowish bill; **broad, black supercilium**. Neck feathers gray with violaceous tinge; black streaking on foreneck. Thighs feathered chestnut; legs brownish green. Rare white phase, entirely white with **yellow bill and yellowish legs**. Dark-phase immatures overall more grayish brown; **entire crown black**. White form of Great Blue Heron distinguished from Great Egret by larger size and yellowish legs. Voice a deep, throaty croak, *guarr* or *braak*, often repeated 3–4 times. Shy and solitary; often stands motionless in search of prey. In flight, flies with folded neck and deep, slow wingbeats.

Little Blue Heron *Egretta caerulea*
Breeding Resident; Nonbreeding Visitor

Common and occasionally abundant at lakes, rivers, marshes, and lagoons islandwide; principally in lowlands but ranges to inland waters at higher elevations more than other herons. Medium-sized, uniquely plumaged heron (65 cm; 340 g) with all-white immatures and all-dark adults. Adult uniformly **slaty blue-gray** body and wings; purplish-brown head and neck. Immature initially entirely white; late in first year becomes mottled with dark feathers of adult plumage. In all plumages **bill bluish gray with black tip; legs pale, dull green**. White immature resembles Snowy Egret but distinguished by pale gray base of bill, lack of yellow lores, and greenish legs. Voice a hoarse, complaining, drawn-out *rraa-aahh* or *gruuh-uhh*. Relatively inactive feeder, moves slowly and methodically or stands motionless.

Tricolored Heron *Egretta tricolor*
Breeding Resident; Nonbreeding Visitor

Common islandwide in mangroves, lagoons, river mouths, and lakes near the coast. An active, slender, medium-sized (65 cm; male 415 g, female 335 g) heron with **very long bill** and neck. Adult has slaty bluish-gray head, neck, and upperparts, **contrasting with white belly**, undertail coverts, and underwing coverts. **Throat and foreneck white** with narrow chestnut median stripe. Immature has chestnut nape and upperwing coverts. Bill yellowish with dark tip but turns bluish with dark tip in breeding adults. Legs usually greenish yellow but turn pinkish red in breeding adults. Similar Little Blue Heron and Reddish Egret have dark bellies, entirely dark neck, and more conspicuously bicolored bill. Voice a guttural, drawn-out *aahhrr* or *guarr*, similar to Snowy Egret. Tends to forage actively, singly or in loose groups, by running and chasing, sometimes flapping wings.

Reddish Egret *Egretta rufescens*
Breeding Resident

Locally common at coastal lagoons, salt ponds, and bays. Medium-sized, active heron (75 cm; 825 g); dark and white color phases. Dark form slate gray; head and neck reddish brown. More common white-phase birds entirely white. Long, heavy **bill pinkish with black tip in both forms**. **Legs and feet slaty blue gray**. Head and neck plumes give adults a shaggy appearance when breeding. Dark-form immature pale, buffy gray overall, pinkish-cinnamon tint on neck; white-form immature is entirely white. All immatures have dark bills, lores, and legs. Similar adult Little Blue Heron has smaller, black-tipped bill, blue-gray at base. Immature Little Blue Heron similar to white-phase Reddish Egret but has gray bill. Voice a low, nasal grunting. Distinctive foraging behavior includes dashing pursuit of prey, often with wings spread to form canopy.

Great Blue Heron

imm

white phase

dark phase

Little Blue Heron

imm
molting

imm

Tricolored Heron

imm

imm

white phase

Reddish Egret

dark phase

Great Egret *Ardea alba*
Breeding Resident; Nonbreeding Visitor
Common to abundant at lower elevations in large freshwater and
saltwater swamps, grassy marshes, riverbanks, and turtlegrass
beds in shallows behind reefs. Large, slender, *entirely white* egret
(100 cm; 1,000 g) with *yellow bill* and *black legs and feet*. Similar

white form of Great Blue Heron is rare but somewhat larger, with heavier bill and yellowish legs.
Cattle Egret is much smaller, stockier, and prefers drier habitat. Voice a deep, hoarse, throaty,
drawn-out croak, *karrr* or *ahrr-rr*.

Little Egret *Egretta garzetta*
Vagrant
Possible at coastal areas, lagoons, and ponds at low elevations. Small, slender egret (60 cm;
450 g) with entirely white plumage. Breeding adult has *two long head plumes*, stringy breast
plumes, nearly straight back plumes, *black legs with yellowish feet*, and grayish-yellow lores.
Nonbreeding adults and immatures have yellowish extending onto lower legs, and dark lores.
Difficult to distinguish from common Snowy Egret, but Little Egret appears larger, with longer,
thicker bill; head flatter; lores and feet slightly duller. Head plumes of breeding adult Little Egret
are longer, back plumes are straighter; nonbreeding birds have dark lores and darker legs. Voice
a nasal, croaking *kark*.

Snowy Egret *Egretta thula*
Breeding Resident; Nonbreeding Visitor
Common at coastal and interior wetlands of all types islandwide,
principally in lowlands. Medium-sized, slender, *entirely white
heron* (60 cm; 370 g). Note *black legs, yellow feet and lores*, and
thin, pure black bill. Adult breeders have many elongated, wispy

plumes on head, neck, and back. Legs of nonbreeding adult and immature dark in front, greenish
yellow in back. Similar immature Little Blue Heron has bicolored bill, lacks yellow on lores, and
has greenish legs. See vagrant Little Egret. Voice a hoarse, rasping *guarr* or *raarr*, higher-pitched
and more nasal than Great Egret. Very active while foraging, running and jumping to seize prey;
often stirring bottom sediments with feet.

Cattle Egret *Bubulcus ibis*
Breeding Resident; Nonbreeding Visitor
Common to abundant islandwide except at highest elevations.
Stocky, white, short-legged, thick-necked heron (51 cm; 365 g).
Distinguished by small size and *short, thick, yellowish bill*.
Breeding individuals have reddish legs and eyes, reddish tinted

bill, and buffy-orange wash on crown, breast, and upper back. Nonbreeding birds have black legs
and yellow bill; buffy-orange wash reduced or absent. Immatures have blackish bill. Generally
silent. The only heron regularly occurring in uplands; gregarious, often alongside cattle in
pastures. Seldom visits water. Flies in formations to and from communal roosts.

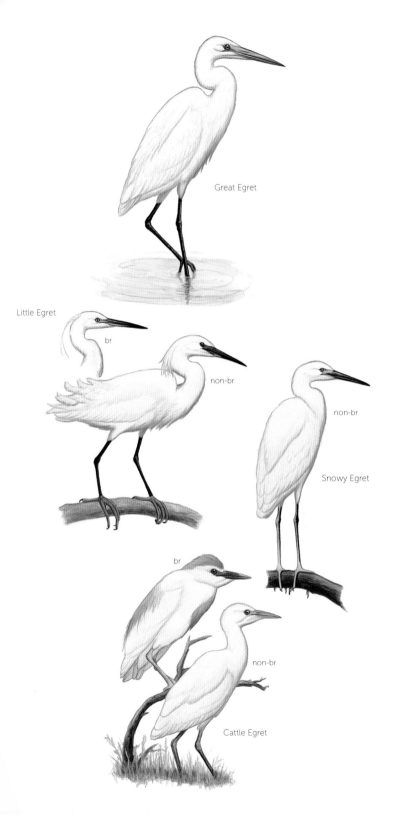

Great Egret

Little Egret

br

non-br

non-br

Snowy Egret

br

non-br

Cattle Egret

American Flamingo *Phoenicopterus ruber*
Nonbreeding Visitor; Breeding Resident

Regular but local at shallow lagoons and coastal estuaries with high salinity. Tall, slender wading bird (115 cm; 2,550 g) with *orangish-pink coloration overall*, very long legs and neck, and *uniquely curved bill* with pronounced black tip. Immature much paler. Runs when taking off and landing. In flight, head and neck outstretched and drooping; flight feathers black. Somewhat similar Roseate Spoonbill smaller, paler, lacks black on wings, and has longer, spatulate bill. Distinctive gooselike honks in flight; feeding birds often give low, conversational gabble. Typically occurs in flocks at feeding localities with low human disturbance. Hispaniolan birds are mostly seasonal migrants from breeding colony at Great Inagua, Bahamas. Occasionally breeds in small colonies at remote, undisturbed sites.

White Ibis *Eudocimus albus*
Breeding Resident

Fairly common near the coast islandwide. Striking, medium-sized wading bird (62 cm; male 1,035 g, female 765 g) with long, distinctively decurved bill. Adult entirely white with *black wing tips*; *reddish bill*; face and legs also red. Immature primarily brown with *white belly* and rump; bill and legs orangish. Similar Glossy Ibis entirely dark. Voice a series of low, hoarse grunts; a nasal *oohh-oohh*. Typically occurs in flocks; flies in lines with neck extended. Often nomadic; disperses widely.

Glossy Ibis *Plegadis falcinellus*
Breeding Resident; Nonbreeding Visitor

Fairly common in coastal lowlands nearly islandwide, including mudflats, marshy savannas, and rice fields; sparingly inland along rivers and lake edges. Relatively small ibis (58 cm; 650 g), *entirely dark*; may appear black, but is metallic bronze and green in good light. Long, *brownish-olive, decurved bill*. Legs grayish but may be reddish when breeding. Immature lighter and duller than adult. Similar immature White Ibis has white, rather than dark belly and rump. Generally silent but occasionally gives repeated, nasal grunt, *urnn urnn urnn*, o quacking *waa waa waa*. Typically flocks; may wander widely after breeding.

Roseate Spoonbill *Platalea ajaja*
Breeding Resident

Locally common in shallow lagoons and edges of mudflats in coastal lowlands islandwide; also at some inland lakes. Unmistakable, large, *pink wader* (78 cm; 1,500 g). Plumage bright pink, with carmine red upperwing coverts; white neck, upper mantle, and upper chest. Head unfeathered and pale greenish white, with band of black skin from ea across nape. Tail orangish with reddish-pink coverts. Note unique grayish-white, *spatula-like bil* Legs reddish. Immature almost entirely white but displays pink wash and yellowish bill. General silent; emits low, soft grunts and rapid, dry, rasping *rrek-ek-ek-ek-ek* when breeding. Typical occurs in small flocks. Feeds by wading through shallow water sweeping head from side to sid straining organisms from bottom sediments.

American Flamingo

White Ibis

imm

imm

Glossy Ibis

imm

Roseate Spoonbill

imm

Turkey Vulture *Cathartes aura*
Breeding Resident

Increasingly widespread in open areas, including scrublands, cane fields, pasturelands, cities, and towns. Large size (72 cm; 2,000 g), blackish-brown coloration, small bare head diagnostic. Adult **head reddish** at close range; immature has blackish head. In flight, ***dark wings distinctly two-toned*** with lighter flight feathers; ***wings held above horizontal in broad V***. Frequently soars, rocking and tilting from side to side. Usually silent. Often sunbathes on exposed perches with wings outstretched.

Swallow-tailed Kite *Elanoides forficatus*
Passage Migrant; Nonbreeding Visitor

Rare but increasingly regular near coastal swamps, savannas, and river mouths. Unmistakable. ***Medium-sized, bicolored raptor*** (58 cm; 465 g) with long, pointed wings and ***deeply forked tail***. White head and underparts contrast with black back, wings, and tail. Flight graceful and buoyant. Voice a high, shrill, whistled *ke-wee-wee*, *hewee-we*, the first note short. When hunting, glides slowly, low to ground, with steady wings but tail constantly balancing; plucks insects and lizards from treetops. In migration, often soars more than 500 m above ground, often in small flocks.

Northern Harrier *Circus hudsonius*
Nonbreeding Visitor; Passage Migrant?

Rare visitor to marshes, swamps, open savannas, and rice fields. Large, slender hawk (50 cm; male 370 g, female 515 g) with long wings and tail, long legs; ***distinctive white rump*** and facial disk. Adult male pale gray above, whitish below, with chest and sides flecked reddish brown. Adult female dark brown above, white below, with underparts heavily streaked with brown. Immature brown above, entirely reddish brown below with dark brown streaks limited to upper breast. Usually flies low over fields or marshes with erratic heavy flaps and distinctive ***tilting glides***; ***wings uptilted in a dihedral*** much like a Turkey Vulture. Soars only occasionally. Similar hawks have heavier build and broader wings, and often soar at fairly high altitudes. Generally silent on Hispaniola.

Mississippi Kite *Ictinia mississippiensis*
Vagrant

Most likely to occur in open areas, such as savannas, pasture lands, sugarcane, or scrub during migratory periods. Sleek, medium-sized raptor (35 cm; male 260 g, female 325 g), somewhat falconlike with pointed wings, long tail. Adult light to medium-gray overall, with back and upperwing coverts darker gray to near-black. Flight feathers black except secondaries, which are pale gray to silvery white above. ***Tail uniformly black***. Head and nape of male grayish white, paler than female. Immatures have head, neck, and underparts white or pale buff, streaked heavily with brown, rufous, and gray. Upperparts dull black, feathers edged narrowly with white to brown. Wing-linings barred or mottled brown, dark gray, and white. ***All birds have dark patch around scarlet eye***. Similar falcons have patterned tails and more complex face patterns. Call high, thin, descending whistle *pee-teeer*, often in flight. May occur in small flocks; often soars.

Swallow-tailed Kite

Turkey Vulture

imm

Northern Harrier

♂

♀

♂

Mississippi Kite

Osprey *Pandion haliaetus*
Nonbreeding Visitor; Passage Migrant

Regular and sometimes relatively common at coastal lagoons, rivers, and major lakes and ponds islandwide. Large, lean bird of prey (58 cm; male 1,400 g, female 1,570 g). In all plumages, birds appear white below with ***dark wrist patch***. Adults uniformly dark brown above with white breast and belly. Two races occur: more widespread North American race has ***white crown and forecrown with dark bar through eye***. The more restricted Caribbean race, breeding in Bahamas and Cuba, has whiter head with only a trace of an eye-line. Voice a series of short, piercing whistles. Distinctive flight silhouette features long, narrow wings ***angled at the wrist*** and bowed down. This is the only fish-eating hawk in Hispaniola; will hover over water, dropping feet-first to catch fish.

Sharp-shinned Hawk *Accipiter striatus*
Threatened Breeding Resident

Uncommon, increasingly local resident of mature forests in interior hills and mountains, most often in pine, shade coffee, or broadleaf forest. Small forest hawk (male 26 cm, 100 g; female 32 cm, 180 g); ***short, rounded wings***; relatively small head; ***long, narrow, squared-off tail***, boldly barred with black. Adults dark steel blue above with ***narrow rufous bars on whitish underparts***. Immatures brown above; buffy white below, ***thickly streaked with dark brown***. In flight, note short, rounded wings and long, narrow tail. Similar Broad-winged Hawk is much larger, chunkier, and with shorter tail and broader wings. Voice a series of short, sharp, high-pitched notes, *que-que-que-que*. Sharp-shinned Hawks fly rapidly through the forest with alternate bursts of shallow wing flaps and glides.

Swainson's Hawk *Buteo swainsoni*
Vagrant

Large (51 cm; male 815 g, female 1,150 g), slender, long-tailed, long-winged hawk of open habitats; possible during migration or the nonbreeding season. Variably plumaged, but adult generally dark brown above, whitish below, with ***rufous to dark brown bib***. Less common darker-phase birds may have bib extending through breast and belly. Immature similar to adult but underparts variably streaked and spotted brown. In flight, soars like Turkey Vulture on ***wings held in a dihedral***; ***dark flight feathers contrast with lighter underwing coverts***. Gray tail with numerous thin black bands; wide subterminal black band; buffy tip. Similar Broad-winged Hawk has broad black-and-white tail bands, and light flight feathers contrasting with darker underwing coverts. Voice a high, drawn-out scream.

Osprey

migratory race

resident race

Sharp-shinned Hawk

imm

imm light phase

Swainson's Hawk

adult dark phase

adult light phase

American Kestrel *Falco sparverius*
Breeding Resident

Common to abundant in many open or semiopen habitats including suburbs and parks, from lowlands into the pine zone, but especially in dry forest and scrub. Small falcon (26 cm; 120 g) with ***reddish-brown, barred back***; ***reddish-brown tail*** with black terminal band; boldly patterned head with ***two black facial bars***. Underparts vary from whitish to reddish brown, spotted brown to black. Adult males have blue-gray wings; adult females reddish-brown wings. Immatures similar to adults but more streaked than spotted on breast. Similar Merlin is heavily streaked below, and has single black facial bar. Voice a high-pitched *killi-killi-killi* or *kli-kli-kli-kli-kli*. Often perches along roadsides, bobbing tail; may hover while hunting.

Merlin *Falco columbarius*
Passage Migrant; Nonbreeding Visitor

Regularly occurring in semiopen areas, especially near lakes and lagoons where shorebird prey abound. Small, dark, compact falcon (28 cm; male 165 g, female 230 g) with ***pale tan supercilium***. Adult male has pale blue-gray to blackish-gray upperparts; rufous feathering on legs. Underparts heavily streaked; ***tail black with 2–5 contrasting, narrow gray or buffy bands***. Adult female has dark brown upperparts; tail barred black with brown or buff. Immatures resemble females. Much larger Peregrine Falcon has wide, dark malar stripe; tail has more than 5 light bands. American Kestrel has rufous on back or tail. Voice a rapid, accelerating series of strident, trilling calls, *ki-ki-kee*. In flight, Merlin's great speed and agility, rapid wingbeats, long, pointed wings, and long, narrow tail are characteristic.

Peregrine Falcon *Falco peregrinus*
Passage Migrant; Nonbreeding Visitor

Uncommon but regularly seen near the coast, offshore cays, and other localities with abundant shorebirds, seabirds, or waterfowl prey. Large, stocky falcon (male 42 cm, 725 g; female 52 cm, 1,100 g) with pointed wings; long, tapered tail; rapid, powerful flight. When perched, its ***wide, dark malar stripe and crown*** give a distinctive "helmeted" appearance. Adult dark brown to slaty gray above, cream-colored to whitish below with dark barring. Immature brown above; underparts heavily streaked brown. Similar Merlin is distinctly smaller, with less pronounced facial markings. Voice a harsh, scolding *kak-kak-kak-kak*.

American Kestrel

Merlin

Peregrine Falcon

imm

Ridgway's Hawk *Buteo ridgwayi*
Critically Endangered Endemic Breeding Resident

Rare with a restricted distribution; found historically in undisturbed forested foothills and other wooded habitats. Medium-sized raptor (38 cm; male 320 g, female 400 g), with dark brownish upperparts, gray underparts washed brownish red, ***reddish-brown thighs***, and dark gray tail with ***3–4 thin whitish bars***. Males grayer than females, with more horizontal barring on chest, and bright ***reddish-brown bend of wing***. Females browner overall with ***brown bend of wing***, lighter breast, gray belly tinted reddish pink, and more heavily barred tail. Immature brownish above; buffy-white underparts with pale gray and tan streaks; tail less distinctly barred. Similar Broad-winged Hawk has boldly banded tail with wide bands. See Swainson's Hawk. Voice includes three distinct calls: a plaintive squealing *kleeah*; a short nasal yelping *weeup*; and a 2-syllable whistle-squeal. In flight, soars on broad wings with fan-shaped tail; wings display light patches. Natural populations occur in Los Haitises, Dominican Republic and the Cayemites islands, Haiti, with reintroduced birds now breeding at Punta Cana; in 2019, 25 birds were released at Aniana Vargas National Park.

Broad-winged Hawk *Buteo platypterus*
Vagrant

Possible in dense broadleaf, mixed broadleaf and pine forests during nonbreeding season. Medium-sized (39 cm; male 375 g, female 430 g), chunky, soaring hawk with relatively short tail and broad wings with slightly pointed tips. Adult dark brown above, whitish below, with reddish-brown barring; ***tail boldly banded with broad black-and-white bars***. Pale underwings have dark border on trailing edge. Immature has white underparts heavily streaked with dark brown; tail bands and dark border of underwing less distinct. Similar Swainson's Hawk has gray tail with many thin, black bands and wide subterminal black band. Sharp-shinned Hawk has similar color pattern but tail is long and narrow rather than fan-shaped; seldom soars. Voice a thin, high, shrill whistle, *pweeeeeeeeee*.

Red-tailed Hawk *Buteo jamaicensis*
Breeding Resident; Nonbreeding Visitor

Common in nearly all habitat types islandwide. Large, conspicuous hawk (male 50 cm, 995 g; female 58 cm, 1,175 g), most often seen soaring on broad, rounded wings. Adult dark brown above, buffy to whitish below, with distinctly contrasting ***dark belly band*** and ***reddish tail***; belly band tends to be light and diffuse in resident Hispaniolan subspecies. Wings have dark bar and wrist patch on leading edge. Immature has faintly barred, grayish brown tail; underparts more heavily streaked. Similar immature Broad-winged Hawk is smaller, has broad tail bands, and flaps more in flight. Smaller Ridgway's Hawk has barred tail. Voice a sharp, raspy scream, *keeer-r-r-r*, slurring downward.

Ridgway's Hawk

Broad-winged Hawk

imm

imm

Red-tailed Hawk

imm

imm

Barn Owl *Tyto alba*
Breeding Resident; Nonbreeding Visitor

Moderately common islandwide, especially in relatively open areas, rice fields, dry scrub, open woodlands, and human settlements. Large (36 cm; 525 g), long-legged nocturnal owl with *flat, white, heart-shaped face*; dark eyes. Generally pale overall, with light orangish-brown upperparts and mostly white underparts. Very similar Ashy-faced Owl is darker overall; heart-shaped face silver gray rather than white. Voice a drawn-out scream, *karr-r-r-r-ick*. Also emits long hissing screech; loud clicks.

Ashy-faced Owl *Tyto glaucops*
Endemic Breeding Resident

Locally common and fairly widespread in open woodlands and dry and moist broadleaf forest. Large (30 cm; male 300 g, female 500 g), long-legged, nocturnal owl. Upperparts dark grayish brown with light brown or tawny mottling; underparts tawny with fine barring; *silvery-gray, heart-shaped face*. Similar Barn Owl has white facial disk and underparts, paler upperparts. Ashy-faced tends to be found in more heavily forested sites than Barn Owl; less likely to be found around cities and towns than Barn Owl. Voice a series of high-pitched, ratchety clicks, sometimes followed by hissing cry.

Burrowing Owl *Athene cunicularia*
Breeding Resident

Locally common in semiopen dry habitats, scrubby areas, pine savannas, pastures, and limestone ravines. *Small, long-legged owl* (22 cm; 160 g), often seen standing on open ground; conspicuously bobs when approached. Round head lacks tufts; broad pale eyebrows, yellow eyes. Upperparts of adult brown, profusely spotted with white; underparts white with broad brown barring. Juveniles similar but underparts buffy and unbarred. Voice a soft, high-pitched, 2-note *coo-cooo*. When alarmed or agitated, gives clucking chatter or scream. May hover while hunting; sometimes flycatches. Active day and night; nests in underground burrows.

Stygian Owl *Asio stygius*
Endangered Breeding Resident

Rare in dense deciduous and pine forests in remote areas; never near human dwellings or in second-growth habitats. Identified by *large size* (42 cm; 675 g), dark overall coloration, and *conspicuous ear tufts*. Upperparts have cream-colored and white spots; underparts streaked. Facial disk dark; eyes yellowish orange. Juvenile pale buff overall with barred belly. Unmistakable; all other Hispaniolan owls are smaller, lighter colored, and lack or have very short ear tufts. Voice a single deep, emphatic *hu* or *whu*. During breeding season, male calls a short, low-pitched *fool*, and female answers with higher-pitched *niek* or *quick*.

Short-eared Owl *Asio flammeus*
Threatened Breeding Resident

Uncommon and local in lowlands, including pastures, short-grass marshlands, savannas, rice fields, and citrus plantations. Medium-sized owl (38 cm; 345 g), tan or buffy below; heavy dark streaking on breast reduced on lower belly. *Whitish facial disk* distinct and round, with *blackish feathering around yellow eyes*. Small ear tufts often concealed. In flight, shows conspicuous *black wrist patches* on whitish underwings and large buff patches on upperwings. Voice a short, emphatic barking call, *bow-wow* or *uh-uh*; wing-claps given during courtship and nest defense sound like rapid, cracking whip. Most active at dawn and dusk, when it flies low over open areas. Buoyant flight of slow, deliberate flaps and alternating glides.

Barn Owl

Ashy-faced Owl

Burrowing Owl

Stygian Owl

Short-eared Owl

Hispaniolan Trogon *Priotelus roseigaster*
Threatened Endemic Breeding Resident

Locally common in undisturbed humid forest, both deciduous broadleaf and pine, in foothills and mountains. Brightly colored and unmistakable, often seen perched upright with tail pointing straight down (29 cm; 77 g). Glossy green crown and upperparts, **bright red belly**, yellow bill, and gray chin, throat, and breast. Facial mask blackish. Long, graduated, **dark blue tail** conspicuously **tipped with white below**. Male has wings with fine black and white barring; prominent white notches on outer edges of primaries. Female has gray-green wing; lacks fine white barring; red on belly less vivid. Voice a hollow *coc, ca-rao*; or *cock-craow*, repeated several times, but ventriloquial nature makes calling birds difficult to find. Relatively inactive, strictly arboreal, most often perches on horizontal branches between foliage and trunk. This is the national bird of Haiti.

Broad-billed Tody *Todus subulatus*
Endemic Breeding Resident

Common to abundant in variety of forest types, including lowland and montane second-growth, and deciduous understory of pine forest; often near earthen embankments. Diminutive (12 cm; 8.5 g), chunky and short-tailed; bright green above with red throat. **Underparts grayish white washed yellow and pink**, creating dirty appearance; sides reddish pink. Underside of lower mandible **entirely reddish. Iris brown**. Juveniles briefly lack red on throat; breast streaked pale green. Similar Narrow-billed Tody is slightly smaller, cleaner white below, with pale blue iris; underside of lower mandible usually red with black tip. Voice a monotonous, often repeated *terp, terp, terp*. A single call note in the same tone contrasts with Narrow-billed Tody's 2-note call. May also be located by unique *burrrrrrrr* made by the wings in short flights.

Narrow-billed Tody *Todus angustirostris*
Endemic Breeding Resident

Common in mature montane forests, moist ravines, and coffee plantations; locally common at some forested lower-elevation sites. Small, chunky bird (11 cm; 7.5 g) with brilliant green upperparts, red throat, **whitish underparts**, and reddish-pink sides. **Iris pale blue**. Underside of lower mandible **reddish, usually with black tip**. Juveniles briefly lack red on throat; breast streaked pale green. Similar Broad-billed Tody slightly larger, grayish white below, with entirely red underside of lower mandible; iris brown. Call a frequently repeated *chick-kweee*, accented on second syllable. Also chattering *chippy-chippy-chippy-chip*, dropping in pitch but not in tone. Perches with tail pointed down, bill pointed up, scanning above for insects that it captures with a quick sallying flight on whirring wings and audible snap of its bill.

Hispaniolan Trogon

♂

♀

Broad-billed Tody

Narrow-billed Tody

Belted Kingfisher *Megaceryle alcyon*
Nonbreeding Visitor; Passage Migrant

Regular and moderately common along coastline, edges of fresh and saline lakes and ponds in lowlands, and courses of rivers and streams. Unmistakable aquatic bird (32 cm; 155 g) distinguished by *large, shaggy-crested head*; stout, sharply pointed bill; *bluish gray upperparts and head*; and nearly complete white collar. Legs very short. Male has single blue-gray breast band; female has one blue-gray and one rufous breast band, with rufous on flanks. Immature has rusty spotting in a slaty breast band. Voice a loud, reverberating, dry rattle. Frequents conspicuous perches, usually near or over water; often hovers before plunging into water for prey.

Antillean Piculet *Nesoctites micromegas*
Endemic Breeding Resident

Locally common in dry and humid forest, semiarid scrub, and pines mixed with broadleaf trees. Unmistakable; small and chunky (15 cm; 30 g). Bill fairly small, *sharply pointed*. Adults *olive above*, pale yellowish below with *heavy dark spots and streaks*. Pale auriculars streaked dark. Male has bright orange-red patch in center of yellow crown; female lacks this red. Juvenile duller green above with duller yellow crown; abdomen more heavily barred. Voice surprisingly loud; staccato, *tu-tu-lu-feo*, accented on last note; noisy chatter *yeh-yeh-yeh* during flight. Flight direct and even, not undulating. Often shy and difficult to see, but also noisy and easy to hear. Both sexes frequently call to one another. Does not hammer like a woodpecker, but persistent pecking of tree trunks, branches, and vines is audible; probes fruit, flowers, dense leaf clusters, and vine tangles.

Hispaniolan Woodpecker *Melanerpes striatus*
Endemic Breeding Resident

Common resident in virtually all habitats containing some trees; most numerous in partly wooded areas with palms scattered across pastures. Conspicuous, medium-sized woodpecker (23 cm; male 88 g, female 70 g). Upperparts *barred blackish and greenish yellow*; underparts unmarked dark buffy olive. Forehead and face grayish; black-and-white patches on lower nape. *Uppertail coverts red; tail black*. Eye whitish to yellow. Male with crown entirely red; female has black crown, red nape. Similar Yellow-bellied Sapsucker is smaller, with distinct black-and-white facial markings, barred upperparts, and conspicuous white wing patch. Strong, variable vocalizations include loud, rolling call interrupted with throaty noises. Call notes include *wup* and *ta-a*; also a short *b-d-d-d-t* with 3–5 distinct notes. Forages at all levels but not on the ground.

Yellow-bellied Sapsucker *Sphyrapicus varius*
Nonbreeding Visitor

Uncommon but regular in montane forests, woodlands, and gardens; most often recorded in pine forest. Medium-sized woodpecker (22 cm; 50 g), identified by large, *white upperwing covert patch*, especially visible in flight. Adult has red forecrown and crown, with black border at rear, prominent *black and white striped facial pattern*, and broad black breast band. Chin and throat red in adult male; white in adult female, which may also have crown partially or wholly black. Immature resembles adult but with brownish head, indistinct facial stripes, usually faint red mottling on crown; chest and sides pale brown with dusky barring. Distinguished from Hispaniolan Woodpecker by white wing patch and black-and-white facial pattern. Mostly silent, but may give nasal mewing, *wah*. Drills series of horizontal holes in live trees to feed on sap and insects attracted to it.

Belted Kingfisher

Antillean Piculet

Hispaniolan Woodpecker

imm

Yellow-bellied Sapsucker

Olive-throated Parakeet *Eupsittula nana*
Breeding Resident

Locally common at lower elevations in Sierra de Bahoruco, where found in pine forests, broadleaf scrub, croplands, and gardens; elsewhere rare in scattered coastal cities. Small, slender, dark green parakeet (24 cm; 77 g), with *blue primaries* and *long, pointed tail. Underparts dark brownish olive*. Eye-ring and *bill grayish to creamy yellow*. Similar Hispaniolan Parakeet is larger with slightly lighter green plumage and yellowish-green underparts; lacks blue primaries, and has distinctive red bend of wing; bill a mix of pinks and oranges. Voice a screeching call of paired notes, such as *creek-creek* or *clack-clack*, repeated often in flight. Olive-throated Parakeet has more erratic, rapid flight than Hispaniolan Parakeet. First documented in 1995; genetically derived from Jamaican birds but unknown if introduction was natural or human-assisted.

Hispaniolan Parakeet *Psittacara chloropterus*
Threatened Endemic Breeding Resident

Locally common in undisturbed habitat; most often seen in pine zone of interior mountains, but also feeds in adjacent agricultural habitats and shade coffee plantations; surprisingly common in urban parks of Santo Domingo. Large parakeet (32 cm; 145 g).
Bright green overall, with yellowish-green underparts; *long, pointed tail*, white eye-ring, and *red edge along bend of wing*. In flight, note red underwing coverts. Similar Hispaniolan Parrot is more robust, larger, and with shorter, squared tail. See Olive-throated Parakeet. Screeching calls, often repeated in groups of 3–4 notes in flight, such as *creek-creek-creek-creek* or *clack-clack-clack-clack*. Travels and forages in flocks, often feeding on corn and other crops.

Hispaniolan Parrot *Amazona ventralis*
Endangered Endemic Breeding Resident

Locally common only in major reserves of interior montane forests where suitable fruits and seeds are available, and where free from human persecution. Distinguished by large size (30 cm; 250 g), chunky shape, and short, *squared tail*. Bright green overall, with *white forecrown and eye-ring, dark auricular spot*, and *maroon belly*. In flight, shows *bright blue primaries and secondaries*. Flies with rapid wingbeats, with wings moving below the plane of back. Similar Hispaniolan and Olive-throated parakeets are smaller with long, pointed tails. Loud bugling calls in flight; perch calls consist of loud squawkings and screeches. Normally feeds on seeds and fruits at middle to high levels in trees. Forms foraging flocks that sometimes depredate crops. Often roosts at higher elevations, descending to lower elevations to feed.

Olive-throated Parakeet

Hispaniolan Parakeet

Hispaniolan Parrot

Hispaniolan Elaenia *Elaenia cherriei*
Endemic Breeding Resident

Locally common, primarily in pine forests with fruit-bearing shrub understory, but also open country with scattered trees, and moist broadleaf forests. Small, nondescript flycatcher (15 cm; 14 g). Note faint dark eye-line, **two distinct whitish wingbars**, and **small bill with pinkish base**. Head and upperparts grayish olive, underparts pale gray, lightly washed yellowish. Neck and breast faintly streaked gray. Erectile crest usually held flat, concealing white crown patch. Immature lacks crown patch. Similar Hispaniolan Pewee slightly darker below and lacks wingbars. See Stolid Flycatcher. Commonly heard call is an emphatic *wheep!* frequently repeated; also high chip notes. Song a fast, descending *pwee-chi-chi-chi-chi-chi*; also a trilling dawn song. Some authorities treat *E. cherriei* as part of the Greater Antillean Elaenia, *E. fallax*.

Great Crested Flycatcher *Myiarchus crinitus*
Vagrant

Possible in woodlands and semiopen habitats during migratory periods. Large, noisy flycatcher (19 cm; 33 g). Upperparts olive brown, **wings reddish brown** with whitish wingbars, **tail also reddish brown**. Throat and **upper breast gray**, **belly bright yellow**. Bill dark with pink base. Often raises crown feathers to form crest when excited. Similar Stolid Flycatcher darker above, especially on head, with wings and tail less rufous; belly paler yellow. Voice a loud, harsh *wheeep* with a rising inflection; also a rolling *prrrrreeet*.

Stolid Flycatcher *Myiarchus stolidus*
Breeding Resident

Common islandwide in lower-elevation desert scrub and dry forest, but also regular at higher elevations in pine and moist broadleaf forest. Medium-sized (20 cm; 23 g), large-headed, dark-backed flycatcher with two pale white wingbars and primaries **strongly fringed white**. Upperparts olive brown, darker on head; **tail brownish with reddish-brown inner webs**. Throat and breast grayish white, **belly pale yellow**. Bill black and moderately heavy. Raised crest noticeable. Similar pewees and elaenia are substantially smaller; kingbirds are larger, more robust, lack yellowish belly. See vagrant Great Crested Flycatcher. Voice a prolonged, rolling, ascending *whee-ee-ee*, *swee-ip*, *bzzrt*; also a plaintive *jui*. Often snaps bill loudly and repeatedly.

Eastern Wood-Pewee *Contopus virens*
Vagrant

Tends to frequent coastal and urban woodlands, forest edge, scrub, and gardens during migratory periods. Medium-sized flycatcher (15 cm; 14 g). Grayish olive above, pale below with slightly darker wash on breast and sides; whitish wingbars. Upper mandible dark, lower pale orange with dark tip. Distinguished from very similar Hispaniolan Pewee by more distinct and whitish wingbars, paler breast washed grayish rather than olive brown, belly and undertail coverts pale gray to whitish **without dusky olive-brown wash**. See Hispaniolan Elaenia. Calls include a flat, dry *chip* note and a plaintive *pee-ah-weee*. Sits upright but **does not flick wings or wag tail**.

Hispaniolan Pewee *Contopus hispaniolensis*
Endemic Breeding Resident

Common and widespread, most frequently in pine forest, but also dry and humid broadleaf forest, scrubby woodlands, shade coffee, orchards, and karst forests. Small flycatcher (15 cm; 11 g), with drab grayish-olive upperparts, somewhat darker on head. **Inconspicuous wingbars** light gray to buffy. Underparts light gray with olive, yellow, or brown wash. Bill relatively long and broad, blackish above, **pinkish yellow or pale orangish below**. Similar Hispaniolan Elaenia paler below, has two distinct wingbars. See vagrant Eastern Wood-Pewee. Voice a mournful *purr*, *pip-pip-pip-pip*. Dawn song a loud, rapid-fire volley of short notes, *shurr, pet-pet, pit-pit, peet-peet*, with paired syllables successively rising in pitch. Often flicks tail when perched.

Hispaniolan Elaenia

Great Crested Flycatcher

Stolid Flycatcher

Eastern Wood-Pewee

Hispaniolan Pewee

Gray Kingbird *Tyrannus dominicensis*
Breeding Resident

Conspicuous, common, boisterous species of open habitats in lowlands; most numerous in dry forest, cactus scrub, agricultural areas. Large flycatcher (24 cm; 44 g). *Gray above, pale grayish white below*, with distinct *blackish mask*. Faint whitish wingbars present; tail notched. Small yellowish-orange or reddish-orange crown patch usually concealed. Immature has pale brownish wingbars; lacks crown patch. Similar Hispaniolan Kingbird brown above, has entirely dark crown extending below eye, squared tail. Northern Mockingbird also gray and white but cocks long tail upward; pronounced white wing and tail patches. Voice a loud, emphatic *pe-ti-gre*; song a more musical variation of call, *pe-ti-grée, pe-ti-grro*. Note harsh *peet* and *burr*. Usually seen on exposed perches, telephone lines, and treetops. Very aggressive; sometimes attacks larger species such as hawks.

Hispaniolan Kingbird *Tyrannus gabbii*
Endangered Endemic Breeding Resident

Very uncommon and local in densely forested broadleaf and pine habitats at mid- to upper elevations. Large flycatcher (25 cm; 42 g) with large bill. *Crown and facial mask blackish*, contrasting with *dark gray-brown back, wings, and tail*; wings and tail edged rufous. Underparts whitish, lightly washed gray or brown. Tail squared. Yellow or pale orange crown patch usually concealed. Juvenile gray above, buffy white below, with buffy or brownish upperwing coverts; lacks crown patch. Similar Gray Kingbird has lighter crown, lighter gray upperparts, black facial mask distinct from crown. Stolid Flycatcher has smaller bill; yellowish wash on underparts. Calls variable, but note long, loud, rolling trill, *br-r-r-r-r-r-r*, often terminating with several explosive, sputtering notes. Snaps bill loudly. Some authorities treat *T. gabbii* as part of the Loggerhead Kingbird, *T. caudifasciatus*.

Fork-tailed Flycatcher *Tyrannus savana*
Vagrant

Possible in semiopen country with scattered trees during nonbreeding season. Grayish flycatcher with dark head and *conspicuously long, forked tail* (male 39 cm, female 29 cm; 31 g). Adult male has gray back, blackish-brown wings, *black crown and nape*, and entirely white underparts. Long tail, all-black and edged white; may be shorter during molt. Females and immatures similar but duller, head browner, tail shorter. Similar Scissor-tailed Flycatcher is paler gray, including head; has salmon pink wash on sides, flanks, and undertail coverts. Seldom vocalizes, but may give high, hard chips and twittering notes, and a high *jeek*.

Scissor-tailed Flycatcher *Tyrannus forficatus*
Vagrant

Possible in semiopen country with scattered trees during nonbreeding season. Pale grayish flycatcher with *conspicuously long, forked tail* (male 42 cm, female 30 cm; 39 g). *Pearl gray head* and upperparts, wings and tail dusky brown; underparts whitish with *salmon pink wash on sides, flanks, and undertail coverts*. *Axillaries reddish*. White outer tail feathers broadly tipped black. Females and immatures generally paler with less intense salmon and reddish coloration than males; tail shorter. Similar Fork-tailed Flycatcher somewhat darker, has black head, lacks salmon pink wash. Voice a variable chattering.

Gray Kingbird

Hispaniolan Kingbird

Fork-tailed Flycatcher

♂

♀

Scissor-tailed Flycatcher

White-eyed Vireo *Vireo griseus*
Vagrant

Possible in thick, dry scrub and dense undergrowth at low elevations during nonbreeding season. Small vireo (12 cm; 12 g), grayish green tinged yellow above, ***whitish below*** with yellowish sides and flanks. Neck more grayish than rest of upperparts. Note ***broad yellow spectacles***, dusky lores, and ***two white to yellowish-white wingbars***. Adult has ***white iris***; immature a duller, brownish iris. Bill black. Similar Thick-billed and Yellow-throated vireos have yellow spectacles, but both have dark iris. Thick-billed entirely pale yellow below; Yellow-throated has bright yellow chin, throat, and breast. Adults give soft *pick* and *mew* calls in nonbreeding season. Alarm call a series of nasal, churring notes. Song a loud, nasal, slurred 3- to 7-syllabled song, often beginning and ending with sharp *chip*.

Flat-billed Vireo *Vireo nanus*
Endemic Breeding Resident

Uncommon; locally distributed from lowlands to mid-elevation in dry scrub, limestone hills, and occasionally mesic forest. Small vireo (13 cm; 11 g), grayish green above, dull grayish white below, washed with pale yellow. ***Outer tail feathers tipped white***, two white wingbars, ***dull white iris***. Similar White-eyed Vireo has yellow spectacles and clean white chin, throat, and breast. Black-whiskered Vireo has narrow malar stripe, white supercilium, dark line through eye, lacks wingbars. Voice a chattering, high-pitched *weet-weet-weet-weet* or clear, whistled *wi-wi-wi-wi*; may give harsh scolding call notes. Moves deliberately in low vegetation, sometimes foraging on ground.

Yellow-throated Vireo *Vireo flavifrons*
Nonbreeding Visitor

Regular but uncommon in mid- and upper canopy of a wide variety of forest types. Fairly large vireo (14 cm; 18 g). Upperparts olive green with contrasting gray rump; ***bright yellow chin, throat, and breast***; white belly and undertail coverts. Note ***bold yellow spectacles***, two white wingbars, and dark iris and lores. Similar White-eyed Vireo has white chin, throat, and breast. Thick-billed Vireo entirely buffy below, with more distinct black lores and grayish crown. Flat-billed Vireo dull whitish on breast, lacks yellow spectacles, has white iris. See Pine Warbler. Song a variable series of wheezy, slurred, short phrases separated by pauses, *chee-wee*, *chee-woo*, *u-wee*, *chee-wee*. Scolding call a harsh, descending series, *chi-chi-chi-chi*. Occasionally sings in nonbreeding season.

Thick-billed Vireo *Vireo crassirostris*
Breeding Resident

Moderately common throughout Île de la Tortue, Haiti. Heavy billed, medium-sized vireo (14 cm; 13 g); generally olive upperparts, grayish-green crown and nape, ***blackish lores***, ***dark iris***, two white wingbars. ***Bright yellow spectacles***, sometimes broken around eye. ***Underparts dingy whitish to buffy yellow***. Immature has poorly defined wingbars; lacks blackish lores. Similar White-eyed Vireo has white iris; smaller, thinner bill; whitish on throat, breast, and belly. Yellow-throated Vireo has bright yellow chin, throat, and breast, with white belly; olive green rather than grayish crown; lacks black lores. Bubbly, variable song *chik-didle-wer-chip*, slower and less emphatic than White-eyed Vireo. Calls include buzzy, low, nasal notes. More often heard than seen; often perches motionless in dense vegetation while singing.

White-eyed Vireo

Flat-billed Vireo

Yellow-throated Vireo

Thick-billed Vireo

Philadelphia Vireo *Vireo philadelphicus*
Vagrant

Possible in young, early-successional woodlands and similar habitats during the nonbreeding period. Small, *plain-winged* vireo (11 cm; 12 g) with *pale yellowish underparts*, palest on throat and deepest on breast; grayish-olive upperparts; grayish cap; *dusky lores and postocular stripe*; white supercilium. Very similar Warbling Vireo has pale lores creating "blank-faced" look, less pronounced supercilium, pale yellowish wash limited to sides and flanks. Noticeably larger Black-whiskered and Red-eyed vireos have larger bills, more distinct supercilium and eye-stripe. All other vireos on Hispaniola have pronounced wingbars. Tennessee Warbler is smaller, with brighter green upperparts, thinner and more finely pointed bill, less well-defined postocular stripe. Calls include soft, nasal *ehhh* or descending, twittering series of *cheeur* notes. May sing repetitive, deliberate song during spring migration; reminiscent of Black-whiskered Vireo.

Warbling Vireo *Vireo gilvus*
Vagrant

Possible in broadleaf forests, especially near water courses, during migration. Medium-sized, pale, unmarked vireo (12 cm; 13 g). Upperparts grayish olive, with crown slightly grayer. *No wingbars.* *Underparts dingy white*, with cleaner *white breast and belly*. Sides of neck and flanks lightly washed yellow; buffier on neck. *Lores pale*; *whitish supercilium without black borders arches over eye*; indistinct grayish eye-line. Similar Philadelphia Vireo has more pronounced supercilium, and more extensive yellow wash across upper breast. Red-eyed and Black-whiskered vireos are larger, greener, and have distinct white supercilium bordered narrowly above and below by black. Voice a variety of harsh, nasal mews; also a short, dry *git* or *vit*. Song is a soft, burry, rapid, run-on warble.

Red-eyed Vireo *Vireo olivaceus*
Vagrant

Possible in extensive broadleaf forests and shaded coffee plantations during migration and the nonbreeding season. Large vireo (14 cm; 18 g), distinguished by *gray crown* contrasting with olive green upperparts. Underparts white. Note prominent *white supercilium bordered by blackish eye-line below and distinct, thin, blackish lateral crown stripe above*. Adult has *red iris*; immature has dull brown iris and yellower tints on flanks and undertail coverts. Similar Black-whiskered Vireo has larger bill, black malar stripe, more buffy yellow underparts, duller green on back, paler gray on crown. Call a nasal, *myaahh*. Song consists of abrupt phrases separated by deliberate pauses *here-I-am ... up-here ... see-me? ... see me?*

Black-whiskered Vireo *Vireo altiloquus*
Breeding Visitor; Breeding Resident

Common to abundant in variety of woodlands and forested habitats at low- to mid-elevations. Large vireo (16 cm; 18 g); olive brownish upperparts, whitish underparts washed pale olive on sides and flanks, pale yellowish undertail coverts. *White supercilium contrasts with dusky eye-line and grayish crown*. Note narrow *black malar stripe*. Adult has red iris. Immature has brown iris, duller upperparts, more buffy underparts, and faint wingbar. See similar Red-eyed Vireo. Repetitive, monotonous song consists of short, 3-syllabled phrases, separated by distinct pause, *julián chi-ví*. Calls include a thin mewing *tsit* and a sharp, nasal, *yeeea*. Most nonbreeding birds thought to migrate to South America, but some appear to remain year-round.

Yellow-breasted Chat *Icteria virens*
Vagrant

Possible in dense scrub-shrub habitat or thick forest undergrowth in the nonbreeding season. Unmistakable. Robust build (18 cm; 25 g), *heavy bill*, and *long tail*. Upperparts, wings, and tail olive green. *Throat, breast, and upper belly bright yellow*; lower belly and undertail coverts white. Note *white spectacles*. Lores black in males, gray in females, bordered above and below by white. Calls variable; includes a harsh, nasal *cheow*, a sharp *cuk*, and a soft *tuk*. Song extremely varied collection of whistles, mews, squawks, and gurgles.

Philadelphia Vireo

Warbling Vireo

Red-eyed Vireo

Black-whiskered Vireo

Yellow-breasted Chat

Hispaniolan Palm Crow *Corvus palmarum*
Threatened Endemic Breeding Resident

Locally common, especially in remote areas; known mostly from pine forests, but recorded irregularly in dry scrub, dry forest, and humid broadleaf forest. Small, completely black corvid (36 cm; 300 g). In good light, purplish-blue sheen on back and upperwing coverts, fades to dull brownish black in worn plumage. Similar White-necked Crow is considerably larger, and has a less steady flapping flight. Hispaniolan Palm Crow **best identified by distinctive voice**: a harsh and nasal *aaar*, or *cao cao*, with complaining quality. Call usually given in pairs or in a series. Vocalizations less variable and more distinctly nasal than those of White-necked Crow. May flick tail downward, with wing tips lowered, while calling.

White-necked Crow *Corvus leucognaphalus*
Threatened Endemic Breeding Resident

Locally common to uncommon, most often occurring in lowland swamps, cactus forest, coastal mangroves, and broadleaf forests; occasionally in pine woodlands. Large, entirely black corvid (44 cm; mass unavailable), with large bill and **red-orange eye**. Upperparts have violet sheen, and base of neck is white, but these features rarely visible. Best distinguished from smaller Hispaniolan Palm Crow by reddish eye and **unique, variable voice**. Wide variety of vocalizations, including a *caw* and clucking, gurgling, bubbling, and laughlike calls and squawks; described as a comical *culic calao calao*. Flight tends to be less direct than Hispaniolan Palm Crow; will occasionally soar. Often flicks tail downward. Considered an endemic because extirpated from Puerto Rico.

Hispaniolan Palm Crow

White-necked Crow

White-necked Crow

Purple Martin *Progne subis*
Vagrant

Vagrant passage migrant over semiopen country, most likely near water. Large swallow (19 cm; 50 g) with forked tail. Adult male ***entirely glossy bluish black***; adult female and immature have ***scaled pattern on grayish-brown breast, a light gray forecrown and collar***, and an ***indistinct border*** between the grayish-brown breast and dingy whitish belly. See very similar Cuban and Caribbean martins. Male Purple and Cuban martins cannot be distinguished in the field; male Caribbean Martin has white belly. Female Cuban Martin has pale gray upper breast extending onto flanks, but shows a sharper demarcation with the white belly than in Purple Martin. Caribbean Martin has brown wash on breast rather than scaled pattern, with brown blending into white belly. Song of male Purple Martin is a rich, liquid gurgling; includes a high *twick-twick*. Calls include high, melodious warbles and low whistles.

Cuban Martin *Progne cryptoleuca*
Vagrant

Inhabits semiopen areas, especially near water and along coast, such as scrub, farmland, mangroves; also human habitations. Large, fork-tailed swallow (19 cm, 40 g). Male glossy steel blue, with ***concealed white band on lower belly***; wings and tail sooty black, tail forked. Female duller, sooty brown with blue feather margins above, greenish-blue gloss on wings and tail, sooty gray from side of head to breast and sides. ***Belly unmarked white***, but with a ***sharp demarcation*** with the pale gray upper breast and flanks. Extremely similar male Purple Martin has longer and more deeply forked tail, no concealed white abdominal band. Female Purple Martin has more scaled appearance to breast, and an indistinct border between the breast and belly. See also Caribbean Martin. Vocalizations very similar to those of other martins, include liquid gurgling, strong melodious warbling, and a high-pitched *twick-twick*.

Caribbean Martin *Progne dominicensis*
Breeding Visitor

Fairly common at low to mid-elevations, along coastlines and in open country, wherever abandoned woodpecker cavities are available for nesting. Large, bicolored swallow (20 cm; 40 g) with forked tail. Male upperparts, head, and throat metallic blue;  ***belly white*** with dark band across vent. Female and immature similar to adult male, but blue of underparts replaced by ***brownish wash blending into white belly***. Similar female Purple Martin has scaled pattern on breast rather than brownish wash; female Cuban Martin has pale gray upper breast extending onto flanks, but with a sharp demarcation with the white belly. Male Purple and Cuban martins entirely bluish black. Voice a rich, liquid gurgling, including a high *twick-twick*. Also melodious warble and gritty *churr*. Vocalizations similar to Purple Martin.

Purple Martin and Cuban Martin ♂

Caribbean Martin ♂

Purple Martin ♀

Cuban Martin ♀

Caribbean Martin ♀

Bank Swallow *Riparia riparia*
Passage Migrant

Rare, but probably overlooked; most likely near water. Small, slender swallow (12 cm; 15 g), **grayish-brown upperparts**, white underparts, with a **dark band across breast**. Forecrown pale; tail slightly notched. Immature has buffy wingbars. Similar Northern Rough-winged Swallow has pale brownish wash across breast; squared tail. Antillean Palm-Swift has a white rump; longer, narrower wings; flight more rapid and darting. Voice a rolling, buzzy series of repeated, short notes, *chirr* or *bzrrrt*. Typically found with other swallows; often seen perched on utility wires.

Tree Swallow *Tachycineta bicolor*
Passage Migrant; Nonbreeding Visitor

Regularly occurring in small numbers in open country near water, lakes, marshes, meadows. Medium-sized swallow (14 cm; 20 g) with **moderately forked tail**. Adult male and older females **iridescent greenish blue above**; entirely white underparts. Yearling females and immatures have brownish upperparts; underwing coverts pale gray. Similar but smaller Golden Swallow has golden sheen above, more forked tail, longer wings, more graceful flight. Mostly silent on Hispaniola, but sometimes gives a high, liquid twittering.

Golden Swallow *Tachycineta euchrysea*
Endangered Endemic Breeding Resident

Uncommon; increasingly rare and local. Occurs primarily at higher elevations over pine forest; occasionally over open fields and humid broadleaf forest. Small swallow (12 cm; 13 g) with moderately forked tail. Adults **iridescent bluish-green upperparts with golden sheen**; white underparts. Females duller above than males, with grayish wash on breast. Immatures similar to females but duller above, with gray breast band. Similar Tree Swallow has shallower tail notch, relatively shorter and broader wings, less graceful flight. Voice a soft twittering *chi-weet* during the breeding season. Often seen foraging over pine forests or perched in small groups in large, dead pine snags. Considered an endemic because believed to be extirpated from Jamaica.

Northern Rough-winged Swallow
Stelgidopteryx serripennis
Nonbreeding Visitor

Unusual but regularly occurring near lakes and rivers; probably often overlooked. Small, drab, somewhat stocky swallow (13 cm; 15 g), uniform **warm brown above**, white below, with **pale brownish wash on chin, throat, and chest**. Tail square. Immature has cinnamon wingbars. Similar Bank Swallow has well-defined dark breast band; shallower and faster wingbeats. Voice a repetitive series of low, coarse *prriit* or *brrrtt* notes, slightly rising in inflection. Often occurs in the company of other swallows.

Bank Swallow

Tree Swallow

imm

Golden Swallow

♂

♂

imm

♀

Northern Rough-winged Swallow

Barn Swallow *Hirundo rustica*
Passage Migrant; Nonbreeding Visitor

Common passage migrant and regular nonbreeding visitor, primarily near coast, but also in lowlands over agricultural lands and wetlands. An elegant swallow (18 cm; 20 g), with long, slender, pointed wings and *long, deeply forked tail* with *white spots* on inner webs. Adults dark bluish black above, tan to orangish underneath, with dark chestnut throat and forecrown. Females average paler below with shorter tail than males. Immature has throat and upper breast tan, remainder of underparts white, tail less deeply forked. Deeply forked tail and uniformly tan or orangish underparts distinguish this species from all other swallows. Voice a short, husky *chit* or *chit-chit*. Typically seen in flocks zigzagging low to ground over fields or water, or perched on utility wires.

Cliff Swallow *Petrochelidon pyrrhonota*
Vagrant

Possible as a passage migrant near coasts, lakes, and open and semiopen land. Stocky, pale-rumped swallow (13 cm; 23 g), distinguished by *dark reddish-brown chin, throat, and auriculars*; *buff-colored forecrown, collar, and rump*. Rest of upperparts metallic bluish black; underparts dull white. Chestnut throat patch often contains dark patch of greenish or bluish black. *Tail short and squared*. Immatures variable but show much paler throat and auriculars; duller and browner upperparts. Similar Cave Swallow has darker, more extensive patch on forecrown; much paler buffy throat and auriculars. Calls include low, burry, nasal *vrrrt* and drier rolled *chrri-chrri*, repeated in flight. Often occurs in the company of other swallows, but almost certainly overlooked because of similarity to common Cave Swallow.

Cave Swallow *Petrochelidon fulva*
Breeding Resident

Common islandwide near cliffs along coast; inland over fields, open areas, and wetlands; occasionally in towns. Small, stocky (13 cm; 20 g), pale-rumped swallow. Identified by *dark, rufous-buff rump and forecrown*; *paler buffy auriculars and throat, extending around nape, across breast, and down sides*, giving dark-capped appearance. Tail short and square to slightly notched. Similar Cliff Swallow has dark reddish-brown throat and auriculars and lighter forecrown. Song a mix of twittering notes and nasal buzzes. Common flight call a soft, rising *twit* or *pwid*. Highly gregarious; typically seen in flocks, often perched on utility wires.

Barn Swallow

imm

Cliff Swallow

Cave Swallow

Rufous-throated Solitaire *Myadestes genibarbis*
Breeding Resident

Locally common in moist broadleaf forest of foothills and mountains; usually not found in pine forest or shade coffee except when associated with humid broadleaf habitat. Unmistakable, slender, arboreal thrush (19 cm; 27 g), mostly gray above with **white chin, reddish-brown throat and undertail coverts**; rest of underparts pale gray. Note **white crescent** below eye. Tail fairly long with white outer feathers visible when fanned. Legs and feet yellow. Sings one of the most beautiful songs on Hispaniola; haunting, clear, minor-key whistled notes of different tones, typically ending in higher-pitched trill. Most often heard at dawn and dusk.

American Robin *Turdus migratorius*
Vagrant

Possible on lawns, in parks, and other open habitats during nonbreeding season. Large, conspicuous thrush (25 cm; 77 g); slaty-gray upperparts and **dull orangish-red underparts**. Throat is white streaked black; undertail coverts white. Bill yellow. Males have blackish head and tail; females paler overall. Similar Red-legged Thrush has bright reddish bill and legs; gray breast. La Selle Thrush has darker slaty head and upperparts, dark gray breast, and white streak on belly. Voice a staccato, clucking *puk-puk-puk*; also a low, mellow *pup*. Song a series of short, happy phrases, followed by pauses, *cheer-up … cheer-ey*.

Red-legged Thrush *Turdus plumbeus*
Breeding Resident

Fairly common in wide variety of habitats from dry forest and second-growth woodland to pines and humid forest; most numerous in moist broadleaf forest. Large thrush (26 cm; 72 g); slaty-gray upperparts, **reddish legs and bill, red eye-ring, white tail tips**. Breast gray, throat white with black stripes, belly and undertail coverts whitish. Juvenile duller overall with gray throat spotted black. See similar American Robin and La Selle Thrush; both lack red bill and legs. Call notes a low *wéecha* and a rapid, high-pitched *chu-wéek, chu-wéek, chu-wéek*. Alarm call a loud *chuá-chuá*. Song a melodious but monotonous series of 1- to 3-syllable phrases, often uttered in pairs, with distinct pause between each note, *chirruit … chir-ruit* or *pert … squeer*. Forages mainly on ground. Often seen at dawn, darting from roadsides or forest openings.

La Selle Thrush *Turdus swalesi*
Endangered Endemic Breeding Resident

Uncommon and very local; restricted to remaining montane forest fragments where confined to dense undergrowth of moist broadleaf forest, and pine forest with dense broadleaf understory; often found with thick stands of climbing bamboo. Large, extremely secretive thrush (26 cm; 97 g); slaty-black head and upperparts, **slaty-gray upper breast, rich rufous lower breast and sides**, **white belly** and undertail coverts. Auriculars silvery; throat streaked white. **Eye-ring yellowish orange**; bill reddish orange. Legs dark. See similar Red-legged Thrush and American Robin. Voice a series of deliberate *tu-re-oo* and *cho-ho-cho* calls, often given at dawn and dusk. Also a loud *wheury-wheury-wheury* alarm call. Song a quiet, mellow mix of gurgling notes. Sings from exposed perches at dawn and dusk; otherwise quiet, inconspicuous, and largely terrestrial.

Rufous-throated Solitaire

American Robin

Red-legged Thrush

La Selle Thrush

Veery *Catharus fuscescens*
Vagrant
Possible in second-growth woodlands and other forested habitats, where most often seen on the ground or in forest understory. May occur as a passage migrant or nonbreeding visitor. Medium-sized thrush (18 cm; 30 g), generally with ***uniformly reddish-brown upperparts***. Throat and chest buffy with ***indistinct brownish spots***; rest of underparts white. Has inconspicuous pale eye-ring. Other similar *Catharus* thrushes lack the uniform, warm reddish brown above, and are more distinctly spotted below. Call a low, nasal *pheu* or *veer*. Song, rarely heard outside of breeding season, a rich downward spiral with an ethereal quality.

Bicknell's Thrush *Catharus bicknelli*
Threatened Nonbreeding Visitor
Uncommon to rare, locally distributed in dense understory of moist broadleaf forest, or broadleaf forest mixed with relatively few pines, mostly at mid- to higher elevations. Smallish, slender *Catharus* thrush (16 cm; 28 g), with olive-brown upperparts and  contrasting ***chestnut-tinged tail***, whitish underparts; ***sides of throat and breast creamy buff prominently spotted black***. Auriculars and lores grayish. Similar Veery is more finely spotted below; more reddish brown above. Generally silent on Hispaniola except for brief dawn and dusk calling. Calls typically a downward slurred whistle, *beer* or *pee-irt*, occasionally a softer *chook* or *chuck*. Song a high-pitched *chook-chook, wee-o, wee-o, wee-o-tee-t-ter-ee*, slurring downward, infrequent and subdued in nonbreeding season. Typically shy and wary. Males predominate in undisturbed montane forests, females and yearlings in younger, more disturbed, mid-elevation forest.

Swainson's Thrush *Catharus ustulatus*
Vagrant
Possible in moist forests and other woodlands with dense understory during migratory period. Medium-sized *Catharus* thrush (17 cm; 30 g) with uniform, olive-brownish upperparts, ***distinct buffy eye-ring and lores forming spectacles***, whitish underparts but ***buffier across the breast***, and brownish-black ***spotting on throat and breast***. Similar Bicknell's Thrush has grayish face, upperparts warmer brownish gray with contrasting rufous-brown tail. Veery is more finely spotted below; more reddish brown above; lacks eye-ring. Rarely vocalizes at southbound stopover sites, but most common and distinctive call a single, sharp *whit*. Often sings during spring stopover; song flutelike, rolling and spiraling upward. Nocturnal migrants give characteristic clear, emphatic *peeep* or *queep* call.

Wood Thrush *Hylocichla mustelina*
Vagrant
Possible in understory of primary broadleaf and older second-growth forest during nonbreeding season. Largest of the spotted thrushes (20 cm; 45 g), distinguished by ***bright cinnamon-brown crown and nape***, slightly duller on back, wings, and tail; conspicuous ***white eye-ring***; white underparts with ***heavy blackish spots on breast, sides, and flanks***. No other thrush is as heavily spotted below or as distinctly reddish brown on upperparts. Typical call of rapid, staccato *pit-pit-pit* notes; also a lower, clucking *bup-bup* or *tut-tut*. Outside of breeding season, rarely sings its clear, flutelike song of 3–5 syllables, ending with a trill.

Veery

Bicknell's Thrush

Swainson's Thrush

Wood Thrush

Gray Catbird *Dumetella carolinensis*
Nonbreeding Visitor

Rare; occurring in thickets and dense undergrowth at low to mid-elevations. Small mimid (23 cm; 38 g), **almost entirely dark gray** with **black cap**, **reddish-brown undertail coverts**, and long tail often cocked slightly upward. Similar Rufous-throated Solitaire has reddish-brown throat, white outer tail feathers. Voice a hoarse, catlike *meew*; also soft, low-pitched *quirt* or *turrr*. Alarm note a loud, harsh chatter, *chek-chek-chek*. Song a rambling series of disconnected phrases, including meews, squeaks, gurgles, and imitations. More often heard than seen; generally forages near or on ground.

Pearly-eyed Thrasher *Margarops fuscatus*
Breeding Resident

Local and uncommon but increasingly widespread in low- to mid-elevation thickets, woodlands, and coastal forests. Large mimid (28 cm; 100 g) with brown upperparts; **dull white underparts streaked with brown**. **Iris distinctly white**; bill large and yellowish; tail has large, **white tips**. Somewhat similar to Eastern and Western chat-tanagers but ranges do not overlap. Voice a series of 1- to 3-syllabled phrases, *pío-tareeu-tsee*, with fairly lengthy pauses separating each. Often sings well into day and during clear nights. Also many raucous call notes, including a guttural *craw-craw* and a harsh *chook-chook*. Arboreal and extraordinarily aggressive. Competes with other birds for cavity nest sites; known to eat eggs and young of other birds.

Northern Mockingbird *Mimus polyglottos*
Breeding Resident

Common resident in nearly every low-elevation habitat, including open country, semiarid scrub, gardens, parks. Conspicuous bird (24 cm; 49 g), pale gray or gray brown above, grayish white below. **Wings and tail with conspicuous white patches**, show clearly in flight. **Long tail often cocked upward**. Thin dark line through yellowish eye. Juvenile has brownish-gray upperparts; buffy-white underparts with faint brownish breast spots. Similar Gray Kingbird lacks white patches; does not cock its shorter tail. Voice a clear, melodious series of varied phrases, each phrase repeated 2–6 times. Alarm call a loud, explosive *tchak*. An expert mimic, often incorporates calls of other species in diverse repertoire. Sings night and day.

Palmchat *Dulus dominicus*
Endemic Breeding Resident

Common and locally abundant resident islandwide in nearly all lowlands and mid-elevation habitats, especially where royal palms present. Unmistakable. Conspicuous, flocking bird (20 cm; 48 g), most often seen flying to and from treetops in semiopen country. Upperparts dark brown; underparts creamy white, **heavily streaked brown**. Tail medium-long and squared. **Heavy bill yellow**; **eye reddish**. Quite noisy, particularly around its nest, producing array of strange, slurring, whistled call notes. Large twiggy nest structure is up to 2 m wide; built and used communally by many pairs; each nest chamber has a separate entrance. Nests most often built in royal palms. This is the Dominican national bird.

American Pipit *Anthus rubescens*
Vagrant

Possible in open fields and sandy areas during nonbreeding period. **Slender, thin-billed**, long-tailed, ground-dwelling bird (16 cm; 21 g). Habitually **bobs tail while walking**. Upon taking flight, displays conspicuous **white outer tail feathers**. In nonbreeding adult, note buffy supercilium, two faint wingbars; underparts vary from pinkish buff to pale gray, with **blackish streaks concentrated on breast**. Distinguished from sparrows by more slender bill and body, longer legs and longer tail. Flight call a high, distinctive *sip-it* or *sip*; song a high-pitched *pip-pip*.

Gray Catbird

Pearly-eyed Thrasher

Northern Mockingbird

Palmchat

American Pipit

Village Weaver *Ploceus cucullatus*
Breeding Resident

Introduced; moderately common throughout coastal lowlands in open dry forest, desert scrub, agricultural areas, and vegetation near water and villages. Chunky (17 cm; male 40 g, female 34 g), heavy-billed finch. Male orange-yellow overall with **black hood, chestnut-brown nape, red iris**. Female yellowish green, brightest on face and breast; darker wings and mantle; **yellow supercilium and wingbars**. Eye red. Immature similar to female but iris brownish. Similar adult male Baltimore Oriole also black and orange-yellow but slimmer with longer bill and tail. Voice a steady high-pitched chatter with musical whistling calls. Often flocks. Nests colonially.

Pin-tailed Whydah *Vidua macroura*
Breeding Resident?

Rare, introduced resident of grassy and open shrubby habitats, cultivated lands and gardens. Small finch (12 cm, breeding male 30 cm; 15 g) with stubby bill. Breeding male unmistakable with **extremely long tail feathers**, black forehead and crown, white face and collar, black upperparts, and **large white wing patch**. **Bill red**. Female's head and face distinctly striped, with **dark stripes on side of crown and through eye**, separated by **rufous to buff supercilium**. Upperparts rufous buff with blackish streaks; underparts buffy white with dark streaks on sides. Tail relatively short; bill black in breeding season, red in nonbreeding season. Calls include harsh alarm chatter, low *peeee* and double *chip-chip* in flight. Song a jerky series with hissing quality, interspersed with trills and rapid tinny jingling. Brood parasite assumed to breed on Hispaniola but not yet documented.

Red Avadavat *Amandava amandava*
Breeding Resident? Extirpated?

Introduced but possibly extirpated. Expected primarily in grassy margins of freshwater swamps, sugarcane fields, and drainage canals. Small finch (10 cm; 9 g). Breeding male primarily **deep red overall** with brownish-black upperwing and tail; small **white spots on wings, flanks, and sides**. Adult female and nonbreeding male brownish above, paler below; note **red uppertail coverts and bill**, white spots on wing, dark eye-line. Immature similar to adult female but lacks red and has buff-colored wing spots. See similar Scaly-breasted and Tricolored munias. Call notes are a musical *sweet* and *sweet-eet*; also variety of melodious whistles and warbles.

Scaly-breasted Munia *Lonchura punctulata*
Breeding Resident

Introduced; common, spreading islandwide in lowland open areas with seeding grass, borders of sugarcane, agricultural areas, road edges, and parks. Small finch (12 cm; 14 g); adult deep reddish brown above, whitish below, with **cinnamon-colored hood** and **scalloped black-and-white underparts**. Immatures lack adult markings; cinnamon-colored above, paler below. Immature can be confused with several species, but **heavy, blackish bill** and light cinnamon coloration unique. Separated from immature Tricolored Munia by being less pale below. Voice a soft, plaintive, whistled *peet,* dropping in pitch and fading. Typically flocks; often with Tricolored Munia. Also known as Nutmeg Mannikin and Checkered Munia.

Tricolored Munia *Lonchura malacca*
Breeding Resident

Introduced; locally common in low-elevation grassy areas bordering sugarcane, marshes, rice plantations, and agricultural fields. Small finch (12 cm; 12 g); adults strikingly patterned with **cinnamon-colored back and wings**, **full black hood**, white underparts with black belly patch. Bill pale grayish. Immatures cinnamon brown above, buffy below; dark bill. Immature similar to Scaly-breasted Munia, but Tricolored is more cinnamon-colored and has **paler bill and underparts**. Call note a thin, nasal honk, *neat*, less plaintive, clear, and melodious than Scaly-breasted Munia. Also known as Tricolored Mannikin and Black-headed Munia.

Village Weaver

♀

♂

Pin-tailed Whydah

♂

♀

Red Avadavat

br ♂

imm

♀ & non-br ♂

Scaly-breasted Munia

imm

Tricolored Munia

imm

Cedar Waxwing *Bombycilla cedrorum*
Nonbreeding Visitor

Rare visitor to forests and woodlands. Unmistakable; sleek bird (16 cm; 32 g) with overall grayish-brown plumage. Crown and back warm cinnamon brown; wings, rump, and uppertail coverts plain gray. Underparts tan, fading to pale yellowish on belly; undertail coverts whitish. Note sharp **black facial mask** edged white, **black chin patch**, conspicuous **back-pointed crest**, and **yellow-tipped tail** (occasionally orange). Secondaries may have variable numbers of red, waxlike tips. Voice a thin, high-pitched, slightly trilled *sreee*. Typically occurs in small flocks, often visiting trees or shrubs with ripe berries.

Antillean Euphonia *Chlorophonia musica*
Breeding Resident

Locally common in dense forest canopy where mistletoe is present; typically includes tropical evergreen, moist broadleaf, and deciduous forest, shade coffee, and occasionally pine forest. Unmistakable. Small, compact bird (11 cm; 13 g), with **sky blue crown and nape**. Males primarily blackish above, orangish yellow below and on rump and forehead. **Chin and throat dark violet**. Female duller overall, mostly greenish above, yellowish green below. **Rump and forecrown yellowish**. A variety of call notes, including a rapid, scolding *ti-tit* (sometimes 1 or 3 syllables); a hard, metallic *chi-chink*; a plaintive whistle, *whee*. Also a jumbled, tinkling song, *tuc-tuc-tuc* punctuated with explosive whistles. Despite colorful appearance, most readily located in canopy by its calls.

Hispaniolan Crossbill *Loxia megaplaga*
Endangered Endemic Breeding Resident

Uncommon and local in high pine forests of Cordillera Central, Sierra de Bahoruco, Massif de la Selle, and Massif de la Hotte. Remarkable, unmistakable finch (16 cm; 28 g) noteworthy for **uniquely crossed bill tips**. Adult male dusky brown, **washed pale red overall** but concentrated on head, upper back, and upper breast. Adult female dusky brown with finely streaked breast, with **yellow wash on upper breast**; **yellowish rump**. Adults of both sexes have **two broad white bars on blackish wings**. Juvenile similar to female but browner and more heavily streaked, especially on breast. Voice high-pitched, emphatic, *chu-chu-chu-chu*, similar to typewriter keys, heard often in short flights between pines; also soft, whistling warble. Breeding pairs give *chit-chit* contact calls. Restricted to mature Hispaniolan pine habitat; may wander as pinecone supply varies. Often quiet and secretive, but listen for telltale cracking of pine seeds.

Antillean Siskin *Spinus dominicensis*
Endemic Breeding Resident

Locally common in pine forest and associated weedy clearings of interior hills and mountains; occasionally in nearby moist broadleaf forest. Small, chunky finch (11 cm; 9 g) with **light yellow, conical bill**. Male with yellow body, olive-green back, **black head and throat**, two diffuse yellow patches on black tail. Female olive green above, yellowish white below, with faint pale gray streaking, pale yellowish rump, **two yellowish wingbars**. Similar female Village Weaver is larger, darker, has more massive bill and yellow supercilium. Female Yellow-faced Grassquit has dark bill, lacks wingbars, and has no streaks on underparts. Calls include *seee-ip*, a higher-pitched *swee-ee*, and a soft *chut-chut* when flushed. Song a low, jumbled trill. Small flocks forage from tree to tree and in bushes or grassy patches.

Cedar Waxwing

imm

Antillean Euphonia

imm

♀

♂

Hispaniolan Crossbill

♀

♂

Antillean Siskin

♂

♀

House Sparrow *Passer domesticus*
Breeding Resident

Introduced; locally occurring but increasingly common in urban areas and villages. Stocky (16 cm; 28 g), with shorter legs and thicker bill than native sparrows. Male brown above with blackish streaks; ***single white wingbar***; rump grayish. Note ***chestnut nape***, gray crown, ***pale gray auriculars***, ***black patch on face and throat forming a bib***. Underparts grayish. Female and immature much duller; crown grayish brown. ***Pale buffy supercilium and thin dusky eye-line present behind the eye only***. Underparts dingy grayish brown; black bib lacking. Similar Grasshopper Sparrow has pale central crown stripe and buffy underparts. Adult Rufous-collared Sparrow has gray and brown stripes on head and narrow black neck band. Call notes include loud *chirp* or *cheep*, also husky rattle or chatter. Song a monotonous series of *chirp* notes. Gregarious; may flock any time of year.

Rufous-collared Sparrow *Zonotrichia capensis*
Breeding Resident

Common in scrub and understory in the high-elevation pine zone of Sierra de Neiba and Cordillera Central. Distinctive, medium-sized, stocky sparrow (13 cm; 24 g); brown upperparts with coarse dark streaks; grayish white underparts, whiter on throat. Note ***black neck band***, ***reddish-brown nape***, and ***gray crown with black stripes***. Often displays slight crest. Juvenile duller, somewhat spotted below; lacks black or reddish-brown markings. Similar Grasshopper Sparrow lacks black band on foreneck, reddish-brown nape, and gray on crown. Song and Lincoln's sparrows streaked above and below. Voice an accelerating trill, *whis-whis-whis-whis-whiswhisu-whiswhis*, often given from prominent perch. Shy and retiring; often in pairs. Usually feeds on seeds from the ground.

Song Sparrow *Melospiza melodia*
Vagrant

Possible in thickets, brush, and gardens during nonbreeding season. Medium-sized, stocky sparrow (16 cm; 21 g) with fairly long, rounded tail. Upperparts grayish with coarse brown streaks; underparts whitish with ***coarse brown streaks converging into central breast spot***. Wings and tail brownish. Crown has broad brown lateral stripes bordering paler central stripe. Also note broad gray supercilium, and conspicuous brown malar stripes bordering unmarked whitish throat. Similar Lincoln's Sparrow smaller, less heavily streaked above and below, and has buffy wash on breast. Savannah Sparrow has shorter, notched tail; yellowish lores and supercilium; legs distinctly pinker. Call notes include sharp, husky *tchunk*; also high-pitched contact note, *tseep* or *seeet*. Variable song often begins with 3–4 short notes, followed by long trill and buzzes. Often feeds on ground with tail cocked.

Lincoln's Sparrow *Melospiza lincolnii*
Vagrant

Possible in understory of high-elevation moist broadleaf forest, or bracken fern tangles at forest edge during nonbreeding period. Small sparrow (14 cm; 18 g); upperparts grayish brown finely streaked black; ***breast and sides washed buffy and finely streaked black***. Throat and belly whitish; wings and tail brown. Crown brown streaked black, with narrow grayish median stripe, broad supercilium and sides of face mostly gray; malar stripes buffy. Similar Song Sparrow larger, more boldly streaked above and below, lacks buffy wash on breast. Calls include sharp low-pitched *chip* and soft, high-pitched *zeet*. Song, unlikely on Hispaniola, a complex gurgling rising in middle and dropping sharply at end. Because of shy, skulking habits, may occur more frequently than recorded.

House Sparrow

♂

♀ & imm

Rufous-collared Sparrow

Song Sparrow

Lincoln's Sparrow

Grasshopper Sparrow *Ammodramus savannarum*
Breeding Resident

Locally common in small colonies in open fields, cattle ranches, savannas, rice fields, and tall grass habitat of lowlands. Small, *flat-headed* sparrow (11 cm; 17 g), intricately patterned with rufous, buff, and gray above; *yellow-orange lores*; white eye-ring; and whitish central stripe on dark crown. *Plain buffy white below*. Juveniles possess paler mark by bill and have fine streaks on breast and flanks. Similar Savannah Sparrow more heavily streaked than immature Grasshopper Sparrow. Two distinct songs. Long, thin, insectlike buzz, followed by what sounds like a hiccup, *zzzzzzz-hic*. Also thin, high-pitched twitter or tinkling song, like fairy bells. Call note is high-pitched, gritty, insectlike *kr-r-it*. Generally very secretive; much more often heard than seen.

Savannah Sparrow *Passerculus sandwichensis*
Vagrant

Possible in open fields, pastures, bushy savannas, and sparse thickets near the coast during the nonbreeding season. Slender sparrow (13 cm; 20 g), with upperparts and underparts heavily streaked brown. *Supercilium and lores yellowish or buff*, *pale central crown stripe*, dark malar stripe, pink legs. *Tail short and slightly notched*. Similar Song Sparrow has heavier breast stripes merging into central spot; longer, rounded tail. Grasshopper Sparrow has more golden supercilium; lacks malar stripe. Immature Grasshopper Sparrow has finer, paler streaks below. Song a high-pitched, buzzy, insectlike series of 3 *chips* followed by 2 wispy notes, the last one shorter and lower, *chip-chip-chip-tisisiiii-tisi*. Call a high, sharp *tsip*. Typically seen on ground.

Yellow-faced Grassquit *Tiaris olivaceus*
Breeding Resident

Common to abundant in open grassy areas, abandoned fields and pastures, edges of clearings, agricultural areas, and sun coffee. Small finch (10 cm; 9 g), greenish olive above, slightly grayer below. Male recognized by *golden yellow throat, supercilium, and crescent below eye*, and by black upper breast. Female and immature usually show faint yellowish supercilium, crescent, and chin; lack black on breast. Similar female and immature Black-faced Grassquit generally more olive in coloration; facial markings are faint at best. Female Antillean Siskin has pale yellow bill and yellow wingbars. Call note usually a high, soft *tek* or *sik*. Song a rapid, thin, buzzy trill, sometimes uttered sequentially on different pitches.

Black-faced Grassquit *Melanospiza bicolor*
Breeding Resident

Locally common in grassy patches and open areas, including pastures, cane fields, clearings, agricultural areas, streamsides, and open broadleaf woodland. Small (11 cm; 10 g), dark olive finch. Male identified by *black head and underparts*. Female and immature uniformly drab brownish olive. Young males show progressive development of black hood and bib. Similar female and immature drabber than Yellow-faced Grassquit counterparts and lack faint yellowish facial markings. Male much smaller than immature Greater Antillean Bullfinch, which can also combine black and olive-brown plumages. Song an emphatic buzz; also a weak buzzing series. Call note a soft musical *tsip*.

imm

Grasshopper Sparrow

Savannah Sparrow

♀ & imm

Yellow-faced Grassquit

♂

Black-faced Grassquit

♂

♀ & imm

Black-crowned Palm-Tanager
Phaenicophilus palmarum
Endemic Breeding Resident

Common in all habitats from lowland desert scrub to pine forest. Distinctive, robust songbird (18 cm; 28 g), with bright yellow-green upperparts, gray nape, **black crown and facial mask**. Mask contrasts with **three bold white spots around eye**. Underparts pale gray, with **diffuse white chin and throat**. Immature duller than adult; crown varies from gray to dark gray or mostly black. See Similar Gray-crowned Palm-Tanager. Song varies geographically, typically consists of jumbled squeaky notes that grow louder, then diminish and slow to short *chit* notes at end. Call a low *chep*, frequently given while foraging; also a nasal, buzzy *pi-au*. Usually moves slowly and deliberately, probing into crevices, holes, and bromeliads, hopping among branches, and hanging acrobatically from trees.

Gray-crowned Palm-Tanager
Phaenicophilus poliocephalus
Endemic Breeding Resident

Locally common but restricted to western end of Tiburón Peninsula and satellite islands. Inhabits dry, moist broadleaf forest, and pine forests; mangroves, lowland scrub, and second growth on islands. Robust songbird (18 cm; 27 g) with adult unmarked yellow-green above, light gray below, with **gray crown and nape**, **blackish facial mask**, and **sharply defined white chin and throat**. **Three white spots** contrast with black mask. Immature duller than adult. Similar immature Black-crowned Palm-Tanager may have a gray crown but will not have the sharply defined white chin and throat. Call is *peee-u*. During courtship, an extended melodic song is given and, less often, a canarylike "whisper song."

Hispaniolan Highland-Tanager *Xenoligea montana*
Endangered Endemic Breeding Resident

Locally common in high-elevation moist broadleaf forest, or mixed broadleaf and pines. Small, robust songbird (13 cm; 12 g), with fairly long tail and heavy bill. Back and rump bright green. Underparts white, washed gray on sides of breast and flanks. Head and nape gray, with **blackish spot between eye and bill bordered above by white line**; narrow white crescents above and below eye. Wings and tail blackish; outer primaries edged white, forming **prominent white patch in closed wing**. White spots on outer tail feathers. Similar Green-tailed Ground-Tanager has red iris and lacks white in wing, tail, and in front of eye. Calls a low chattering *suit-suit-suit-chir-suit-suit-suit-suit-chir-chi*; also a thin, low-pitched *tseep*. Song a series of high-pitched, accelerating, squeaky notes. Usually in pairs or mixed-species flocks, actively foraging from understory to high canopy. Also known as White-winged Warbler.

Green-tailed Ground-Tanager *Microligea palustris*
Endemic Breeding Resident

Locally common in lowland dry scrub and dry broadleaf forest, higher-elevation moist broadleaf forest, and the dense understory of pine forest; population density greatest at middle and higher-elevation habitats. Small, slender, active bird (13 cm; 13 g) with long tail. Upperparts unmarked olive greenish, except **head, face, and nape grayish**. Underparts uniformly dull white. Note **incomplete white eye-ring**. Adults have **red iris**; immatures have brown iris and greenish wash on head and nape. Similar Hispaniolan Highland Tanager has small white patch on outer primaries and in front of eye, white tail spots, and lacks red iris. Call a varied series of short, rasping and squeaking notes; song a high *sip sip-sip*. Feed low to ground and in tangles of brush and vines. Inquisitive; often responds to *pishing* noises. Also known as Green-tailed Warbler.

Black-crowned Palm-Tanager

ray-crowned Palm-Tanager

Hispaniolan Highland-Tanager

Green-tailed Ground-Tanager

Western Chat-Tanager *Calyptophilus tertius*
Endangered Endemic Breeding Resident

Uncommon and local in dense understory of high-elevation, moist broadleaf, and pine forest, frequently in heavily vegetated ravines. Restricted to Massif de la Hotte, Massif de la Selle, and western Sierra de Bahoruco to at least Polo. Mockingbird-shaped endemic (21 cm; 49 g), with *long, rounded tail*. Dark *chocolate brown above*, mostly *white below*, with bright *yellow spot in front of eye*, yellow fringe on bend of wing. Legs and feet are robust. Very similar but slightly smaller Eastern Chat-Tanager has brighter yellow eye-spot, yellow eye-ring, and more extensive yellow-orange patches at bend of wing and on underwing coverts. Ranges of the two species probably do not overlap, but some question remains. Melodious song heard especially at dawn: emphatic, clear whistling *chirri-chirri-chirri-chip-chip-chip*, repeated many times. Call a sharp *chin-chin-chin*. Also a *tick, tick, tick* contact call. Mostly ground-dwelling; shy and difficult to observe.

Eastern Chat-Tanager *Calyptophilus frugivorus*
Endangered Endemic Breeding Resident

Uncommon and local in dense understory of high-elevation, moist broadleaf and pine forest, frequently in heavily vegetated ravines. Restricted to most remote, undisturbed areas of Sierra de Neiba, Cordillera Central, Sierra de Ocoa, Sierra de Martín García, and extreme eastern Sierra de Bahoruco between Polo and Barahona. Low-elevation populations in dense swampy undergrowth of Samaná Peninsula, and dense semiarid scrub on Île de la Gonâve likely extirpated. Mockingbird-shaped (19 cm; 32 g), with long, rounded tail. Dark *chocolate brown above*, mostly *white below* with bright *yellow spot in front of eye*, yellow fringe on bend of wing, and *yellow eye-ring* broken anteriorly and posteriorly. Legs and feet robust. See very similar Western Chat-Tanager. Song similar to Western Chat-Tanager with subtle differences; an emphatic, clear whistling *chip-chip-swerp-swerp-swerp* or *chirri-chirri-chirri-chip-chip-chip*, repeated many times; given mostly at dawn. Call a sharp *chin chin chin*, heard especially in early morning. Mainly terrestrial; very secretive and difficult to observe.

Hispaniolan Spindalis *Spindalis dominicensis*
Endemic Breeding Resident

Locally common in mid-elevation evergreen, and montane broadleaf and pine forests. Unmistakable. Small-billed tanager (16 cm; 29 g) with striking plumage differences between sexes. Male has *black head boldly striped with white*. Nape brilliant yellow with orange tinge; yellow back broken by dark yellow-green mantle. Underparts yellow with reddish-brown wash on breast. Tail and wings black, edged whitish; bold chestnut patch at bend of wing. Female relatively nondescript with olive-brown upperparts, *whitish mustache stripe*, yellowish rump. Underparts dull whitish with *fine dusky streaks*. Immatures similar overall to adult females, but males more heavily streaked, including indistinct black streaks or dark green back. Rump of immature male yellowish tinged chestnut. Call a very high-pitched *seep*, feeble and insectlike. Dawn song a thin, high-pitched whistle or prolonged weak *tsee see see see*. Arboreal; tends to move frequently in search of large fruit crops.

Western Chat-Tanager

ern Chat-Tanager

Hispaniolan Spindalis

Bobolink *Dolichonyx oryzivorus*
Passage Migrant
Rarely encountered; possible in rice fields, pastures, and areas where grass is seeding. Medium-sized blackbird (18 cm; male 45 g, female 39 g). Nonbreeding adult warm buffy brown overall with streaked back, rump, and sides. Note **unmarked, buff-colored throat** and **buffy central crown stripe**. **Wings and tail feathers noticeably pointed**. Breeding male black below with a distinctive **yellowish-buff hindneck** and **white patches on wings and rump**. Breeding female similar to nonbreeding birds but paler, with whitish rather than buff-colored throat. Nonbreeding adult Bobolink differs from similar sparrows by larger size, streaked sides and lower belly, and pointed tail feathers. Call heard on migration a distinctive, musical *pink*; may also give soft, low *chuk*. Song a boisterous series of bubbling notes and gurgling phrases. Typically flocks in nonbreeding season.

Hispaniolan Oriole *Icterus dominicensis*
Threatened Endemic Breeding Resident
Common in the lowlands, broadleaf forest edges, and shade coffee plantations, but primarily wherever palms occur. A showy oriole (21 cm; 36 g); adult black overall with **yellow shoulders, lower belly, undertail coverts, and rump**. Immature has mainly
olive upperparts and dull olive-yellow underparts. Wings black; throat is sometimes black or reddish brown. Similar Tawny-shouldered Blackbird has tan patch on shoulder. Immature similar to female Shiny Cowbird, but oriole more olive with longer bill. Call note a hard, sharp *keek* or *check* and a harsh *chrr*. A melodic but rarely heard dawn song consists of exclamatory and querulous high-pitched whistles.

Orchard Oriole *Icterus spurius*
Vagrant
Possible in woodlands, forest edges, orchards, and parks in nonbreeding season. Small, compact oriole (17 cm; 20 g), with short tail and bill. Adult male has entirely black head, upper breast, back, and tail; **chestnut lower breast, belly, undertail coverts, and rump**. Wings mostly black with narrow white lower wingbar and broad chestnut upper wingbar. Female olive green above, greenish yellow below, with grayish-brown wings with two narrow white wingbars. Immature similar to female, but first-year male has variable black on throat and chest; occasional chestnut feathers on body. See similar Baltimore Oriole. Call a soft *chut* or *chuck*, also rapid, scolding chatter. Song a long, rich warbling, often including harsh notes with a down-slurred ending.

Baltimore Oriole *Icterus galbula*
Nonbreeding Visitor
Rarely encountered; possible at all elevations in treed gardens, semiarid scrubland, open woodlands, and forest edges during the nonbreeding period. Medium-sized oriole (18 cm; 34 g). Adult male has **vibrant orange and black plumage**, white wingbar, and orange outer tail patches. Adult female and immature drab olive brownish to brownish orange above, with two whitish wingbars. Underparts orange yellow, brightest on breast; lower belly and sides often pale grayish white. Similar male Village Weaver is yellow and black, and chunkier with heavier bill and shorter tail. Calls include repetitive chatter and sharp *chuk* notes. Song a distinctive, rich flutelike, double-noted whistle, infrequently heard on Hispaniola.

Bobolink

br ♀, non-br & imm

br ♂

Hispaniolan Oriole

♀

♂

Orchard Oriole

♂

♀

imm ♂

Baltimore Oriole

♂

♀

imm

Tawny-shouldered Blackbird *Agelaius humeralis*
Breeding Resident

Locally common in Haitian coastal marshes and scrub; also may be found near lowland woodlands, gardens, pastures, and rice fields. Medium-sized blackbird (21 cm; 36 g); black overall with a **tawny shoulder patch**, most conspicuous when flying. Shoulder patch of immature birds much smaller; sometimes not visible in perched birds. Similar Greater Antillean Grackle is larger, has long V-shaped tail, lacks shoulder patch. Sometimes emits harsh call, *wiii-wiiii-wiiii*. Typical call a strong, short *chic-chic*; also nasal and metallic notes. Song given by both sexes, 1–2 protracted buzzing notes. Usually in flocks. Sometimes enters open restaurants for food scraps.

Shiny Cowbird *Molothrus bonariensis*
Breeding Resident

Increasingly common and widespread; found primarily in disturbed habitats, open areas in lowlands, especially near rice fields, livestock, woodland edges, and scrub. Medium-sized blackbird (18 cm; 35 g) with **conical bill**. Adult male **uniformly glossy black with purplish sheen**. Adult female drab grayish brown above, paler below; faint supercilium. Immature resembles adult female, but underparts streaked pale gray; supercilium very faint. Similar Greater Antillean Grackle is much larger, with heavier bill and longer tail. See similar-sized Tawny-shouldered Blackbird. Song consists of bubbling *purr* notes, followed by three high, thin notes, the third drawn-out and fading. Varied calls include *chuk*, a chattering flight call, and a high, clear, whistled flight call. Shiny Cowbird is a brood parasite, confirmed to lay eggs in nests of Palmchat, Yellow Warbler, Hispaniolan Oriole, and Village Weaver.

Great-tailed Grackle *Quiscalus mexicanus*
Breeding Resident

Rare recent immigrant, now breeding on Hispaniola. Possible in wetlands, irrigated agriculture and other croplands, and near human settlements, especially along central south coast of Dominican Republic. Currently known only from Nigua, but expected to expand range. Very large grackle (male 43 cm, 220 g; female 33 cm, 115 g). Adult male black with purple gloss to head, back, and underparts; green gloss to flight feathers. **Tail very long and deeply V-shaped**. **Eye pale**, white to yellowish. Adult female and immatures brownish, paler brown on head and throat, and warmer brown across breast. Tail much shorter than adult male; eye pale. Similar Greater Antillean Grackle smaller, with shorter tail, and bright yellow eye. Voice a wide variety of loud cracks, whistles, hard notes, and guttural sounds. Highly social; may occur in large flocks and communal roosts.

Greater Antillean Grackle *Quiscalus niger*
Breeding Resident

Moderately common in lowland mangroves, marshes, savannas, open fields, and agricultural areas. Fairly large, strongly dimorphic blackbird (28 cm; male 80 g, female 65 g) with dark plumage, long tail, and **long, conical, sharply pointed bill**. Adult male has glossy metallic blue to violet-black plumage and **deep V-shaped tail**. Adult female duller than male; tail has smaller V. Adults of both sexes have **yellow iris**. Immatures dull brownish black, tail flat, iris light brown. Similar Great-tailed Grackle is considerably larger, with a longer tail and a pale or yellowish-white eye. Song consists of clear, musical notes *chin-chin-chilin*. Highly variable repertoire of calls, wheezy gasps, and a *chuk*. Typically moves and roosts in flocks. May forage around livestock, on lawns, in parks; commonly scavenges food scraps from humans.

Tawny-shouldered Blackbird

♂ Shiny Cowbird
♀

Great-tailed Grackle
♀
♂

Greater Antillean Grackle

Blue-gray Gnatcatcher *Polioptila caerulea*
Vagrant

May occur in a variety of habitats from forests to scrublands, mangroves, and gardens during nonbreeding season. Tiny, active bird (11 cm; 6 g) with ***long, thin tail*** with white outer feathers, ***often cocked upward*** or fanned. Upperparts ***bluish gray***, underparts white. Note prominent ***white eye-ring***. Bill fine-tipped and narrow. Sexes similar in nonbreeding season. In breeding plumage, male distinguished by fine black eyebrow stripe. Similar to warblers but smaller, slimmer, and longer-tailed. Voice a thin, mewing, nasal call of 2–6 syllables, *zee-zeet*. Thin, soft, complex song of mews, chips, and whistles, seldom given during nonbreeding season.

Ruby-crowned Kinglet *Corthylio calendula*
Vagrant

Possible in low, scrubby vegetation or other wooded habitats in the nonbreeding season. Very active, ***tiny bird*** (10 cm; 7 g), with olive-green to gray upperparts, dusky white underparts. Note bold, ***slightly broken, white eye-ring***, and ***two whitish wingbars*** with one ***dark bar*** below lower whitish bar. Male's red crown patch usually concealed; female lacks crown patch. Voice a short, dry *chet* note, often strung together in prolonged chatter. Actively hops and flits through vegetation in search of insects, often with conspicuous ***flicking of the wings***; sometimes hovers while foraging.

Black-and-white Warbler *Mniotilta varia*
Nonbreeding Visitor

Moderately common; most numerous at mid- and upper elevations in dry forest, moist broadleaf forest, shade coffee, and pine. Unmistakable. Medium-sized (12 cm; 11 g), distinctively patterned warbler. Male has upperparts and sides conspicuously streaked black and white, underparts white, crown with bold black-and-white stripes, blackish auriculars. Female has buffy white underparts, less distinct streaking on sides, and grayer auriculars. Breeding plumage similar but bolder. Bill long and slightly decurved. Call a sharp, buzzy *chit* or *spik*; also a thin, weak *tsit* or *tseep*. Song, occasionally heard late in nonbreeding season, is a high-pitched, *weesee weesee weesee*. Forages by creeping across branches and up and down tree trunks.

American Redstart *Setophaga ruticilla*
Nonbreeding Visitor

Common to locally abundant; older males occur primarily in moist forests, shade coffee, and mangroves; females and young males tend toward scrubby second-growth and dry forest. Slim, active warbler (12 cm; 8 g). Adult male unmistakable with black upperparts, throat, and breast; ***large orange patches on wings, tail, and sides***. Belly and undertail coverts white. Adult female olive gray above, grayer on head, dull white below; ***large pale yellow patches on wings, tail, and sides***. Immature male similar to female, but yellow patches are more orange; some irregular black flecking on head, throat, and breast. Call a clear high *tschip*; also a weak, rising *tsip*. Male song rarely heard; emphatic, buzzy, *tsee tsee tsee tsee tseeo* often with down-slurred ending. Forages with acrobatic flycatching.

Northern Parula *Setophaga americana*
Nonbreeding Visitor

Common in dry broadleaf forest, scrub, and second growth; regularly occurs in small numbers in shade coffee; rare in higher-elevation forests. Small warbler (11 cm; 9 g); ***upperparts bluish gray*** washed green; distinct ***greenish-yellow patch on mantle***. Chin, throat, and breast yellow; belly and undertail coverts white. Note two white wingbars, white tail spots, and ***broken white eye-ring***. Male variably marked across chest with narrow black and chestnut band. Female and immatures duller overall with breast band indistinct or lacking. Breeding birds similar, but brighter. Breeding male also has black lores. Call note a distinct *tsch*, frequently repeated. Rarely heard song an ascending buzz, *zeeeeeeee-tsup*.

Ruby-crowned Kinglet

Blue-gray Gnatcatcher

♂

Black-and-white Warbler

♀

♀

imm ♂

♂

American Redstart

♂

♀

Northern Parula

Ovenbird *Seiurus aurocapilla*
Nonbreeding Visitor

Often abundant; most numerous in mid-elevation dry forest, moist broadleaf forest, and shade coffee plantations; common in pine zone. Large, ground-dwelling warbler (15 cm; 20 g). Upperparts uniformly grayish olive above; ***orangish crown bordered by blackish stripes*** and a ***bold buffy-white eye-ring***. Underparts white ***boldly streaked blackish*** on throat, breast, and sides. Legs pinkish. Sexes identical; immature similar to adults. See similar Northern and Louisiana waterthrushes. Fairly vocal, giving a loud, sharp *chup* or *chek*. Song, rarely heard late in nonbreeding season; an explosive, ringing *teacher teacher teacher*.

Worm-eating Warbler *Helmitheros vermivorum*
Nonbreeding Visitor

Uncommon in dry forest, wet limestone forest, sun coffee plantations, or transitional broadleaf forest. Medium-sized, stocky warbler (12 cm; 13 g) with large bill and flat head. Upperparts olive brown; ***head buffy with bold black lateral crown stripes and eye-stripes***. Underparts buffy, but slightly whiter on throat and belly. Tail fairly short and squared. Sexes identical. See similar Swainson's Warbler. Call a sharp, loud *chip* or *tchik*; flight call a short, high buzz *dzt*. Song, rarely heard in nonbreeding season, a rapid, flat, buzzy trill.

Louisiana Waterthrush *Parkesia motacilla*
Nonbreeding Visitor

Uncommon but regular along flowing streams with wooded margins in hills and mountains of the interior. Large, terrestrial warbler (14 cm; 20 g); uniformly dark olive brown above, white below, with dark brown streaks on breast and sides, flanks washed buffy. Bold ***white supercilium flares and broadens behind eye***. Throat white and ***unspotted***. Sexes identical. Similar Northern Waterthrush washed with yellow or buffy below, has fine streaks on throat, and buffier supercilium narrows behind eye. Call note a loud, metallic *chink* or *chip*. Song a ringing, musical series of slurred whistles, *seeup seeup seeup*, followed by complex jumble of shorter rapid chips. Habitually teeters and rhythmically pumps its tail.

Northern Waterthrush *Parkesia noveboracensis*
Passage Migrant; Nonbreeding Visitor

Moderately common to abundant. Occurs near water; most often close to mangroves, but also low-elevation streams, rivers, lagoons, or lakes. Large, terrestrial warbler (14 cm; 18 g); dark olive brown above, buffy white below, with well-defined dark brown streaks; finer ***streaks on throat***. ***Supercilium buffy white, narrows behind eye***. Sexes identical. See similar Louisiana Waterthrush. Call note a loud, metallic *chink*. Song, rarely heard on wintering grounds, loud series of notes, falling in pitch and accelerating, *sweet sweet sweet swee-wee-wee chew chew chew chew*. Particularly common in fall migration. Teeters and rhythmically pumps tail when walking.

Swainson's Warbler *Limnothlypis swainsonii*
Nonbreeding Visitor

Rare but regular; inhabits dense understory of vines and shrubs in mature, montane moist broadleaf forest. Plain, medium-sized warbler (13 cm; 15 g) with long, heavy, sharply pointed bill. Upperparts unmarked brown or olive brown. ***Crown chestnut brown*** with contrasting pale white or ***creamy buff supercilium***; dusky line through eye. Unmarked underparts yellowish white to white, grayer on sides. Sexes identical. Similar Worm-eating Warbler has bold black stripes on head. Call note a strong, liquid, descending *chip* or *ssh*, also a short, metallic *ziip* and a high, thin *zeep* flight call. Song a loud, ringing series of clear, slurred notes, *whee whee whee whip-poor-will*.

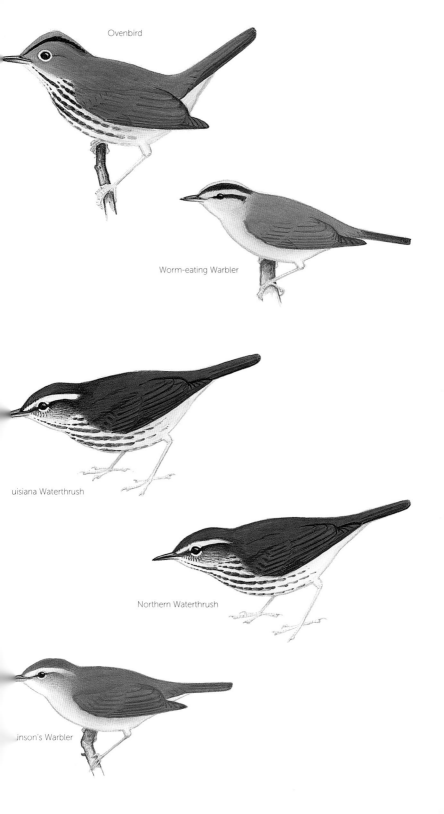

Ovenbird

Worm-eating Warbler

uisiana Waterthrush

Northern Waterthrush

nson's Warbler

Golden-winged Warbler *Vermivora chrysoptera*
Vagrant

Has occurred in semiopen forests, forest borders, or gaps in nonbreeding season. Small (13 cm; 9 g), boldly plumaged warbler with yellow crown, grayish nape and back, and *large yellow wing patch*. Head boldly patterned with broad *black auriculars* bordered above and below by white, and by *black throat*. Rest of underparts grayish white; undertail coverts white. Female and immature birds duller; throat and auriculars pale gray; yellow wing patch smaller. Similar Blue-winged Warbler is yellow below, with black eye-line and two white wingbars. Hybrids of these two species ("Brewster's Warbler") have been recorded on Hispaniola. Call note a sharp, loud *chip* or *jeet*; also thin *tzip* calls. Primary song a fine, high buzz, *zeee bee-bee-bee*. Frequents mid- to upper tree-canopy levels; probes dead leaves for insects.

Blue-winged Warbler *Vermivora cyanoptera*
Nonbreeding Visitor

Rarely occurring in highland habitats during nonbreeding period. Small warbler (11 cm; 8 g); bright yellow on crown and underparts, greenish-yellow back and nape, bluish-gray wings and tail. *Bold black eye-line*; *two distinct white wingbars*. Female slightly duller overall than male, with more olive crown and grayer eye-line; wingbars less distinct. Breeding plumage similar but brighter. See similar Golden-winged Warbler. Prothonotary Warbler lacks white wingbars and black eye-line. Pine Warbler larger and less boldly marked, lacks eye-line, has duller wingbars and underparts. Yellow Warbler lacks dark eye-line, has olivaceous wings, yellow tail spots. Call notes include a sharp, dry *chik* or *jeet*; also short, high, slightly buzzy *tzip* or *dzit*. Primary song a buzzy *beeee-BZZZZ*.

Prothonotary Warbler *Protonotaria citrea*
Passage Migrant; Nonbreeding Visitor?

Uncommon passage migrant; usually found in mangroves and adjacent coastal lowlands. Fairly large (14 cm; 15 g), *strikingly golden yellow warbler* with large bill; *prominent black eye*. Male has bright golden-yellow head, breast, and belly; greenish-yellow back; unmarked bluish-gray wings and tail. Lower belly and undertail coverts white; tail has conspicuous white outer webs. Females and immatures duller, washed greenish, especially on crown and nape. Breeding birds similar, but male a rich golden yellow. Females strongly washed green above, with yellow on head and underparts less intense than males. Similar Blue-winged Warbler has white wingbars and black eye-line. See also Yellow Warbler. Call a loud, metallic *tink* or *tschip*; also quieter, thin *tsip*. Song a repeated series of high-pitched, metallic, upslurred notes, *tsweet tsweet tsweet tsweet*. Some birds may overwinter.

Yellow Warbler *Setophaga petechia*
Breeding Resident; Passage Migrant

Locally common to abundant in coastal mangroves and adjacent dry scrub. Medium-sized (12 cm; 10 g), *strikingly yellow warbler*. Nonbreeding birds have olive-yellow upperparts, yellow head, bright yellow underparts. Wingbars, inner webs of tail, and tail spots are yellow. Male shows *light chestnut-red streaking on breast*. Female similar but less bright, with no streaking below. Females may show gray on nape. Breeding birds similar to nonbreeding birds but brighter. Compare to similar Wilson's, Hooded, Prothonotary, and Blue-winged warblers. Call notes include a loud *chip*. Song variable, but typically clear, rapid *sweet-sweet-sweet-ti-ti-ti-weet*. Some North American breeding birds pass through as migrants.

Golden-winged Warbler

♀

♂

Blue-winged Warbler

hybrid "Brewster's Warbler"

Prothonotary Warbler

♀ & imm

♂

♂

♀

Yellow Warbler

imm

Nashville Warbler *Leiothlypis ruficapilla*
Vagrant

Possible in shrubby woodlands, forest edges, and scrub during nonbreeding season. Small warbler (11 cm; 9 g) with unmarked olive-green upperparts; grayish head washed brownish gray in nonbreeding season; **white eye-ring**. Underparts, including **throat and undertail coverts, are yellow**; belly white. Adults may have concealed chestnut crown patch. Breeding birds similar, but head more distinctly gray. Similar female or immature Mourning Warbler and Connecticut Warbler are larger, with entirely gray hood, including chin and throat; solid yellow belly. Call a sharp, metallic *pink*. Loud, 2-part song unlikely heard on Hispaniola, *teebit-teebit-teebit, chipper-chipper-chipper*. Often bobs tail.

Connecticut Warbler *Oporornis agilis*
Passage Migrant

Rare but regular; typically stays near the ground in dense understory of moist woodlands, but most Hispaniola records during migration are from low-elevation thorn scrub and acacia woodlands. Large, terrestrial warbler with stocky build (14 cm; 15 g). Olive to olive brown above, with **pale gray to brownish hood** extending to lower throat. **Complete white eye-ring** in all plumages. Remaining underparts pale yellow with **long undertail coverts extending nearly to tip of tail**. Adult male has bluish-gray hood; adult female and immature have grayish-brown hood; throat whitish or pale buffy. Similar Mourning Warbler has narrow, broken white eye-ring and shorter undertail coverts. Usually silent in nonbreeding season, but call note a soft *pwik* or *poit*; song a loud, ringing *beecher-beecher-beecher-beecher*. Shy skulker; typically walks (rather than hops) on the ground.

Mourning Warbler *Geothlypis philadelphia*
Vagrant

Possible in wet habitats, including dense thickets, second growth, and old fields during nonbreeding period. Large, sturdy warbler (13 cm; 13 g) with olive-green upperparts and bright yellow underparts. In nonbreeding plumage, **gray to brownish-gray hood** extends to lower throat; sometimes interrupted by yellowish upper throat. Females and immatures show thin, white, broken eye-ring. Legs and feet pinkish. In breeding plumage, male has bluish-gray hood, broad black bib on lower edge; lacks eye-ring. Female similar to male but has pale gray or brownish-gray hood without black on lower edge, and a broken eye-ring. See similar Connecticut Warbler. Voice a harsh, metallic *chik* or *jink*. Song unlikely on Hispaniola, a ringing *teedle-teedle, turtle-turtle* with second pair of notes lower. Typically found on or near ground where it hops rather than walks.

Kentucky Warbler *Geothlypis formosa*
Passage Migrant; Nonbreeding Visitor

Rare but regular in understory of moist broadleaf and karst forests. Medium-sized (13 cm; 14 g), ground-dwelling warbler. Adult male has plain olive-green upperparts; solid bright yellow underparts. **Black crown, forecrown, and side of head form drooping mask**; yellow supercilium and partial eye-ring form **bold yellow spectacles**. Tail fairly short; legs pinkish. Adult female and immature male similar but with less extensive black on face and crown. Immature female has grayish-olive face. Breeding plumage similar. Similar Hooded Warbler has variable black hood, entirely yellow face, white tail spots. See Common Yellowthroat. Calls vary from low, hollow *chok* or *chup* to higher, sharper *chip* or *chek* when agitated. Song a rolling series of 2-syllable phrases *prr-reet prr-reet prr-reet*.

Nashville Warbler

♂

♀

♂

Connecticut Warbler

♀, non-br, & imm

♀

Mourning Warbler

non-br & imm

♂

♂

Kentucky Warbler

Common Yellowthroat *Geothlypis trichas*
Nonbreeding Visitor

Common to abundant at almost any elevation in dry scrub, overgrown fields, regenerating thickets, borders of lowland marshes, and scrub understory of pine forest. Medium-sized, compact warbler (12 cm; 10 g). Adult male plain olive-green upperparts, with **black facial mask edged white or gray above**. Throat, breast, and undertail coverts bright yellow; **belly and sides dusky white**. Adult female similar but lacks facial mask; underparts paler buffy yellow. Immature duller and browner than adult female; male may have traces of mask. Similar Kentucky Warbler entirely bright yellow below; yellow spectacles. Female and immature Connecticut and Mourning warblers have underparts entirely yellow; grayish or pale brownish hood. Call note a dry *tchep*. Clear song, *witchety, witchety, witchety, witch*, rarely heard. May segregate by sex; males more common in second growth and scrub; females in open pasture and regenerating fields.

Hooded Warbler *Setophaga citrina*
Nonbreeding Visitor

Uncommon but regular. Segregates by sex; males in mature forest, females in scrub, secondary forest, and disturbed habitats. Medium-sized warbler (13 cm; 11 g). Adult males olive-green above, black hood and throat contrasting with **bright yellow forecrown, face, and auriculars**; rest of underparts bright yellow. Adult female similar to male, but extent of black hood varies. Immature male similar to adult but olive-yellow tipping on throat and crown feathers. Immature female lacks black hood; yellow face contrasts with olive-green crown and nape. Note **large, dark eye**; tail-fanning behavior exposes **large white spots in outer tail feathers**. Similar Kentucky Warbler has variable black on face, yellow spectacles, lacks white tail spots. Call a loud, metallic *chip* or *chink*. Song a loud, clear, musical series of slurred notes, *ta-wit ta-wit ta-wit teeoo*.

Canada Warbler *Cardellina canadensis*
Vagrant

Possible in dense undergrowth of woodlands during nonbreeding season. Medium-sized warbler (14 cm; 11 g). Male bluish gray above; black forecrown contrasts with **complete white eye-ring and yellow lores forming spectacles**. Underparts yellow with bold **black necklace of breast streaks**; undertail coverts white. Adult female similar but duller overall; immatures duller still. Breeding birds similar to nonbreeding male but with bolder black markings. Similar Kentucky Warbler has olive upperparts, yellow undertail coverts, lacks streaking on breast. Female Hooded Warbler has yellow mask, yellow undertail coverts, conspicuous white tail spots. Calls include low, subdued *chip* or *tchup* and loud, sharp *check*. Variable song starts with a *chip* followed by a series of sputtering warbling notes.

Wilson's Warbler *Cardellina pusilla*
Vagrant

Possible in dense, moist broadleaf forests during nonbreeding season. Small, spry warbler (11 cm; 8 g). Male upperparts uniformly yellowish olive green, underparts entirely yellow. Note **glossy black crown; bright yellow forecrown and supercilium**. Adult female and immature male similar to adult male, but duller with little or no black in crown. Immature female lacks black cap and has more olive forecrown. See similar adult female and immature Hooded Warblers, immature Yellow Warbler. Call a husky, nasal *chip* or *jip*. Song rarely heard, a staccato series of *chip*s dropping at end. Characteristically flicks tail upward; hops restlessly from perch to perch.

Common
Yellowthroat

♂

♀ & imm

imm ♂

Hooded Warbler

imm

♀

♂

♀ & imm

Canada Warbler

♂

♂

Wilson's Warbler

♀ & imm

Cape May Warbler *Setophaga tigrina*
Nonbreeding Visitor

Common to abundant in many habitats from thorn scrub and dry forest, to shade coffee, broadleaf, and pine forests. Medium-sized warbler (13 cm; 11 g) with short tail, thin, decurved bill, *yellowish rump*. Nonbreeding adult male has grayish-green back with dark streaks, *chestnut-tinged auriculars* bordered by yellow, *yellow patch on sides of neck*, white wing patch. Underparts yellow heavily streaked black. Adult female and immatures similar but duller, with gray auriculars, *blurred yellow spot on side of neck*, greenish rump, two whitish wingbars. In breeding plumage, male's chestnut auriculars more pronounced. Similar Yellow-rumped Warbler browner above with brighter, more sharply defined rump patch; small yellow patches on sides. See Magnolia, Prairie, and Palm warblers. Calls include a high-pitched *tsit*. Rarely sings thin, high, buzzy, ascending song, *tseet-tseet-tseet-tseet*. Territorial around favored feeding sites which include nectar sources.

Bay-breasted Warbler *Setophaga castanea*
Passage Migrant

Rare; possible in coastal areas in October. Fairly large, nondescript warbler in nonbreeding plumage (14 cm; 13 g); greenish-gray upperparts faintly streaked blackish; *buffy white, unstreaked underparts*. *Undertail coverts buffy*; two bold, white wingbars. Adult males have variable amounts of chestnut on sides, but females and immatures have yellowish wash. *Legs and feet grayish*. Breeding male has *dark chestnut cap, and band* across chin, throat, and sides; black mask; buffy patch on sides of neck. Breeding female duller; crown, breast, and sides are only *washed with chestnut*. See similar nonbreeding Blackpoll, Pine, and Cape May warblers. Call notes include a clear, metallic *chip*; a high, buzzy *tsip* in flight or while foraging; rarely heard song a thin *tsee-tsee-tsee*.

Chestnut-sided Warbler *Setophaga pensylvanica*
Nonbreeding Visitor; Passage Migrant

Uncommon in scrub and early-successional forest habitats, especially during migration. Distinctive, medium-sized warbler (12 cm; 9 g). *Bright yellowish green above* with 2 yellowish-white wingbars and variable black spotting; *pale gray below*. Note conspicuous *white eye-ring on gray face*. Males often show some chestnut on sides. In breeding plumage, male has yellow forecrown, black eye-line and malar stripe, distinct *chestnut band along sides*, white underparts. Female duller with less extensive chestnut. Similar Bay-breasted and Blackpoll warblers in nonbreeding plumage have more olive-gray and streaked upperparts, more yellowish underparts, and lack eye-ring. Call note a loud *chip* not unlike Yellow Warbler. Song a clear, rapid *please please pleased to MEETyou*, dropping off at end.

Blackpoll Warbler *Setophaga striata*
Passage Migrant

Common southbound migrant in fall, much less common northbound in spring; almost always in dry scrub habitat near coast. Distinctive, larger warbler (14 cm; 12 g). Grayish-olive *upperparts variably streaked black*; whitish underparts washed yellow on throat, breast, and sides; diffuse olive streaking on sides. Lower belly and *undertail coverts pure white*; 2 wingbars also white. Legs (sometimes) and *feet yellowish*. Female and immatures similar but have reduced streaking. Breeding male has *black cap and malar stripe*; *broad white auriculars*. Similar nonbreeding adult and immature Bay-breasted Warblers lack streaking below, have buffy undertail coverts, and grayish legs. Call a sharp, clear *chip*. Song a thin, high *tsit-tsit-tsit-tsit-tsit-tsit* on same pitch, usually louder in middle and softer at end.

br ♂

non-br ♀ & imm ♂

Cape May Warbler

♀

Bay-breasted Warbler

br ♀ & non-br ♂

non-br ♀ & imm

br ♂

br ♂

& non-br ♂

Chestnut-sided Warbler

Blackpoll Warbler

br ♀ & imm

br ♀ & non-br ♂

non-br ♀ & imm

br ♂

Magnolia Warbler *Setophaga magnolia*
Nonbreeding Visitor

Regular but uncommon; in mangroves, thorn scrub, dry forest, and shade coffee. Medium-sized warbler (12 cm; 9 g); upperparts grayish olive streaked black, **rump yellow**, two white wingbars. Head and nape gray; eye-ring and thin supercilium white. Underparts bright yellow with variable black streaking on sides; pale gray neck band often present. Lower belly and undertail coverts white. Note large **white spots in middle of all but the two central tail feathers**. Breeding male has black auricular, prominent white supercilium, bold white wing patch; heavy black "necklace" across breast. Breeding female paler than male. Call note a hard, nasal *enk*; also a dry, high-pitched *chip*. Song short, musical *sweeter sweeter sweetest*, accentuated at end.

Blackburnian Warbler *Setophaga fusca*
Passage Migrant; Nonbreeding Visitor

Uncommon in woodlands during migration; occurs rarely during overwintering period. Fairly small warbler (11 cm; 10 g). Nonbreeding male dusky-olive to blackish above with **pale buffy streaks on back**; **black auriculars bordered by yellowish orange**; two bold white wingbars. **Chin, throat, and breast yellowish orange**; belly buffy white; sides streaked black; white spots in outer web of outermost tail feathers. Female and immature similar but duller; yellow replaces orange; less prominent streaking on back and sides. Breeding male unmistakable with **brilliant orange throat and facial markings**; breeding female has yellowish-orange facial markings. Call a thin but sharp *tchip* or *tsip*, often 2-syllabled. Variable song of high, thin notes rising towards end.

Yellow-throated Warbler *Setophaga dominica*
Nonbreeding Visitor

Moderately common; occurs primarily in pine forests; also found at lower elevations in palms, especially during migration. Medium-sized (13 cm; 10 g), strikingly patterned warbler with a long bill. **Upperparts gray**, **throat and upper breast yellow**, belly white with black streaks on sides. Two white wingbars. Note triangular **black auriculars broken by white crescent below eye**, white supercilium, white patch on side of neck. Female and immature similar but duller, with black markings slightly reduced. See similar Blackburnian Warbler. Call note a soft, clear, high-pitched, slightly descending *chip* or *clip*. Song a series of clear ringing notes, increasing in speed, dropping in pitch, but rising abruptly at the end.

Black-throated Green Warbler *Setophaga virens*
Nonbreeding Visitor

Uncommon but regular in broadleaf forest, pine forest, and shade coffee. Fairly small (11 cm; 9 g), foliage-gleaning warbler. Male bright olive green above, **bright yellow face**, dull olive-gray auriculars. **Black chin and throat patch** extends onto upper breast; two white wingbars; white tail spots. Underparts whitish, sides streaked black, undertail coverts washed yellowish. Adult female and immature male duller, with yellowish chin and throat. Immature female duller still. Breeding plumage similar but bolder. Voice a short, sharp *tsip* or *tek*. Rarely heard song has distinct patterns of short, level buzzes.

Tennessee Warbler *Leiothlypis peregrina*
Nonbreeding Visitor

Rarely occurring; most often reported from shade coffee plantations and montane broadleaf forests. Small to medium-sized warbler (11 cm; 10 g), lacking distinctive markings. Adults in nonbreeding plumage grayish green above, dull grayish white below, with **white undertail coverts**; rest of underparts often tinged yellow. Note distinct **dusky eye-line**; **narrow whitish supercilium**. Male tends to have grayer crown, brighter olive-green upperparts, and less yellowish wash on underparts, especially in breeding season. Voice a sharp, high *tsip* or *tseet*, also short, fine *tsit* calls. Ringing, repetitive, staccato song, increasing in loudness and pitch.

Magnolia Warbler

br ♂

♀

non-br & imm

Blackburnian Warbler

♀ & non-br ♂

non-br & imm

br ♂

Yellow-throated Warbler

br ♂

Black-throated
Green Warbler

♀ & non-br ♂

non-br & imm

♀

non-br & imm

Tennessee Warbler

♂

Black-throated Blue Warbler *Setophaga caerulescens*
Nonbreeding Visitor

Common in wide range of habitats; most numerous in mid-elevation broadleaf forests and shade coffee. Medium-sized warbler (13 cm; 10 g). Male **dark blue above** with small **white patch at base of primaries**; **black face and throat**. Underparts white with black band along flanks. Female drab olive gray above with small **white spot at base of primaries**, narrow whitish supercilium, slightly **grayer auriculars**. Underparts dull buffy white. Immature male like adult but upperparts washed greenish; immature female similar to adult, but wing spot reduced. Voice a sharp, dry *tsik* or *ctuk*. Song a rising, buzzy *zwee zwee zwee*.

Palm Warbler *Setophaga palmarum*
Nonbreeding Visitor

Common to abundant near or on ground in areas without thick ground cover. Medium-sized warbler (13 cm; 10 g); grayish brown to **cinnamon brown above**, dull whitish to pale buff below, with faint streaking on breast and flanks. Note **brick-red crown patch**, pale supercilium, dark eye-line, yellow chin and throat, and two indistinct buffy wingbars. **Rump yellow olive; undertail coverts yellow**. Sexes alike; breeding plumage similar but brighter. Call a sharp, slightly metallic *chip* or *chik*. Song a dry, weak trill. Frequently pumps its tail. Most individuals occurring on Hispaniola belong to duller-plumaged Western subspecies.

Pine Warbler *Setophaga pinus*
Breeding Resident

Common and sometimes abundant in pine forest of interior hills and mountains. Large warbler (13 cm; 12 g) with fairly stout bill. Adult male has **unstreaked greenish-olive upperparts**, and bright yellow throat and breast with variable **diffuse dark streaking**. **Auriculars greenish olive**, bordered below and toward rear by yellow. Note indistinct yellow eye-ring and supercilium, **two white wingbars**, white spots on outermost two to three tail feathers, and white lower belly and undertail coverts. Adult female similar but generally duller overall. Immatures browner and duller than adults. Song a simple, rapid, musical trill. Call note a strong, sharp *tzip* or *tchik*.

Yellow-rumped Warbler *Setophaga coronata*
Nonbreeding Visitor

Regular and locally common island-wide in wide range of habitats, but most common in pine forest. Large warbler (14 cm; 12 g), grayish brown above with indistinct black streaking on back, **small yellow crown patch**, and **bright yellow rump**. Underparts dull whitish with blurry streaks on breast; **small yellow patches on sides**. Note two narrow white wingbars, white tail spots, pale supercilium, and broken white eye-ring. Females and immatures duller and browner. In breeding plumage, male bluish gray above, whitish below, with black breast band and auriculars; bright yellow crown and side patches. Breeding female duller overall. Call note is flat, emphatic *chek* or *chup*, given frequently while foraging. Rare song is clear, warbling trill.

Prairie Warbler *Setophaga discolor*
Nonbreeding Visitor

Common to abundant in dry thorn scrub, margins of mangroves, and pine forest with a scrubby broadleaf understory. Small warbler (11 cm; 8 g); nonbreeding male olivaceous above with **chestnut streaks on back**, bright yellow below with prominent **black streaks on sides**. Distinctive yellow supercilium, **blackish eye-line**, broad yellow crescent below eye, bordered below by **blackish crescent**; blackish mark on side of neck. Pale yellow wingbars; white tail spots. Nonbreeding female and immature duller. Breeding plumage similar but brighter. Call note a dry *chip* or *chek*. Song a thin, ascending buzzy *zee-zee-zee-ZEEET*.

Black-throated Blue Warbler

♂

♀

Palm Warbler

br western ssp.

non-br western ssp.

♀ & imm

non-br
eastern ssp.

Pine Warbler

♂ & ♀

br ♂

br ♀

Yellow-rumped Warbler

non-br & imm

♂

♀ & imm

Prairie Warbler

Summer Tanager *Piranga rubra*
Vagrant
Possible in woodlands, forest edges, thickets, and gardens, primarily at mid-elevations. Large tanager (18 cm; 30 g) with relatively long, heavy, **pale bill**; head may appear slightly crested. Nonbreeding male yellowish olive green above, **orangish yellow below**, often with scattered red feathers. Nonbreeding female similar to breeding female; yellowish olive green above, **orangish yellow below**, with faint dusky eye-line. Adult male **entirely rose red**, brighter below, with wings and tail subtly darker. Similar Western Tanager has pale wingbars in all plumages. See Scarlet Tanager. Call a distinctive staccato, descending *pit-i-tuck*.

Scarlet Tanager *Piranga olivacea*
Vagrant
Possible in a variety of wooded habitats with tall trees, and in more open woodlands, parks, and gardens; primarily a passage migrant, but may rarely overwinter. Medium-sized, unmarked tanager (16–17 cm; 25 g). Adult female **uniformly olive-green above** with **contrasting dull brownish-olive wings and tail**; olive-yellow underparts. Nonbreeding adult male and immatures resemble female but are brighter with black wings and tail. Adult breeding male unmistakable with brilliant red body, black wings and tail, pale grayish bill. Female and immature distinguished from very similar Summer and Western tanagers by more uniform upperparts, more contrastingly dark wings. Western Tanager has wingbars; Summer Tanager has larger bill. Call of Scarlet Tanager a slightly hoarse, throaty *chik-brrr* or *chip-churr*.

Western Tanager *Piranga ludoviciana*
Vagrant
Possible in wide variety of forest, scrub, and semiopen habitats. Medium-sized tanager (18 cm; 28 g) with **relatively small bill, short tail**, and pronounced wingbars. Adult nonbreeding male has greenish-yellow head, often washed reddish on face; blackish back, wings, and tail; yellow nape, rump, uppertail coverts, and underparts. Note **upper yellow wingbar, lower white wing bar**. Breeding male similar but brighter; most or all of head reddish. Adult female has olive-green upperparts, grayer on back, more yellow on rump. Underparts bright yellow to grayish white; undertail coverts yellow. Wings and tail grayish brown; two yellowish white wingbars. Immatures of both sexes similar to adult female, but males brighter overall. See similar Summer and Scarlet tanagers. Similar female orioles have longer bill and tail. Call a quick, soft, rising chatter, *pit-ick*, *pit-er-ick*, or *pri-di-dit*.

Bananaquit *Coereba flaveola*
Breeding Resident

Locally common in nearly all habitat types; often abundant in mesic scrub and forest, suburban areas, town parks, and gardens. Unmistakable. Small (11 cm; 9 g), colorful bird with short tail, **slender decurved bill**. Adult grayish black above with **yellow rump**, **bold white supercilium**, **small white spot on wing**. Breast and belly yellow; throat gray. Reddish-pink spot at base of bill. Immature paler and duller than adult with yellowish-white supercilium. Song a thin, wheezy, high-pitched series of rapid notes, *tzi-tzi-tzi-tzi-tziit-tzi*. Call note a short, high, unmusical *tsip*. While foraging, Bananaquits commonly pierce the base of flowers to steal nectar, their primary food.

Summer Tanager

♂

♀

Scarlet Tanager

♂

♀

non-br ♂ & imm

Western Tanager

non-br ♂

br ♂

♀

Bananaquit

Rose-breasted Grosbeak *Pheucticus ludovicianus*
Nonbreeding Visitor

Uncommon but regular in broadleaf forest canopy or subcanopy. Unmistakable. Large, robust migratory finch (20 cm; 45 g) with **heavy, pale bill**. Nonbreeding male distinguished by **pinkish breast** which may have considerable buffy wash, black or blackish-brown head and back, white spots on upperwing coverts and primaries, and large white patches on outer tail feathers. Lower breast and belly white; rump white with gray barring. Female has streaked brown upperparts, **head boldly striped whitish and brown**, and underparts whitish, streaked brown. In flight, male displays **rosy underwing coverts; females are yellow**. Breeding male is brighter and more contrasting, with black replacing brown, and red replacing pink. Breeding female similar to nonbreeding female. Call a sharp, metallic *chink* or *eek*. Song is a rich, melodious warble.

Blue Grosbeak *Passerina caerulea*
Nonbreeding Visitor

Rare visitor to weedy fields, rice plantations, dry forest edges, and lowland scrub. Large finch (16 cm; 28 g) with **heavy bill** and long, rounded tail. Both immature male and female are plain **warm rufous brown overall**. Breeding male deep blue with **reddish-brown wingbars** and dull black flight feathers; small black patch on face between eye and bill extends to chin. Bill two-toned, with black upper mandible, silver lower mandible. Female paler gray brown throughout, with occasional blue feathers, and **buffy-brown patch on wing**. Similar Indigo Bunting smaller, with smaller bill; lacks conspicuous wingbars. Call a metallic, hard *tink* or *chink*. Song a long, rich, husky warble. Commonly flicks and spreads tail.

Indigo Bunting *Passerina cyanea*
Nonbreeding Visitor

Uncommon in rice fields, grassy areas bounded by heavy thickets, pasture edges, and fairly dry scrub. Small (13 cm; 15 g), active finch, often encountered in flocks. Nonbreeding male brown overall with variable **patches of blue** in wings and tail. Female entirely dull brown with **pale, blurry, breast streaks**, pale wingbars. Breeding male entirely bright blue. See similar immature munias, but female bunting has faint breast stripes and wingbars. Call note an emphatic, dry *twit* or *spik*. Rarely heard song of paired phrases, *sweet-sweet, chew-chew, sweet-sweet*.

Painted Bunting *Passerina ciris*
Vagrant

Prefers thickets and brushy areas of semiarid forest during nonbreeding season. Small, brightly colored bunting (13 cm, 16 g). Adult male unmistakable with **blue head and nape**, bronze-green back, **red rump and underparts**, contrasting with dark wings and tail. Adult female has **dark greenish upperparts, yellow-green underparts**. Immature plumages similar to adult female. Female and immature distinguished from similar Indigo Bunting by greenish coloration, from female Yellow-faced Grassquit by darker coloration and lack of distinctive facial pattern, from female Antillean Euphonia by larger size, longer tail, lack of yellow forehead. Call a soft *pwich* or *plik* with rising inflection; song a sweet, continuous warble.

Greater Antillean Bullfinch *Melopyrrha violacea*
Breeding Resident

Common in dense thickets and understory of dry broadleaf forest, especially where gumbo limbo (*Bursera simaruba*) fruits are found in season; less common in understory of humid and pine forests. Chunky, **heavy-billed bird** (16 cm; 22 g), with **orange-red supercilium, throat, and undertail coverts**. Adult male black overall; adult female slate gray. Immatures generally olive brown with orange-red markings similar to those of adults; later becoming more mottled with gray or black of adults. Song a repetitive trill of insectlike notes, *tzeet, tseet, tseet, tseet, seet, seet, seet*. Alarm call a thin *spit*. Despite being relatively common, often difficult to detect in dense vegetation.

Rose-breasted Grosbeak

non-br ♂ & imm ♂

Blue Grosbeak

Indigo Bunting

Painted Bunting

Greater Antillean Bullfinch

APPENDIX 1:
LOCAL NAMES OF HISPANIOLAN BIRDS

Table 1. Local Names, Scientific Names, and Alpha Codes of Hispaniolan Birds. A rich and interesting variety of local names is in use, but here we have tried to select those names most widely used in our experience.

Family	English	Scientific	Alpha Code	Dominican	French	Kreyòl
Anatidae						
	White-faced Whistling-Duck	*Dendrocygna viduata*	WFWD	Yaguaza cara blanca	Dendrocygne veuf	Jenjon figi blanch
	Black-bellied Whistling-Duck	*Dendrocygna autumnalis*	BBWD	Yaguaza barriga prieta	Dendrocygne à ventre noir	Jenjon vant nwa
	West Indian Whistling-Duck	*Dendrocygna arborea*	WIWD	Yaguaza	Dendrocygne des Antilles	Jenjon fran
	Fulvous Whistling-Duck	*Dendrocygna bicolor*	FUWD	Yaguasín	Dendrocygne fauve	Jenjon wouj
	Canada Goose	*Branta canadensis*	CANG	Ganso Canadiense	Bernache du Canada	Zwa Kanada
	Wood Duck	*Aix sponsa*	WODU	Huyuyo	Canard branchu	Kanna bwòdè
	Blue-winged Teal	*Spatula discors*	BWTE	Pato de la Florida	Sarcelle à ailes bleues	Kanna zèl ble
	Northern Shoveler	*Spatula clypeata*	NSHO	Pato cuchareta	Canard souchet	Kana tèt vèt fal blan
	Gadwall	*Mareca strepera*	GADW	Pato friso	Canard chipeau	Kanna chipo
	Eurasian Wigeon	*Mareca penelope*	EUWI	Silbon Euroasiatico	Canard siffleur	Faldam etranje
	American Wigeon	*Mareca americana*	AMWI	Pato cabecilargo	Canard d'Amérique	Kanna zèl blanch
	Mallard	*Anas platyrhynchos*	MALL	Pato Inglés	Canard colvert	Kana kolye blan
	White-cheeked Pintail	*Anas bahamensis*	WCHP	Pato de la orilla	Canard des Bahamas	Kana kwen bèk wouj
	Northern Pintail	*Anas acuta*	NOPI	Pato Guineo	Canard pilet	Kanna pilè
	Green-winged Teal	*Anas crecca*	GWTE	Pato de la Carolina	Sarcelle d'hiver	Kana zèl vèt
	Canvasback	*Aythya valisineria*	CANV	Pato lomo blanco	Fuligule à dos blanc	Kanna do blanch
	Redhead	*Aythya americana*	REDH	Pato cabeza roja	Fuligule à tête rouge	Kana tèt wouj
	Ring-necked Duck	*Aythya collaris*	RNDU	Pato negro	Fuligule à collier	Kana tèt nwa
	Greater Scaup	*Aythya marila*	GRSC	Pato Turco mayor	Fuligule milouinan	Kana zèl blan pentle
	Lesser Scaup	*Aythya affinis*	LESC	Pato Turco menor	Petit fuligule	Kana zèl pentle
	Hooded Merganser	*Lophodytes cucullatus*	HOME	Mergansa de caperuza	Harle couronné	Kanna tèt kepi
	Red-breasted Merganser	*Mergus serrator*	RBME	Mergansa pechiroja	Harle huppé	Kanna fal wouj kolye blan
	Masked Duck	*Nomonyx dominicus*	MADU	Pato criollo	Érismature routoutou	Kanna kagoul nwa
	Ruddy Duck	*Oxyura jamaicensis*	RUDU	Pato espinoso	Érismature rousse	Kanna machwè blan takte
Numididae						
	Helmeted Guineafowl	*Numida meleagris*	HELG	Guinea	Pintade de numidie	Pentad mawon
Odontophoridae						
	Northern Bobwhite	*Colinus virginianus*	NOBO	Cordoniz	Colin de Virginie	Kay

Family	English	Scientific	Alpha Code	Dominican	French	Kreyòl
Phasianidae						
	Ring-necked Pheasant	*Phasianus colchicus*	RNEP	Faisán	Faisan de Colchide	Fezan
	Red Junglefowl	*Gallus gallus*	REJU	Gallina; Gallo	Coq bankiva	Poul; Kòk
Phoenicopteridae						
	American Flamingo	*Phoenicopterus ruber*	AMFL	Flamenco	Flamant rose	Flanman wòz
Podicipedidae						
	Least Grebe	*Tachybaptus dominicus*	LEGR	Tigua	Grèbe minime	Plonjon je jòn
	Pied-billed Grebe	*Podilymbus podiceps*	PBGR	Zaramagullón	Grèbe à bec bigarré	Plonjon je nwa
Columbidae						
	Rock Pigeon	*Columba livia*	ROPI	Paloma doméstica	Pigeon biset	Pijon
	Scaly-naped Pigeon	*Patagioenas squamosa*	SNPI	Paloma Turca	Pigeon à cou rouge	Ranmye kou wouj
	White-crowned Pigeon	*Patagioenas leucocephala*	WCPI	Paloma coronita	Pigeon à couronne blanche	Ranmye tèt blanch
	Plain Pigeon	*Patagioenas inornata*	PLAP	Paloma ceniza	Pigeon simple	Ramye miyèt
	Eurasian Collared-Dove	*Streptopelia decaocto*	EUCD	Tórtola de collarina	Tourterelle turque	Toutrèl ak kolye
	Common Ground Dove	*Columbina passerina*	CGDO	Rolita	Colombe à queue noire	Zòtolan
	Ruddy Quail-Dove	*Geotrygon montana*	RUQD	Perdiz colorada	Colombe rouviolette	Pèdri fran
	White-fronted Quail-Dove	*Geotrygon leucometopia*	WFRQ	Perdiz coquito blanco	Colombe d'Hispaniola	Pèdri fron blanch
	Key West Quail-Dove	*Geotrygon chrysia*	KWQD	Perdiz grande	Colombe à joues blanches	Pèdri vant blanch
	White-winged Dove	*Zenaida asiatica*	WWDO	Tortola aliblanca	Tourterelle à ailes blanches	Toutrèl zèl blanch
	Zenaida Dove	*Zenaida aurita*	ZEND	Rolón Turco	Tourterelle à queue carrée	Toutrèl wouj
	Mourning Dove	*Zenaida macroura*	MODO	Rabiche	Tourterelle triste	Toutrèl ke fine
Cuculidae						
	Smooth-billed Ani	*Crotophaga ani*	SBAN	Judío	Ani à bec lisse	Boustabak
	Yellow-billed Cuckoo	*Coccyzus americanus*	YBCU	Pájaro bobo pico amarillo	Coulicou à bec jaune	Ti tako bèk jòn
	Mangrove Cuckoo	*Coccyzus minor*	MACU	Pájaro bobo menor	Coulicou manioc	Ti tako
	Black-billed Cuckoo	*Coccyzus erythropthalmus*	BBCU	Pájaro bobo pico negro	Coulicou à bec noir	Ti tako bèk nwa
	Bay-breasted Cuckoo	*Coccyzus rufigularis*	BBRC	Cúa	Piaye cabrite	Tako Kabrit
	Hispaniolan Lizard-Cuckoo	*Coccyzus longirostris*	HILC	Pájaro bobo	Tacco d'Hispaniola	Tako
Caprimulgidae						
	Common Nighthawk	*Chordeiles minor*	CONI	Querebebé migratorio	Engoulevent d'Amérique	Petonwa etranje
	Antillean Nighthawk	*Chordeiles gundlachii*	ANNI	Querebebé	Engoulevent piramidig	Petonwa

Family	English	Scientific	Alpha Code	Dominican	French	Kreyòl
	Least Pauraque	*Siphonorhis brewsteri*	LEPA	Torico	Engoulevent grouillecor	Petovwa gouye kò
	Chuck-will's-widow	*Antrostomus carolinensis*	CWWI	Don Juán	Engoulevent de Caroline	Petonwa Karolin
	Hispaniolan Nightjar	*Antrostomus eckmani*	HINI	Pitanguá	Engoulevent d'Hispaniola	Petonwa peyi
Nyctibiidae						
	Northern Potoo	*Nyctibius jamaicensis*	NORP	Bruja	Ibijau Jamaïcain	Petonwa ke long
Apodidae						
	Black Swift	*Cypseloides niger*	BLSW	Vencejo negro	Martinet sombre	Chiksol
	White-collared Swift	*Streptoprocne zonaris*	WCSW	Vencejo de collar	Martinet à collier blanc	Zwazo lapli kou blanch
	Chimney Swift	*Chaetura pelagica*	CHSW	Vencejo de chimenea	Martinet ramoneur	Ti irondèl etranje
	Antillean Palm-Swift	*Tachornis phoenicobia*	ANPS	Vencejito palmar	Martinet petit-rollé	Jòljòl
Trochilidae						
	Antillean Mango	*Anthracothorax dominicus*	ANMA	Zumbador grande	Mango doré	Wanga nègès
	Ruby-throated Hummingbird	*Archilochus colubris*	RTHU	Zumbador migratorio	Colibri à gorge rubis	Wanga nègès gòj wouj
	Vervain Hummingbird	*Mellisuga minima*	VEHU	Zumbadorcito	Colibri nain	Ti zwazo wanga
	Hispaniolan Emerald	*Riccordia swainsonii*	HIEM	Zumbador esmeralda	Emeraude d'Hispaniola	Wanga nègès mòn
Rallidae						
	Spotted Rail	*Pardirallus maculatus*	SPRA	Gallito manchado	Râle tacheté	Ral takte
	Clapper Rail	*Rallus crepitans*	CLRA	Pollo de manglar	Râle gris	Ral gri
	Sora	*Porzana carolina*	SORA	Sora	Marouette de Caroline	Ti ral
	Common Gallinule	*Gallinula galeata*	COGA	Gallareta pico rojo	Gallinule poule-d'eau	Poul dlo tèt rouj
	American Coot	*Fulica americana*	AMCO	Gallareta pico blanco	Foulque d'Amérique	Poul dlo tèt blan
	Purple Gallinule	*Porphyrio martinicus*	PUGA	Gallareta azul	Talève violacée	Poul dlo ble
	Yellow-breasted Crake	*Hapalocrex flaviventer*	YBCR	Gallito amarillo	Marouette à sourcils blancs	Ti ral jòn
	Black Rail	*Laterallus jamaicensis*	BLRA	Gallito negro	Râle noir	Ral nwa
Aramidae						
	Limpkin	*Aramus guarauna*	LIMP	Carrao	Courlan brun	Rele
Burhinidae						
	Double-striped Thick-knee	*Burhinus bistriatus*	DSTK	Búcaro	Œdicnème bistrié	Kòk savann
Recurvirostridae						
	Black-necked Stilt	*Himantopus mexicanus*	BNST	Viuda	Échasse d'Amérique	Pèt-pèt

Family	English	Scientific	Alpha Code	Dominican	French	Kreyòl
	American Avocet	*Recurvirostra americana*	AMAV	Avoceta Americana	Avocette d'Amérique	(unknown)
Haematopodidae						
	American Oystercatcher	*Haematopus palliatus*	AMOY	Caracolero	Huîtrier d'Amérique	Gwo bekasin bèk wouj
Charadriidae						
	Black-bellied Plover	*Pluvialis squatarola*	BBPL	Chorlo gris	Pluvier argenté	Bekasin vant nwa
	American Golden-Plover	*Pluvialis dominica*	AMGP	Chorlito dorado Americano	Pluvier bronzé	Bekasin do bronze
	Pacific Golden-Plover	*Pluvialis fulva*	PAGP	Chorlito dorado Siberiano	Pluvier fauve	(unknown)
	Killdeer	*Charadrius vociferus*	KILL	Ti-ito	Pluvier kildir	Bekasin doub kolye
	Semipalmated Plover	*Charadrius semipalmatus*	SEPL	Chorlito semipalmado	Pluvier semipalmé	Bekasin kolye janm jòn
	Piping Plover	*Charadrius melodus*	PIPL	Chorlito silbador	Pluvier siffleur	Ti bekasin siflè
	Wilson's Plover	*Charadrius wilsonia*	WIPL	Chorlito cabezón	Pluvier de Wilson	Bekasin kolye fran
	Snowy Plover	*Charadrius nivosus*	SNPL	Chorlito niveo	Pluvier à collier interrompu	Ti bekasin blanch
Jacanidae						
	Northern Jacana	*Jacana spinosa*	NOJA	Gallito de agua	Jacana du Mexique	Doktè
Scolopacidae						
	Whimbrel	*Numenius phaeopus*	WHIM	Playero picocorvo	Courlis corlieu	Bekasin kouli
	Long-billed Curlew	*Numenius americanus*	LBCU	Zarapito pico largo	Courlis à long bec	Bekasin kouli bèk long
	Hudsonian Godwit	*Limosa haemastica*	HUGO	Barga aliblanca	Barge Hudsinienne	Bekasin kouli vant blanch
	Marbled Godwit	*Limosa fedoa*	MAGO	Barga jaspeada	Barge marbrée	Bekasin kouli takte
	Ruddy Turnstone	*Arenaria interpres*	RUTU	Playero Turco	Tournepierre à collier	Bekasin fal nwa pye rouj
	Red Knot	*Calidris canutus*	REKN	Playero pechirrojo	Bécasseau maubèche	Bekasin mòbèch
	Stilt Sandpiper	*Calidris himantopus*	STSA	Playero zancudo	Bécasseau à échasses	Bekasin janm long
	Sanderling	*Calidris alba*	SAND	Playerito blanquito	Bécasseau sanderling	Bekasin blanch
	Dunlin	*Calidris alpina*	DUNL	Dunlin	Bécasseau variable	Bekasin vant nwa
	Baird's Sandpiper	*Calidris bairdii*	BASA	Playero de Baird	Bécasseau de Baird	Bekasin zèl long
	Least Sandpiper	*Calidris minutilla*	LESA	Playerito menudo	Bécasseau minuscule	Ti bekasin fran
	White-rumped Sandpiper	*Calidris fuscicollis*	WRSA	Playero de rabadilla blanca	Bécasseau à croupion blanc	Bekasin ke blanch
	Buff-breasted Sandpiper	*Calidris subruficollis*	BBSA	Playero de pecho crema	Bécasseau roussâtre	Bekasin savann
	Pectoral Sandpiper	*Calidris melanotos*	PESA	Playero pectoral	Bécassine à poitrine cendrée	Bekasin fal nwa
	Semipalmated Sandpiper	*Calidris pusilla*	SESA	Playerito semipalmado	Bécasseau semipalmé	Ti bekasin janm nwa
	Western Sandpiper	*Calidris mauri*	WESA	Playero occidental	Bécasseau d'Alaska	Ti bekasin bèk long

Family	English	Scientific	Alpha Code	Dominican	French	Kreyòl
	Short-billed Dowitcher	*Limnodromus griseus*	SBDO	Agujeta piquicorta	Bécassin roux	Bekasin mawon bèk long
	Long-billed Dowitcher	*Limnodromus scolopaceus*	LBDO	Agujeta piquilarga	Bécassin à long bec	Bekasin bèk long
	Wilson's Snipe	*Gallinago delicata*	WISN	Guineíto	Bécassine des marais	Bekasin janm kout
	Spotted Sandpiper	*Actitis macularius*	SPSA	Playerito manchado	Chevalier grivelé	Bekasin zèl tranble
	Solitary Sandpiper	*Tringa solitaria*	SOSA	Playero solitario	Chevalier solitaire	Bekasin dlo dous
	Lesser Yellowlegs	*Tringa flavipes*	LEYE	Patas amarillas menor	Petit chevalier	Bekasin janm jòn
	Willet	*Tringa semipalmata*	WILL	Chorlo aliblanco	Chevalier semipalmé	Bekasin zèl blan
	Greater Yellowlegs	*Tringa melanoleuca*	GRYE	Patas amarillas mayor	Gran chevalier	Gwo bekasin janm jòn
	Wilson's Phalarope	*Phalaropus tricolor*	WIPH	Falaropo de Wilson	Phalarope de Wilson	Falawòp
	Red-necked Phalarope	*Phalaropus lobatus*	RNPH	Falaropo de cuello rojo	Phalarope à bec étroit	Falawòp bèk fen
Stercorariidae						
	Pomarine Jaeger	*Stercorarius pomarinus*	POJA	Pagalo pomarino	Labbe pomarin	Lab pirat
	Parasitic Jaeger	*Stercorarius parasiticus*	PAJA	Pagalo parásito	Labbe parsite	Lab parazit
	Long-tailed Jaeger	*Stercorarius longicaudus*	LTJA	Pagalo rabero	Labbe à longue queue	Lab ke long
Laridae						
	Black-legged Kittiwake	*Rissa tridactyla*	BLKI	Gaviota tridactila	Mouette tridactyle	Mòv pye nwa
	Bonaparte's Gull	*Chroicocephalus philadelphia*	BOGU	Gaviota de Bonaparte	Mouette de Bonaparte	Mòv janm wòz
	Laughing Gull	*Leucophaeus atricilla*	LAGU	Gaviota cabecinegra	Mouette atricille	Mòv tèt nwa
	Franklin's Gull	*Leucophaeus pipixcan*	FRGU	Gaviota de Franklin	Mouette de Franklin	Mòv tèt nwa ti bèk
	Ring-billed Gull	*Larus delawarensis*	RBGU	Gaviota piquianillada	Goéland à bec cerclé	Mòv bèk jòn
	Herring Gull	*Larus argentatus*	HERG	Gaviota arenquera	Goéland argenté	Mòv gri
	Lesser Black-backed Gull	*Larus fuscus*	LBBG	Gaviota sombria	Goéland brun	Ti mòv do nwa
	Great Black-backed Gull	*Larus marinus*	GBBG	Gavión	Goéland marin	Mòv pye nwa
	Brown Noddy	*Anous stolidus*	BRNO	Cervera	Noddi brun	Mòv tèt blanch
	Sooty Tern	*Onychoprion fuscatus*	SOTE	Charrán oscuro	Sterne fuligineuse	Mòv vant blanch
	Bridled Tern	*Onychoprion anaethetus*	BRTE	Charrán monja	Sterne bridée	Mòv gri ke blanch
	Least Tern	*Sternula antillarum*	LETE	Charrán menor	Petite sterne	Ti mòv piti
	Gull-billed Tern	*Gelochelidon nilotica*	GBTE	Charrán piquigrueso	Sterne hansel	Mòv bèk nwa
	Caspian Tern	*Hydroprogne caspia*	CATE	Charrán piquiroja	Sterne Caspienne	Gwo mòv bèk jòn
	Black Tern	*Chlidonias niger*	BLTE	Charrán negro	Guifette noire	Mòv nwa
	Roseate Tern	*Sterna dougallii*	ROST	Charrán rosado	Sterne de Dougall	Mòv blanch
	Common Tern	*Sterna hirundo*	COTE	Charrán común	Sterne pierregarin	Mòv bèk wouj

Family	English	Scientific	Alpha Code	Dominican	French	Kreyòl
	Forster's Tern	*Sterna forsteri*	FOTE	Charrán de Forster	Sterne de Forster	Mòv ke fann
	Royal Tern	*Thalasseus maximus*	ROYT	Charrán real	Sterne royale	Mòv wayal
	Sandwich Tern	*Thalasseus sandvicensis*	SATE	Charrán piconegro	Sterne caugek	Mòv kojèk
	Black Skimmer	*Rynchops niger*	BLSK	Pico de tijera	Bec-en-ciseaux noir	Bèk sizo
Phaethontidae						
	White-tailed Tropicbird	*Phaethon lepturus*	WTTR	Rabijunco coliblanco	Phaéton à bec jaune	Payanke bèk jòn
	Red-billed Tropicbird	*Phaethon aethereus*	RBTR	Rabijunco piquirojo	Phaéton à bec rouge	Payanke bèk wouj
Hydrobatidae						
	Wilson's Storm-Petrel	*Oceanites oceanicus*	WISP	Golondrina del mar	Océanite de Wilson	Chanwan oseyani
	Leach's Storm-Petrel	*Hydrobates leucorhous*	LESP	Lavapiés	Océanite cul-blanc	Chanwan dèyè blanch
Procellariidae						
	Black-capped Petrel	*Pterodroma hasitata*	BCPE	Diablotín	Pétrel diablotin	Chanwan Lasèl
	Cory's Shearwater	*Calonectris diomedea*	CORS	Pardela cenicienta	Puffin cendré	(unknown)
	Great Shearwater	*Ardenna gravis*	GRSH	Pardela capirotada	Puffin majeur	Gwo kayen
	Manx Shearwater	*Puffinus puffinus*	MASH	Pardela pichoneta	Puffin des Anglais	Kayen zangle
	Audubon's Shearwater	*Puffinus lherminieri*	AUSH	Pardela de Audubon	Puffin d'Audubon	Kayen Odibon
Ciconiidae						
	Wood Stork	*Mycteria americana*	WOST	Cigüeña Americana	Tantale d'Amérique	Tantal rak bwa
Fregatidae						
	Magnificent Frigatebird	*Fregata magnificens*	MAFR	Tijereta	Frégate superbe	Sizo
Sulidae						
	Masked Booby	*Sula dactylatra*	MABO	Bubí enmascarado	Fou masqué	Fou maske
	Brown Booby	*Sula leucogaster*	BRBO	Bubí pardo	Fou brun	Gwo fou gri
	Red-footed Booby	*Sula sula*	RFBO	Bubí patas rojas	Fou à pieds rouges	Gwo fou blan
Anhingidae						
	Anhinga	*Anhinga anhinga*	ANHI	Anhinga	Anhinga d'Amérique	Aninga
Phalacrocoracidae						
	Double-crested Cormorant	*Nannopterum auritum*	DCCO	Corúa	Cormoran à aigrettes	Kòmoran lanmè
	Neotropic Cormorant	*Nannopterum brasilianum*	NECO	Corúa Neotropical	Cormoran vigua	Kòmoran

Family	English	Scientific	Alpha Code	Dominican	French	Kreyòl
Pelecanidae						
	American White Pelican	*Pelecanus erythrorhynchos*	AWPE	Pelícano blanco	Pélican d'Amérique	Pelikan blan
	Brown Pelican	*Pelecanus occidentalis*	BRPE	Pelícano	Pélican brun	Pelikan mawon
Ardeidae						
	American Bittern	*Botaurus lentiginosus*	AMBI	Martinete	Butor d'Amérique	Rakra ameriken
	Least Bittern	*Ixobrychus exilis*	LEBI	Martinetito	Petit blongios	Ti rakra jon
	Great Blue Heron	*Ardea herodias*	GBHE	Garzón cenizo	Grand héron	Gwo krabye ble
	Great Egret	*Ardea alba*	GREG	Garza real	Grande aigrette	Gwo krabye blanch
	Little Egret	*Egretta garzetta*	LIEG	Garza chiquita	Aigrette garzette	Ti krabye etranje
	Snowy Egret	*Egretta thula*	SNEG	Garza de rizos	Aigrette neigeuse	Zegrèt blan
	Little Blue Heron	*Egretta caerulea*	LBHE	Garza azul	Aigrette bleue	Ti krabye ble
	Tricolored Heron	*Egretta tricolor*	TRHE	Garza tricolor	Aigrette tricolore	Krabye twa koulè
	Reddish Egret	*Egretta rufescens*	REEG	Garza rojiza	Aigrette roussâtre	Krabye tèt wouj
	Cattle Egret	*Bubulcus ibis*	CAEG	Garza ganadera	Héron garde-bœufs	Krabye gad bèf
	Green Heron	*Butorides virescens*	GRHE	Cra-crá	Héron vert	Ti krabye vèt
	Black-crowned Night-Heron	*Nycticorax nycticorax*	BCNH	Rey congo	Bihoreau gris	Kòk lannwit kouwòn nwa
	Yellow-crowned Night-Heron	*Nyctanassa violacea*	YCNH	Yaboa	Bihoreau violacé	Kòk lannwit kouwòn jòn
Threskiornithidae						
	White Ibis	*Eudocimus albus*	WHIB	Coco blanco	Ibis blanc	Ibis blanch
	Glossy Ibis	*Plegadis falcinellus*	GLIB	Coco prieto	Ibis falcinelle	Ibis pechè
	Roseate Spoonbill	*Platalea ajaja*	ROSP	Cuchareta	Spatule rosée	Espatil
Cathartidae						
	Turkey Vulture	*Cathartes aura*	TUVU	Aura tiñosa	Urubu à tête rouge	Malfini karanklou
Pandionidae						
	Osprey	*Pandion haliaetus*	OSPR	Guincho	Balbuzard pêcheur	Malfini lanmè
Accipitridae						
	Swallow-tailed Kite	*Elanoides forficatus*	STKI	Gavilán cola de tijera	Milan à queue fourchue	Malfini ke chankre
	Northern Harrier	*Circus hudsonius*	NOHA	Gavilán de ciénaga	Busard Saint-Martin	Gwo malfini savann
	Sharp-shinned Hawk	*Accipiter striatus*	SSHA	Guaraguaíto de sierra	Épervier brun	Malfini mouche
	Mississippi Kite	*Ictinia mississippiensis*	MIKI	Elanio del Misisipí	Milan du Mississippi	(unknown)
	Ridgway's Hawk	*Buteo ridgwayi*	RIHA	Gavilán de la Hispaniola	Buse de Ridgway	Ti malfini savann

Family	English	Scientific	Alpha Code	Dominican	French	Kreyòl
	Broad-winged Hawk	*Buteo platypterus*	BWHA	Gavilán bobo	Petite buse	Malfini rak bwa
	Swainson's Hawk	*Buteo swainsoni*	SWHA	Gavilán de Swainson	Buse de Swainson	Malfini Swenson
	Red-tailed Hawk	*Buteo jamaicensis*	RTHA	Guaraguao	Buse à queue rousse	Malfini ke rouj
Tytonidae						
	Barn Owl	*Tyto alba*	BANO	Lechuza blanca	Effraie des clochers	Frize komen
	Ashy-faced Owl	*Tyto glaucops*	AFOW	Lechuza cara ceniza	Effraie d'Hispaniola	Frize figi gri
Strigidae						
	Burrowing Owl	*Athene cunicularia*	BUOW	Cucú	Chevêche des terriers	Frize koukou
	Stygian Owl	*Asio stygius*	STOW	Lechuza orejita	Hibou maître-bois	Frize mèt bwa
	Short-eared Owl	*Asio flammeus*	SEOW	Lechuza de sabana	Hibou des marais	Frize savann
Trogonidae						
	Hispaniolan Trogon	*Priotelus roseigaster*	HITR	Papagayo	Trogon damoiseau	Kanson wouj
Todidae						
	Broad-billed Tody	*Todus subulatus*	BBTO	Barrancolí	Todier à bec large	Kolibri fran
	Narrow-billed Tody	*Todus angustirostris*	NBTO	Chi-cuí	Todier à bec étroit	Kolibri mòn
Alcedinidae						
	Belted Kingfisher	*Megaceryle alcyon*	BEKI	Martín pescador	Martin-pêcheur d'Amérique	Pipirit rivyè
Picidae						
	Antillean Piculet	*Nesoctites micromegas*	ANPI	Carpintero de sierra	Picumne des Antilles	Sèpantye bwa
	Hispaniolan Woodpecker	*Melanerpes striatus*	HIWO	Carpintero	Pic d'Hispaniola	Sèpantye
	Yellow-bellied Sapsucker	*Sphyrapicus varius*	YBSA	Carpintero de paso	Pic maculé	Sèpantye etranje
Falconidae						
	American Kestrel	*Falco sparverius*	AMKE	Cuyaya	Crécerelle d'Amérique	Grigri fran
	Merlin	*Falco columbarius*	MERL	Merlin	Faucon émerillon	Grigri etranje
	Peregrine Falcon	*Falco peregrinus*	PEFA	Halcón peregrino	Faucon pèlerin	Grigri pèleren
Psittacidae						
	Olive-throated Parakeet	*Eupsittula nana*	OTPA	Perico amargo	Conure naine	Perich doliv
	Hispaniolan Parakeet	*Psittacara chloropterus*	HPAK	Perico	Conure maîtresse	Perich
	Hispaniolan Parrot	*Amazona ventralis*	HPAT	Cotorra	Amazone d'Hispaniola	Jako

Family	English	Scientific	Alpha Code	Dominican	French	Kreyòl
Tyrannidae						
	Hispaniolan Elaenia	*Elaenia cherriei*	HIEL	Maroíta canosa	Elénie sara	Pipirit sara
	Great Crested Flycatcher	*Myiarchus crinitus*	GCFL	Maroíta de cresta	Tyran huppé	Pipirit gwo krèp
	Stolid Flycatcher	*Myiarchus stolidus*	STOF	Manuelito	Tyran grosse-tête	Pipirit gwo-tèt
	Gray Kingbird	*Tyrannus dominicensis*	GRAK	Petigre	Tyran gris	Pipirit
	Hispaniolan Kingbird	*Tyrannus gabbii*	HIKI	Manjuila	Tyran tête police	Pipirit chandèl
	Scissor-tailed Flycatcher	*Tyrannus forficatus*	STFL	Cola de tijeras	Tyran à longue queue	Pipirit ke long
	Fork-tailed Flycatcher	*Tyrannus savana*	FTFL	Cola ahorquillada	Tyran des savanes	Pipirit ke sizo
	Eastern Wood-Pewee	*Contopus virens*	EAWP	Maroíta oriental	Pioui de l'est	(unknown)
	Hispaniolan Pewee	*Contopus hispaniolensis*	HIPE	Maroíta	Moucherolle d'Hispaniola	Pipirit siflè
Vireonidae						
	White-eyed Vireo	*Vireo griseus*	WEVI	Vireo de ojo blanco	Viréo aux yeux blancs	Ti panach je blanch
	Thick-billed Vireo	*Vireo crassirostris*	TBVI	Vireo de pico ancho	Viréo à bec fort	Ti panach gwo bèk
	Flat-billed Vireo	*Vireo nanus*	FBVI	Ciguita Juliana	Viréo d'Hispaniola	Ti panach bèk plat
	Yellow-throated Vireo	*Vireo flavifrons*	YTVI	Vireo garganta amarilla	Viréo à gorge jaune	Ti panach gòj jòn
	Philadelphia Vireo	*Vireo philadelphicus*	PHVI	Vireo de Filadélfia	Viréo de Philadelphie	Ti panach Filadelfya
	Warbling Vireo	*Vireo gilvus*	WAVI	Vireo cantor	Viréo mélodieux	Ti panach chantè
	Red-eyed Vireo	*Vireo olivaceus*	REVI	Vireo de ojo rojo	Viréo aux yeux rouges	Ti panach je wouj
	Black-whiskered Vireo	*Vireo altiloquus*	BWVI	Julián Chiví	Viréo à moustaches	Ti panach pyas kolèt
Corvidae						
	Hispaniolan Palm Crow	*Corvus palmarum*	HPCR	Cao	Corneille palmiste	Ti Kaw
	White-necked Crow	*Corvus leucognaphalus*	WNCR	Cuervo	Corneille d'Hispaniola	Kaw
Hirundinidae						
	Bank Swallow	*Riparia riparia*	BANS	Golondrina de collar	Hirondelle de rivage	Irondèl kolye senp
	Tree Swallow	*Tachycineta bicolor*	TRES	Golondrina de árboles	Hirondelle bicolore	Irondèl pye bwa
	Golden Swallow	*Tachycineta euchrysea*	GOSW	Golondrina verde	Hirondelle dorée	Irondèl vèt
	Northern Rough-winged Swallow	*Stelgidopteryx serripennis*	NRWS	Golondrina parda	Hirondelle à ailes hérissées	Irondèl fal mawon
	Purple Martin	*Progne subis*	PUMA	Golondrina migratoria	Hirondelle noire	Irondèl vyolèt
	Cuban Martin	*Progne cryptoleuca*	CUMA	Golondrina grande de Cuba	Hirondelle Cubaine	Irondèl Kiben
	Caribbean Martin	*Progne dominicensis*	CAMA	Golondrina grande	Hirondelle à ventre blanc	Irondèl nwa
	Barn Swallow	*Hirundo rustica*	BARS	Golondrina cola de tijera	Hirondelle rustique	Irondèl ke long

Family	English	Scientific	Alpha Code	Dominican	French	Kreyòl
	Cliff Swallow	*Petrochelidon pyrrhonota*	CLSW	Golondrina de farallón	Hirondelle à front blanc	Irondèl fwon blanch
	Cave Swallow	*Petrochelidon fulva*	CASW	Golondrina de cuevas	Hirondelle à front brun	Irondèl falèz
Polioptilidae						
	Blue-gray Gnatcatcher	*Polioptila caerulea*	BGGN	Rabuita	Gobemoucheron gris-bleu	Ti chwichwi
Regulidae						
	Ruby-crowned Kinglet	*Corthylio calendula*	RCKI	Reyezuelo	Roitelet à couronne rubis	Ti kouwòn wouj
Turdidae						
	Rufous-throated Solitaire	*Myadestes genibarbis*	RTSO	Jilguero	Solitaire siffleur	Mizisyen
	Veery	*Catharus fuscescens*	VEER	Zorzal migratorio colorado	Grive fauve	Griv pal
	Bicknell's Thrush	*Catharus bicknelli*	BITH	Zorzal de Bicknell	Grive de Bicknell	Griv Biknel
	Swainson's Thrush	*Catharus ustulatus*	SWTH	Zorzal de Swainson	Grive de Swainson	Griv Swenson
	Wood Thrush	*Hylocichla mustelina*	WOTH	Zorzal migratorio pecoso	Grive des bois	Griv bwa
	American Robin	*Turdus migratorius*	AMRO	Zorzal migratorio	Merle d'Amérique	Kwèt-kwèt etranje
	La Selle Thrush	*Turdus swalesi*	LSTH	Zorzal de La Salle	Merle de La Selle	Kwèt-kwèt Lasèl
	Red-legged Thrush	*Turdus plumbeus*	RLTH	Chua-chuá	Merle vantard	Kwèt-kwèt
Mimidae						
	Gray Catbird	*Dumetella carolinensis*	GRCA	Zorzal gato	Moqueur chat	Zwazo-chat
	Pearly-eyed Thrasher	*Margarops fuscatus*	PETH	Zorzal pardo	Moqueur corossol	Zwazo kowosòl
	Northern Mockingbird	*Mimus polyglottos*	NOMO	Ruiseñor	Moqueur polyglotte	Wosiyòl
Bombycillidae						
	Cedar Waxwing	*Bombycilla cedrorum*	CEDW	Cigua alas de cera	Jaseur d'Amérique	Zwazo pwent ke jòn
Dulidae						
	Palmchat	*Dulus dominicus*	PALM	Cigua palmera	Esclave palmiste	Zwazo palmis
Ploceidae						
	Village Weaver	*Ploceus cucullatus*	VIWE	Madam Sagá	Tisserin gendarme	Madan sara
Viduidae						
	Pin-tailed Whydah	*Vidua macroura*	PTWH	Viuda colicinta	Veuve dominicaine	(unknown)
Estrildidae						
	Red Avadavat	*Amandava amandava*	REAV	Amandava roja	Bengali rouge	Bengali wouj

Family	English	Scientific	Alpha Code	Dominican	French	Kreyòl
	Scaly-breasted Munia	Lonchura punctulata	SBMU	Cigüita pechijabao	Capucin damier	Mannken miskad
	Tricolored Munia	Lonchura malacca	TRMU	Monjita tricolor	Capucin à dos marron	Mannken twa koulè
Passeridae						
	House Sparrow	Passer domesticus	HOSP	Gorrión doméstico	Moineau domestique	Mwano kay
Motacillidae						
	American Pipit	Anthus rubescens	AMPI	Pipit Americano	Pipit d'Amérique	Pipit
Fringillidae						
	Antillean Euphonia	Chlorophonia musica	ANEU	Jilguerillo	Organiste Louis-d'or	Louidò
	Hispaniolan Crossbill	Loxia megaplaga	HICR	Pico cruzado	Bec-croisé d'Hispaniola	Bèk kwaze
	Antillean Siskin	Spinus dominicensis	ANSI	Canario	Chardonneret des Antilles	Ti seren
Passerellidae						
	Grasshopper Sparrow	Ammodramus savannarum	GRSP	Tumbarrocio	Bruant sauterelle	Mwano kann
	Rufous-collared Sparrow	Zonotrichia capensis	RCOS	Cigua de Constanza	Bruant chingolo	Mwano kolèt nwa
	Savannah Sparrow	Passerculus sandwichensis	SAVS	Gorrión de sabana	Bruant des prés	Mwano pwent sousi dore
	Song Sparrow	Melospiza melodia	SOSP	Gorrión	Bruant chanteur	Mwano kann chantè
	Lincoln's Sparrow	Melospiza lincolnii	LISP	Gorrión de Lincoln	Bruant de Lincoln	Mwano tèt arèl dore
Calyptophilidae						
	Western Chat-Tanager	Calyptophilus tertius	WECT	Chirrí de Bahoruco	Tangara d'Haïti	Gwo kònichon
	Eastern Chat-Tanager	Calyptophilus frugivorus	EACT	Chirrí de Cordillera Central	Tangara Cornichon	Ti kònichon
Phaenicophilidae						
	Black-crowned Palm-Tanager	Phaenicophilus palmarum	BPLT	Cuatro ojos	Tangara à couronne noire	Kat je tèt nwa
	Gray-crowned Palm-Tanager	Phaenicophilus poliocephalus	GCPT	Cuatro ojos cabeza gris	Tangara quatre yeux	Kat je tèt gri
	Hispaniolan Highland-Tanager	Xenoligea montana	HIHT	Ciguita aliblanca	Tangara des montagnes	Ti chit je zèl blan
	Green-tailed Ground-Tanager	Microligea palustris	GTGT	Ciguita cola verde	Tangara aux yeux rouges	Ti chit Lasèl
Spindalidae						
	Hispaniolan Spindalis	Spindalis dominicensis	HISP	Cigua amarilla	Zena d'Hispaniola	Bannann mi mòn
Icteriidae						
	Yellow-breasted Chat	Icteria virens	YBCH	Ciguita grande	Paruline polyglotte	Gwo tchit fal jòn

Family	English	Scientific	Alpha Code	Dominican	French	Kreyòl
Icteridae						
	Bobolink	*Dolichonyx oryzivorus*	BOBO	Bobolink	Goglu des prés	Gwo bèk ke pwenti
	Hispaniolan Oriole	*Icterus dominicensis*	HIOR	Cigua canaria	Oriole à capuchon	Bannann mi
	Orchard Oriole	*Icterus spurius*	OROR	Cigua canaria de huertos	Oriole des vergers	Ti mèl
	Baltimore Oriole	*Icterus galbula*	BAOR	Cigua canaria Americana	Oriole de Baltimore	Ti mèl ameriken
	Tawny-shouldered Blackbird	*Agelaius humeralis*	TSBL	Mayito	Petit carouge	Ti mèl zèpolèt
	Shiny Cowbird	*Molothrus bonariensis*	SHCO	Pájaro vaquero	Vacher luisant	Reskiyè
	Great-tailed Grackle	*Quiscalus mexicanus*	GTGR	Chinchilín grande	Quiscale à longue queue	(unknown)
	Greater Antillean Grackle	*Quiscalus niger*	GAGR	Chinchilín	Quiscale noir	Mèl je jòn
Parulidae						
	Ovenbird	*Seiurus aurocapilla*	OVEN	Cigua saltarina	Paruline couronnée	Ti kit tèt dore
	Worm-eating Warbler	*Helmitheros vermivorum*	WEWA	Cigua cabeza rayada	Paruline vermivore	Ti chit tèt plat
	Louisiana Waterthrush	*Parkesia motacilla*	LOWA	Cigua del río	Paruline hochequeue	Ti kit rivyè
	Northern Waterthrush	*Parkesia noveboracensis*	NOWA	Cigua del agua	Paruline des ruisseaux	Ti kit mang lanmè
	Golden-winged Warbler	*Vermivora chrysoptera*	GWWA	Cigua ala de oro	Paruline à ailes dorées	Ti kit zèl dore
	Blue-winged Warbler	*Vermivora cyanoptera*	BWWA	Cigua ala azul	Paruline à ailes bleues	Ti kit zèl ble
	Black-and-white Warbler	*Mniotilta varia*	BAWW	Pegapalo	Paruline noir et blanc	Ti kit demidèy
	Prothonotary Warbler	*Protonotaria citrea*	PROW	Cigua cabeza amarilla	Paruline orangée	Ti kit tèt jòn
	Swainson's Warbler	*Limnothlypis swainsonii*	SWWA	Cigua de Swainson	Paruline de Swainson	Ti kit bèk pwenti
	Tennessee Warbler	*Leiothlypis peregrina*	TEWA	Cigua de Tenesí	Paruline obscure	Ti kit gris
	Nashville Warbler	*Leiothlypis ruficapilla*	NAWA	Cigua de Nashville	Paruline à joues grises	Ti kit tèt gri
	Connecticut Warbler	*Oporornis agilis*	CONW	Cigua de lentes	Paruline à gorge grise	Ti kit fal gri
	Mourning Warbler	*Geothlypis philadelphia*	MOWA	Cigua triste	Paruline triste	Ti kit tris
	Kentucky Warbler	*Geothlypis formosa*	KEWA	Cigua de Kentukí	Paruline du Kentucky	Ti kit tè
	Common Yellowthroat	*Geothlypis trichas*	COYE	Cigua enmascarada	Paruline masquée	Ti kit figi nwa
	Hooded Warbler	*Setophaga citrina*	HOWA	Cigua gorra negra	Paruline à capuchon	Ti kit bonèt nwa
	American Redstart	*Setophaga ruticilla*	AMRE	Candelita	Paruline flamboyante	Ti kit dife
	Cape May Warbler	*Setophaga tigrina*	CMWA	Cigua tigrina	Paruline tigrée	Ti kit kou jòn
	Northern Parula	*Setophaga americana*	NOPA	Cigua parula	Paruline à collier	Ti kit ble pal
	Magnolia Warbler	*Setophaga magnolia*	MAWA	Cigua magnolia	Paruline à tête cendrée	Ti kit ke blanch
	Bay-breasted Warbler	*Setophaga castanea*	BBWA	Cigua castaña	Paruline à poitrine baie	Ti kit fal mawon
	Blackburnian Warbler	*Setophaga fusca*	BLBW	Cigua del frío	Paruline à gorge orangée	Ti kit flanboyan

Family	English	Scientific	Alpha Code	Dominican	French	Kreyòl
	Yellow Warbler	*Setophaga petechia*	YEWA	Canario de manglar	Paruline jaune	Ti kit jòn
	Chestnut-sided Warbler	*Setophaga pensylvanica*	CSWA	Ciguita de costados castaños	Paruline à flancs marron	Tit kò mawon
	Blackpoll Warbler	*Setophaga striata*	BLPW	Ciguita cabeza negra	Paruline rayée	Ti kit séjan
	Black-throated Blue Warbler	*Setophaga caerulescens*	BTBW	Ciguita azul, garganta negra	Paruline bleue	Ti kit ble kou nwa
	Palm Warbler	*Setophaga palmarum*	PAWA	Ciguita palmar	Paruline à couronne rousse	Ti kit palmis
	Pine Warbler	*Setophaga pinus*	PIWA	Ciguita del pinar	Paruline des pins	Ti kit bwa pen
	Yellow-rumped Warbler	*Setophaga coronata*	YRWA	Ciguita mirta	Paruline à croupion jaune	Ti kit dèyè jòn
	Yellow-throated Warbler	*Setophaga dominica*	YTWA	Ciguita garganta amarilla	Paruline à gorge jaune	Ti kit fal jòn
	Prairie Warbler	*Setophaga discolor*	PRAW	Ciguita de los prados	Paruline des prés	Ti kit zèl mawon
	Black-throated Green Warbler	*Setophaga virens*	BTNW	Ciguita pechinegro	Paruline à gorge noire	Ti kit fal nwa
	Canada Warbler	*Cardellina canadensis*	CAWA	Ciguita del Canadá	Paruline du Canada	Ti kit Kanada
	Wilson's Warbler	*Cardellina pusilla*	WIWA	Ciguita de Wilson	Paruline à calotte noire	Ti kit kepi nwa
Cardinalidae						
	Summer Tanager	*Piranga rubra*	SUTA	Tángara roja	Tangara vermillon	Tangara wouj
	Scarlet Tanager	*Piranga olivacea*	SCTA	Tángara escarlata	Tangara écarlate	Tangara wouj zèl nwa
	Western Tanager	*Piranga ludoviciana*	WETA	Tángara carirroja	Tangara à tête rouge	Tangara tèt wouj
	Rose-breasted Grosbeak	*Pheucticus ludovicianus*	RBGR	Degollado	Cardinal à poitrine rose	Kadinal fal wòz
	Blue Grosbeak	*Passerina caerulea*	BLGR	Azulejo real	Guiraca bleu	Giraka ble
	Indigo Bunting	*Passerina cyanea*	INBU	Azulejo	Passerin indigo	Zwazo digo
	Painted Bunting	*Passerina ciris*	PABU	Azulillo multicolor	Passerin nonpareil	(unknown)
Thraupidae						
	Bananaquit	*Coereba flaveola*	BANA	Ciguita común	Sucrier à ventre jaune	Ti kit fal jòn
	Yellow-faced Grassquit	*Tiaris olivaceus*	YFGR	Ciguita de hierba	Sporophile grand chanteur	Ti zèb figi jòn
	Greater Antillean Bullfinch	*Melopyrrha violacea*	GABU	Gallito prieto	Sporophile petit-coq	Ti kòk nwa, Gwo bèk
	Black-faced Grassquit	*Melanospiza bicolor*	BFGR	Juana Maruca	Sporophile cici	Ti zèb figi nwa, Sisi zèb

APPENDIX 2: BIRDS OF HISPANIOLAN OFFSHORE ISLANDS

Table 2. Birds of Hispaniolan Offshore Islands. Occurrence of 194 species of birds reported as having been seen (X) or having bred (B) on satellite islands or island groups associated with Hispaniola. Reports come from published records, personal reports, and eBird checklists. Note that many of the species reported as present on these islands may breed as well, but documentation is often lacking.

English Name	Scientific Name	Navassa Island	Cayemites[1]	Île-à-Vache	Île de la Gonave[2]	Île de la Tortue	Cayos Siete Hermanos	Alto Velo	Beata[3]	Catalina	Saona[4]
West Indian Whistling-Duck	Dendrocygna arborea			X					X	X	X
Blue-winged Teal	Spatula discors			X							
White-cheeked Pintail	Anas bahamensis			X					X	X	X
Masked Duck	Nomonyx dominicus									X	X
Ruddy Duck	Oxyura jamaicensis										X
Helmeted Guineafowl	Numida meleagris										X
American Flamingo	Phoenicopterus ruber			X	B	X					X
Least Grebe	Tachybaptus dominicus								B		X
Pied-billed Grebe	Podilymbus podiceps			X							X
Rock Pigeon	Columba livia										X
Scaly-naped Pigeon	Patagioenas squamosa	X	X	X	X				X		X
White-crowned Pigeon	Patagioenas leucocephala	X	X	X	X	X			B	X	B
Plain Pigeon	Patagioenas inornata					X				X	X
Eurasian Collared-Dove	Streptopelia decaocto										X
Common Ground Dove	Columbina passerina	B	B	B	B	B	B		B	B	B
Ruddy Quail-Dove	Geotrygon montana				B				B	B	B
Key West Quail-Dove	Geotrygon chrysia				B	B					B
White-winged Dove	Zenaida asiatica		X		B	X		X	B		X
Zenaida Dove	Zenaida aurita			X	X	X		X	B	X	X
Mourning Dove	Zenaida macroura		X	X	B	B		X	B	X	X
Smooth-billed Ani	Crotophaga ani	X	X	X	X				X	X	X
Yellow-billed Cuckoo	Coccyzus americanus				X		X		X	X	X
Mangrove Cuckoo	Coccyzus minor	X		X	X	X			X	X	X
Bay-breasted Cuckoo	Coccyzus rufigularis				B						
Hispaniolan Lizard-Cuckoo	Coccyzus longirostris				B	B			B	B	B
Common Nighthawk	Chordeiles minor								X		
Antillean Nighthawk	Chordeiles gundlachii				X	B		X	X	X	X
Least Pauraque	Siphonorhis brewsteri				B				X		
Chuck-will's-widow	Antrostomus carolinensis							X			

English Name	Scientific Name	Navassa Island	Cayemites[1]	Île-à-Vache	Île de la Gonâve[2]	Île de la Tortue	Cayos Siete Hermanos	Alto Velo	Beata[3]	Catalina	Saona[4]
Hispaniolan Nightjar	Antrostomus eckmani								X		
Northern Potoo	Nyctibius jamaicensis				B						
Black Swift	Cypseloides niger		X								
White-collared Swift	Streptoprocne zonaris					X					X
Chimney Swift	Chaetura pelagica					X					
Antillean Palm-Swift	Tachornis phoenicobia		X	X					X	X	X
Antillean Mango	Anthracothorax dominicus	B	B	B	B				B	B	B
Vervain Hummingbird	Mellisuga minima	B	B	B	B					B	B
Hispaniolan Emerald	Riccordia swainsonii			X							
Clapper Rail	Rallus crepitans			X	X						
Common Gallinule	Gallinula galeata		X	X						X	X
American Coot	Fulica americana								X	X	X
Purple Gallinule	Porphyrio martinicus		X								
Limpkin	Aramus guarauna				X	X					X
Double-striped Thick-knee	Burhinus bistriatus								X		
Black-necked Stilt	Himantopus mexicanus	X		X	X	X	X		X	X	X
American Avocet	Recurvirostra americana										X
American Oystercatcher	Haematopus palliatus						X			X	B
Black-bellied Plover	Pluvialis squatarola						X		X	X	X
Killdeer	Charadrius vociferus		X	X	X			X	X	X	X
Semipalmated Plover	Charadrius semipalmatus			X	X				X		X
Piping Plover	Charadrius melodus								X		X
Wilson's Plover	Charadrius wilsonia		X	X	X	X	X		B	X	X
Snowy Plover	Charadrius nivosus			X					X		X
Whimbrel	Numenius phaeopus			X					X		X
Ruddy Turnstone	Arenaria interpres	X		X	X		X		X	X	X
Red Knot	Calidris canutus								X		X
Stilt Sandpiper	Calidris himantopus								X		X
Sanderling	Calidris alba	X		X	X		X		X	X	X
Least Sandpiper	Calidris minutilla		X						X	X	X
White-rumped Sandpiper	Calidris fuscicollis								X		X
Pectoral Sandpiper	Calidris melanotos					X			X	X	X

English Name	Scientific Name	Navassa Island	Cayemites[1]	Île-à-Vache	Île de la Gonâve[2]	Île de la Tortue	Cayos Siete Hermanos	Alto Velo	Beata[3]	Catalina	Saona[4]
Semipalmated Sandpiper	*Calidris pusilla*				X		X		X	X	X
Western Sandpiper	*Calidris mauri*						X				X
Short-billed Dowitcher	*Limnodromus griseus*								X	X	X
Spotted Sandpiper	*Actitis macularius*		X	X	X				X		X
Solitary Sandpiper	*Tringa solitaria*									X	
Lesser Yellowlegs	*Tringa flavipes*	X	X	X	X	X	X	X	X	X	X
Willet	*Tringa semipalmata*			X	X				B	X	X
Greater Yellowlegs	*Tringa melanoleuca*			X	X				X	X	X
Pomarine Jaeger	*Stercorarius pomarinus*	X									
Bonaparte's Gull	*Chroicocephalus philadelphia*	X									
Laughing Gull	*Leucophaeus atricilla*			X				X	X	X	B
Franklin's Gull	*Leucophaeus pipixcan*										X
Ring-billed Gull	*Larus delawarensis*										X
Herring Gull	*Larus argentatus*										X
Lesser Black-backed Gull	*Larus fuscus*										X
Brown Noddy	*Anous stolidus*	B					B		B	X	X
Sooty Tern	*Onychoprion fuscatus*	X					B	B	X		X
Bridled Tern	*Onychoprion anaethetus*	B					B	B	B		
Least Tern	*Sternula antillarum*				X			X	X		X
Gull-billed Tern	*Gelochelidon nilotica*				X				X		X
Caspian Tern	*Hydroprogne caspia*			X							
Black Tern	*Chlidonias niger*								X		X
Roseate Tern	*Sterna dougallii*			X			B	X	B		X
Common Tern	*Sterna hirundo*			X				X	X		X
Royal Tern	*Thalasseus maximus*			X	X		X	X	X	X	X
Sandwich Tern	*Thalasseus sandvicensis*							B	X		
White-tailed Tropicbird	*Phaethon lepturus*	B		X	X	B					
Red-billed Tropicbird	*Phaethon aethereus*						X				
Wilson's Storm-Petrel	*Oceanites oceanicus*								X		X
Black-capped Petrel	*Pterodroma hasitata*							X	X		
Cory's Shearwater	*Calonectris diomedea*	X									
Audubon's Shearwater	*Puffinus lherminieri*	X				X			X		X

English Name	Scientific Name	Navassa Island	Cayemites[1]	Île-à-Vache	Île de la Gonave[2]	Île de la Tortue	Cayos Siete Hermanos	Alto Velo	Beata[3]	Catalina	Saona[4]
Magnificent Frigatebird	Fregata magnificens	B	X	X	B			X	X	X	B
Masked Booby	Sula dactylatra	X									X
Brown Booby	Sula leucogaster	B			X			B	X	X	X
Red-footed Booby	Sula sula	B									X
Brown Pelican	Pelecanus occidentalis	X	X	X	B	X		X	B	X	B
Great Blue Heron	Ardea herodias	X		X	X		X		X	X	X
Great Egret	Ardea alba			X	X			X	X	X	X
Snowy Egret	Egretta thula		X	X	X				X	X	X
Little Blue Heron	Egretta caerulea		X	X	X		X		X		X
Tricolored Heron	Egretta tricolor		X	X	X				X	X	X
Reddish Egret	Egretta rufescens							X			X
Cattle Egret	Bubulcus ibis	X	X	X						X	X
Green Heron	Butorides virescens		X	X					X		B
Black-crowned Night-Heron	Nycticorax nycticorax			X	X				X	X	X
Yellow-crowned Night-Heron	Nyctanassa violacea		X	X	X				X	X	X
White Ibis	Eudocimus albus			X					X		
Glossy Ibis	Plegadis falcinellus			X					X		
Roseate Spoonbill	Platalea ajaja				X						
Turkey Vulture	Cathartes aura		X		X				B	X	
Osprey	Pandion haliaetus	X		X			X	X	X	X	X
Swallow-tailed Kite	Elanoides forficatus									X	X
Northern Harrier	Circus hudsonius					X					
Ridgway's Hawk	Buteo ridgwayi		X	X	B			X	X		
Broad-winged Hawk	Buteo platypterus										X
Red-tailed Hawk	Buteo jamaicensis		X	X	X			X	X		X
Barn Owl	Tyto alba	X						X			X
Ashy-faced Owl	Tyto glaucops	X				X		X			X
Burrowing Owl	Athene cunicularia				B				B		
Stygian Owl	Asio stygius				B						
Broad-billed Tody	Todus subulatus		X		B						
Belted Kingfisher	Megaceryle alcyon	X		X	X			X	X	X	X
Antillean Piculet	Nesoctites micromegas				B						

English Name	Scientific Name	Navassa Island	Cayemites[1]	Île-à-Vache	Île de la Gonave[2]	Île de la Tortue	Cayos Siete Hermanos	Alto Velo	Beata[3]	Catalina	Saona[4]
Hispaniolan Woodpecker	Melanerpes striatus					X			X		X
Yellow-bellied Sapsucker	Sphyrapicus varius				X	X					
American Kestrel	Falco sparverius	X	X	X	X	X		X	B	X	B
Peregrine Falcon	Falco peregrinus	X			X	X		X			
Hispaniolan Parakeet	Psittacara chloropterus				X				X		
Hispaniolan Parrot	Amazona ventralis		X		X				X		X
Stolid Flycatcher	Myiarchus stolidus		B	B	B	B			B	B	B
Gray Kingbird	Tyrannus dominicensis	B	B	B	B	B		X	B	X	B
Hispaniolan Kingbird	Tyrannus gabbii				X						X
Hispaniolan Pewee	Contopus hispaniolensis				X						
White-eyed Vireo	Vireo griseus	X		X	B						
Thick-billed Vireo	Vireo crassirostris					B					
Flat-billed Vireo	Vireo nanus				B					X	B
Red-eyed Vireo	Vireo olivaceus	X	B								
Black-whiskered Vireo	Vireo altiloquus	B	X	X	B	B			B	X	B
White-necked Crow	Corvus leucognaphalus	X	X	X	X						X
Hispaniolan Palm Crow	Corvus palmarum										
Bank Swallow	Riparia riparia			X					X		
Northern Rough-winged Swallow	Stelgidopteryx serripennis										X
Purple Martin	Progne subis	X	X	X					X	X	X
Caribbean Martin	Progne dominicensis	X	X	X					X	X	X
Barn Swallow	Hirundo rustica	X	X	X				X	X	X	X
Cave Swallow	Petrochelidon fulva	X	X	X	X	X		X	X	X	X
Red-legged Thrush	Turdus plumbeus				B	B					B
Gray Catbird	Dumetella carolinensis	X				X					
Pearly-eyed Thrasher	Margarops fuscatus							B	B		
Northern Mockingbird	Mimus polyglottos		B		B	B				B	B
Palmchat	Dulus dominicus		X		B	B					B
Village Weaver	Ploceus cucullatus		X							B	B
Scaly-breasted Munia	Lonchura punctulata	X									
House Sparrow	Passer domesticus									X	X

English Name	Scientific Name	Navassa Island	Cayemites[1]	Île-à-Vache	Île de la Gonâve[2]	Île de la Tortue	Cayos Siete Hermanos	Alto Velo	Beata[3]	Catalina	Saona[4]
Antillean Euphonia	Chlorophonia musica				B						
Antillean Siskin	Spinus dominicensis				X						
Eastern Chat-Tanager	Calyptophilus frugivorus				B						
Black-crowned Palm-Tanager	Phaenicophilus palmarum										B
Gray-crowned Palm-Tanager	Phaenicophilus poliocephalus		X	B	B						
Green-tailed Ground-Tanager	Microligea palustris								B		B
Bobolink	Dolichonyx oryzivorus					X					
Hispaniolan Oriole	Icterus dominicensis			X	B	B			X	X	X
Baltimore Oriole	Icterus galbula								X		X
Shiny Cowbird	Molothrus bonariensis								X		X
Greater Antillean Grackle	Quiscalus niger									B	X
Ovenbird	Seiurus aurocapilla	X	X	X	B	X				X	X
Louisiana Waterthrush	Parkesia motacilla	X		X	X	X					X
Northern Waterthrush	Parkesia noveboracensis	X	X	X	X	X			X		X
Black-and-white Warbler	Mniotilta varia	X		X	X	X					X
Prothonotary Warbler	Protonotaria citrea										X
Nashville Warbler	Leiothlypis ruficapilla	X									
Mourning Warbler	Geothlypis philadelphia	X									
Common Yellowthroat	Geothlypis trichas	X		X	X	X		X			X
Hooded Warbler	Setophaga citrina										X
American Redstart	Setophaga ruticilla	X	X	X	X				X	X	X
Cape May Warbler	Setophaga tigrina	X	X	X	X				X		X
Northern Parula	Setophaga americana	X		X	X	X			X		X
Blackburnian Warbler	Setophaga fusca						X				
Yellow Warbler	Setophaga petechia		B	B	B	B	B		B	X	B
Blackpoll Warbler	Setophaga striata			X	X				X		
Black-throated Blue Warbler	Setophaga caerulescens	X		X	X	X					
Palm Warbler	Setophaga palmarum	X	X	X	X	X				X	X
Pine Warbler	Setophaga pinus	X							X		
Yellow-rumped Warbler	Setophaga coronata		X	X			X			X	X
Yellow-throated Warbler	Setophaga dominica			X	X						X
Prairie Warbler	Setophaga discolor	X	X	X	X	X		X	X		X

English Name	Scientific Name	Navassa Island	Cayemites[1]	Île-à-Vache	Île de la Gonâve[2]	Île de la Tortue	Cayos Siete Hermanos	Alto Velo	Beata[3]	Catalina	Saona[4]
Black-throated Green Warbler	Setophaga virens	X							X		
Rose-breasted Grosbeak	Pheucticus ludovicianus				X						
Bananaquit	Coereba flaveola	X	B	B	B	B			B	X	B
Yellow-faced Grassquit	Tiaris olivaceus	B	B	B	B	B					X
Greater Antillean Bullfinch	Melopyrrha violacea			B	B	B			B	B	B
Black-faced Grassquit	Melanospiza bicolor	B	X	X	B	B					
TOTAL		61	59	90	96	53	24	39	96	74	133

[1] Grand and Petite Cayemites
[2] Île de la Gonave, Petite Gonave, and Fregate Island
[3] Isla Beata and Piedra Negra
[4] Isla Saona and Isla Catalinita

APPENDIX 3:
A CHECKLIST OF BIRDS OF HISPANIOLA

A complete list, in phylogenetic order, of the 318 bird species known to occur on Hispaniola.

Anatidae
☐ White-faced Whistling-Duck
☐ Black-bellied Whistling-Duck
☐ West Indian Whistling-Duck
☐ Fulvous Whistling-Duck
☐ Canada Goose
☐ Wood Duck
☐ Blue-winged Teal
☐ Northern Shoveler
☐ Gadwall
☐ Eurasian Wigeon
☐ American Wigeon
☐ Mallard
☐ White-cheeked Pintail
☐ Northern Pintail
☐ Green-winged Teal
☐ Canvasback
☐ Redhead
☐ Ring-necked Duck
☐ Greater Scaup
☐ Lesser Scaup
☐ Hooded Merganser
☐ Red-breasted Merganser
☐ Masked Duck
☐ Ruddy Duck

Numididae
☐ Helmeted Guineafowl

Odontophoridae
☐ Northern Bobwhite

Phasianidae
☐ Ring-necked Pheasant
☐ Red Junglefowl

Phoenicopteridae
☐ American Flamingo
Podicipedidae
☐ Least Grebe
☐ Pied-billed Grebe
Columbidae
☐ Rock Pigeon
☐ Scaly-naped Pigeon
☐ White-crowned Pigeon
☐ Plain Pigeon
☐ Eurasian Collared-Dove
☐ Common Ground Dove
☐ Ruddy Quail-Dove
☐ White-fronted Quail-Dove
☐ Key West Quail-Dove
☐ White-winged Dove

☐ Zenaida Dove
☐ Mourning Dove

Cuculidae
☐ Smooth-billed Ani
☐ Yellow-billed Cuckoo
☐ Mangrove Cuckoo
☐ Black-billed Cuckoo
☐ Bay-breasted Cuckoo
☐ Hispaniolan Lizard-Cuckoo

Caprimulgidae
☐ Common Nighthawk
☐ Antillean Nighthawk
☐ Least Pauraque
☐ Chuck-will's-widow
☐ Hispaniolan Nightjar

Nyctibiidae
☐ Northern Potoo

Apodidae
☐ Black Swift
☐ White-collared Swift
☐ Chimney Swift
☐ Antillean Palm-Swift

Trochilidae
☐ Antillean Mango
☐ Ruby-throated Hummingbird
☐ Vervain Hummingbird
☐ Hispaniolan Emerald

Rallidae
☐ Spotted Rail
☐ Clapper Rail
☐ Sora
☐ Common Gallinule
☐ American Coot
☐ Purple Gallinule
☐ Yellow-breasted Crake
☐ Black Rail

Aramidae
☐ Limpkin

Burhinidae
☐ Double-striped Thick-knee

Recurvirostridae
☐ Black-necked Stilt
☐ American Avocet

Haematopodidae
- [ ] American Oystercatcher

Charadriidae
- [ ] Black-bellied Plover
- [ ] American Golden-Plover
- [ ] Pacific Golden-Plover
- [ ] Killdeer
- [ ] Semipalmated Plover
- [ ] Piping Plover
- [ ] Wilson's Plover
- [ ] Snowy Plover

Jacanidae
- [ ] Northern Jacana

Scolopacidae
- [ ] Whimbrel
- [ ] Long-billed Curlew
- [ ] Hudsonian Godwit
- [ ] Marbled Godwit
- [ ] Ruddy Turnstone
- [ ] Red Knot
- [ ] Stilt Sandpiper
- [ ] Sanderling
- [ ] Dunlin
- [ ] Baird's Sandpiper
- [ ] Least Sandpiper
- [ ] White-rumped Sandpiper
- [ ] Buff-breasted Sandpiper
- [ ] Pectoral Sandpiper
- [ ] Semipalmated Sandpiper
- [ ] Western Sandpiper
- [ ] Short-billed Dowitcher
- [ ] Long-billed Dowitcher
- [ ] Wilson's Snipe
- [ ] Spotted Sandpiper
- [ ] Solitary Sandpiper
- [ ] Lesser Yellowlegs
- [ ] Willet
- [ ] Greater Yellowlegs
- [ ] Wilson's Phalarope
- [ ] Red-necked Phalarope

Stercorariidae
- [ ] Pomarine Jaeger
- [ ] Parasitic Jaeger
- [ ] Long-tailed Jaeger

Laridae
- [ ] Black-legged Kittiwake
- [ ] Bonaparte's Gull
- [ ] Laughing Gull
- [ ] Franklin's Gull
- [ ] Ring-billed Gull
- [ ] Herring Gull
- [ ] Lesser Black-backed Gull
- [ ] Great Black-backed Gull

- [ ] Brown Noddy
- [ ] Sooty Tern
- [ ] Bridled Tern
- [ ] Least Tern
- [ ] Gull-billed Tern
- [ ] Caspian Tern
- [ ] Black Tern
- [ ] Roseate Tern
- [ ] Common Tern
- [ ] Forster's Tern
- [ ] Royal Tern
- [ ] Sandwich Tern
- [ ] Black Skimmer

Phaethontidae
- [ ] White-tailed Tropicbird
- [ ] Red-billed Tropicbird

Hydrobatidae
- [ ] Wilson's Storm-Petrel
- [ ] Leach's Storm-Petrel

Procellariidae
- [ ] Black-capped Petrel
- [ ] Cory's Shearwater
- [ ] Great Shearwater
- [ ] Manx Shearwater
- [ ] Audubon's Shearwater

Ciconiidae
- [ ] Wood Stork

Fregatidae
- [ ] Magnificent Frigatebird

Sulidae
- [ ] Masked Booby
- [ ] Brown Booby
- [ ] Red-footed Booby

Anhingidae
- [ ] Anhinga

Phalacrocoracidae
- [ ] Double-crested Cormorant
- [ ] Neotropic Cormorant

Pelecanidae
- [ ] American White Pelican
- [ ] Brown Pelican

Ardeidae
- [ ] American Bittern
- [ ] Least Bittern
- [ ] Great Blue Heron
- [ ] Great Egret
- [ ] Little Egret
- [ ] Snowy Egret

- [ ] Little Blue Heron
- [ ] Tricolored Heron
- [ ] Reddish Egret
- [ ] Cattle Egret
- [ ] Green Heron
- [ ] Black-crowned Night-Heron
- [ ] Yellow-crowned Night-Heron

Threskiornithidae
- [ ] White Ibis
- [ ] Glossy Ibis
- [ ] Roseate Spoonbill

Cathartidae
- [ ] Turkey Vulture

Pandionidae
- [ ] Osprey

Accipitridae
- [ ] Swallow-tailed Kite
- [ ] Northern Harrier
- [ ] Sharp-shinned Hawk
- [ ] Mississippi Kite
- [ ] Ridgway's Hawk
- [ ] Broad-winged Hawk
- [ ] Swainson's Hawk
- [ ] Red-tailed Hawk

Tytonidae
- [ ] Barn Owl
- [ ] Ashy-faced Owl

Strigidae
- [ ] Burrowing Owl
- [ ] Stygian Owl
- [ ] Short-eared Owl

Trogonidae
- [ ] Hispaniolan Trogon

Todidae
- [ ] Broad-billed Tody
- [ ] Narrow-billed Tody

Alcedinidae
- [ ] Belted Kingfisher

Picidae
- [ ] Antillean Piculet
- [ ] Hispaniolan Woodpecker
- [ ] Yellow-bellied Sapsucker

Falconidae
- [ ] American Kestrel
- [ ] Merlin
- [ ] Peregrine Falcon

Psittacidae
- [ ] Olive-throated Parakeet
- [ ] Hispaniolan Parakeet
- [ ] Hispaniolan Parrot

Tyrannidae
- [ ] Hispaniolan Elaenia
- [ ] Great Crested Flycatcher
- [ ] Stolid Flycatcher
- [ ] Gray Kingbird
- [ ] Hispaniolan Kingbird
- [ ] Scissor-tailed Flycatcher
- [ ] Fork-tailed Flycatcher
- [ ] Eastern Wood-Pewee
- [ ] Hispaniolan Pewee

Vireonidae
- [ ] White-eyed Vireo
- [ ] Thick-billed Vireo
- [ ] Flat-billed Vireo
- [ ] Yellow-throated Vireo
- [ ] Philadelphia Vireo
- [ ] Warbling Vireo
- [ ] Red-eyed Vireo
- [ ] Black-whiskered Vireo

Corvidae
- [ ] Hispaniolan Palm Crow
- [ ] White-necked Crow

Hirundinidae
- [ ] Bank Swallow
- [ ] Tree Swallow
- [ ] Golden Swallow
- [ ] Northern Rough-winged Swallow
- [ ] Purple Martin
- [ ] Cuban Martin
- [ ] Caribbean Martin
- [ ] Barn Swallow
- [ ] Cliff Swallow
- [ ] Cave Swallow

Polioptilidae
- [ ] Blue-gray Gnatcatcher

Regulidae
- [ ] Ruby-crowned Kinglet

Turdidae
- [ ] Rufous-throated Solitaire
- [ ] Veery
- [ ] Bicknell's Thrush
- [ ] Swainson's Thrush
- [ ] Wood Thrush
- [ ] American Robin
- [ ] La Selle Thrush
- [ ] Red-legged Thrush

Mimidae
- [ ] Gray Catbird
- [ ] Pearly-eyed Thrasher
- [ ] Northern Mockingbird

Bombycillidae
- [ ] Cedar Waxwing

Dulidae
- [ ] Palmchat

Ploceidae
- [ ] Village Weaver

Viduidae
- [ ] Pin-tailed Whydah

Estrildidae
- [ ] Red Avadavat
- [ ] Scaly-breasted Munia
- [ ] Tricolored Munia

Passeridae
- [ ] House Sparrow

Motacillidae
- [ ] American Pipit

Fringillidae
- [ ] Antillean Euphonia
- [ ] Hispaniolan Crossbill
- [ ] Antillean Siskin

Passerellidae
- [ ] Grasshopper Sparrow
- [ ] Rufous-collared Sparrow
- [ ] Savannah Sparrow
- [ ] Song Sparrow
- [ ] Lincoln's Sparrow

Calyptophilidae
- [ ] Western Chat-Tanager
- [ ] Eastern Chat-Tanager

Phaenicophilidae
- [ ] Black-crowned Palm-Tanager
- [ ] Gray-crowned Palm-Tanager
- [ ] Hispaniolan Highland-Tanager
- [ ] Green-tailed Ground-Tanager

Spindalidae
- [ ] Hispaniolan Spindalis

Icteriidae
- [ ] Yellow-breasted Chat

Icteridae
- [ ] Bobolink

- [ ] Hispaniolan Oriole
- [ ] Orchard Oriole
- [ ] Baltimore Oriole
- [ ] Tawny-shouldered Blackbird
- [ ] Shiny Cowbird
- [ ] Great-tailed Grackle
- [ ] Greater Antillean Grackle

Parulidae
- [ ] Ovenbird
- [ ] Worm-eating Warbler
- [ ] Louisiana Waterthrush
- [ ] Northern Waterthrush
- [ ] Golden-winged Warbler
- [ ] Blue-winged Warbler
- [ ] Black-and-white Warbler
- [ ] Prothonotary Warbler
- [ ] Swainson's Warbler
- [ ] Tennessee Warbler
- [ ] Nashville Warbler
- [ ] Connecticut Warbler
- [ ] Mourning Warbler
- [ ] Kentucky Warbler
- [ ] Common Yellowthroat
- [ ] Hooded Warbler
- [ ] American Redstart
- [ ] Cape May Warbler
- [ ] Northern Parula
- [ ] Magnolia Warbler
- [ ] Bay-breasted Warbler
- [ ] Blackburnian Warbler
- [ ] Yellow Warbler
- [ ] Chestnut-sided Warbler
- [ ] Blackpoll Warbler
- [ ] Black-throated Blue Warbler
- [ ] Palm Warbler
- [ ] Pine Warbler
- [ ] Yellow-rumped Warbler
- [ ] Yellow-throated Warbler
- [ ] Prairie Warbler
- [ ] Black-throated Green Warbler
- [ ] Canada Warbler
- [ ] Wilson's Warbler

Cardinalidae
- [ ] Summer Tanager
- [ ] Scarlet Tanager
- [ ] Western Tanager
- [ ] Rose-breasted Grosbeak
- [ ] Blue Grosbeak
- [ ] Indigo Bunting
- [ ] Painted Bunting

Thraupidae
- [ ] Bananaquit
- [ ] Yellow-faced Grassquit
- [ ] Greater Antillean Bullfinch
- [ ] Black-faced Grassquit

SELECTED REFERENCES

Here we focus on literature referenced in the text, and original research published since the first edition of this book (2006) that has contributed in particular to our current understanding of distribution, abundance, and ecology of the birds of Hispaniola.

Almonte-Espinosa, H. 2015. Contribución al conocimiento de las aves en Hoyo de Pelempito, Sierra de Bahoruco, República Dominicana. Novitates Caribaea 8:138–141.

Almonte-Espinosa, H. 2017. Caracterización de la comunidad de aves en el Parque Nacional Sierra Martín García, República Dominicana. Novitates Caribaea 11:79–88.

Almonte-Espinosa, H. 2018. Composición, riqueza, diversidad y abundancia de aves en cuatro áreas verdes de Santo Domingo. Novitates Caribaea 12:14–24.

Almonte-Espinosa, H., and S. C. Latta. 2011. Aspectos del comportamiento de forrajeo de la cigüita del río *Parkesia motacilla* (Aves: Passeriformes: Parulidae) en época no reproductiva. Novitates Caribaea 4:100–108.

[AOU] American Ornithologists' Union. 1998. *Check-list of North American Birds*. Seventh edition. American Ornithologists' Union. Washington, DC.

Arendt, W. J., M. M. Paulino, L. R. Paulino, M. A. Tórrez, and O. P. Lane. 2019. Colonization of Hispaniola by *Margarops fuscatus* Vieillot (Pearly-eyed Thrasher). Urban Naturalist 23:1–24.

Billerman, S. M., B. K. Keeney, P. G. Rodewald, and T. S. Schulenberg (eds.). 2020. Birds of the World. Cornell Laboratory of Ornithology, Ithaca, NY. https://birdsoftheworld.org/bow/home

BirdLife International. 2000. *Threatened Birds of the World.* Lynx Edicions and BirdLife International, Barcelona, Spain, and Cambridge, U.K.

Campbell, J. D., M. A. Taylor, T. S. Stephenson, R. A. Watson, and F. S. Whyte. 2011. Future climate of the Caribbean from a regional climate model. International Journal of Climatology 31:1866–1878.

CATHALAC. 2008. Potential impacts of climate change on biodiversity in Central America, Mexico and the Dominican Republic. Panama City: Water Centre for Humid Tropics of Latin America and the Caribbean.

Curti, M., H. Polanco, T. Hayes, J. Brocca, J. Gañan, and S. Latta. 2014. First record of Turkey Vultures (*Cathartes aura*) nesting on Hispaniola. Journal of Caribbean Ornithology 27:22–24.

Dhondt, A. A., and K. V. Dhondt. 2008. Two bird species new for Hispaniola. Journal of Caribbean Ornithology 21:46–47.

Dod, A. S. 1978. *Aves de la República Dominicana.* Museo Nacional de Historia Natural, Santo Domingo.

Dod, A. S. 1981. *Guía de campo para las aves de la República Dominicana*. Editora Horizontes, Santo Domingo.

Dunning Jr, J. B. 1993. *CRC handbook of avian body masses*. CRC Press, Boca Raton, FL.

Dunning Jr, J. B. 2007. *CRC handbook of avian body masses*. Second edition. CRC Press, Boca Raton, FL.

Earsom, S. D., C. Lombard, J. Schwagerl, J. P. Oland, and L. Miranda-Castro. 2008. Avifauna and human disturbance observations on Navassa Island. Caribbean Journal of Science 44:246–251.

Fahey, A. L., R. E. Ricklefs, J. A. DeWoody, and S. C. Latta. 2012. Comparative historical demography of migratory and nonmigratory birds from the Caribbean island of Hispaniola. Journal of Evolutionary Biology 39:400–414.

FAO. 2015. Forest cover in Dominican Republic. Accessed through Global Forest Watch. www.globalforestwatch.org.

FAO. 2015. Forest cover in Haiti. Accessed through Global Forest Watch. www.globalforestwatch.org.

Foden, W. B., S. H. Butchart, S. N. Stuart, J. C. Vié, H. R. Akçakaya, et al. 2013. Identifying the world's most climate change vulnerable species: a systematic trait-based assessment of all birds, amphibians and corals. PLoS One, 8(6), e65427.

Garrido, E., Y. M. León, Y. Arias, and L. Perdomo. 2010. Nidificación reciente del flamenco (*Phoenicopterus ruber*) en República Dominicana. Journal of Caribbean Ornithology 23:50–51.

Garrido, O. H., and G. B. Reynard. 1993. The Greater Antillean Nightjar: is it one species? Pitirre 7:5.

Garrido, O. H., G. B. Reynard, and A. Kirkconnell. 1997. Is the Palm Crow, *Corvus palmarum* (Aves Corvidae), a monotypic species? Ornitología Neotropical 8:15–21.

Garrido, O. H., J. W. Wiley, and G. B. Reynard. 2009. Taxonomy of the Loggerhead Kingbird (*Tyrannus caudifasciatus*) complex (Aves: Tyrannidae). Wilson Journal of Ornithology 121:703–713.

GFW. 2021a. Dominican Republic. Global Forest Watch. Available at https://gfw.global/3aYKbFa.

GFW. 2021b. Haiti. Global Forest Watch. Available at https://gfw.global/3gZ82bq.

Hardy, J. W., B. B. Coffey, Jr., and G. B. Reynard. 1988. *Voices of New World Nightbirds, Owls, Nightjars, and Their Allies*. 3rd ed. ARA Records, Gainesville, FL.

IUCN. 2020. The IUCN Red List of Threatened Species. Version 2020–3. Available at http://www.iucnredlist.org.

Keith, A., J. Wiley, S. Latta, and J. Ottenwalder. 2003. *The Birds of Hispaniola: Haiti and the Dominican Republic*. British Ornithologists' Union, Tring, UK.

Kirwan, G. W., A. Levesque, M. Oberle, and C. J. Sharpe. 2019. *Birds of the West Indies*. Lynx and BirdLife International Field Guides, Lynx Edicions, Barcelona, Spain.

Landestoy, M. A. 2017. New observations of two rare rallids (Aves: Gruiformes: Rallidae) on Hispaniola. Novitates Caribaea 11:106–114.

Latta, S. C. 2019. Not all pine habitat is the same: how bird communities vary among mature Hispaniolan Pine forests shaped by fire. Caribbean Naturalist 65:1–19.

Latta, S. C., and R. Lorenzo (eds.). 2000. *Results of the National Planning Workshop for Avian Conservation in the Dominican Republic*. Dirección Nacional de Parques, Santo Domingo.

Latta, S. C., and P. G. Rodriguez. 2018. Notable bird records from Hispaniola and associated islands, including four new species. Journal of Caribbean Ornithology 31:34–37.

Latta, S. C., and K. J. Wallace. 2012. *Ruta Barrancolí: A Bird-finding Guide to the Dominican Republic*. The National Aviary, Pittsburgh, PA.

Latta, S. C., C. C. Rimmer, A. R. Keith, J. W. Wiley, H. A. Raffaele, K. P. McFarland, and E. M. Fernandez. 2006. *Birds of the Dominican Republic and Haiti*. Princeton University Press, Princeton, NJ.

Latta, S. C., A. K. Townsend, and I. J. Lovette. 2012. The origins of the recently discovered Hispaniolan Olive-throated Parakeet: a phylogeographic perspective on a conservation conundrum. Caribbean Journal of Science 46:143–149.

Latta, S. C., S. Cabezas, D. A. Mejía, M. M. Paulino, H. Almonte, C. Miller-Butterworth, and G. R. Bortolotti. 2016. Carry-over effects provide linkages across the annual cycle of a Neotropical migratory bird, the Louisiana Waterthrush. Ibis 158:395–406.

Lloyd, J. D., C. C. Rimmer, and K. P. McFarland. 2016. Assessing conservation status of resident and migrant birds on Hispaniola with mist-netting. PeerJ 3:e1541.

Luna, Á., P. Romero-Vidal, F. Hiraldo, and J. L. Tella. 2018. Cities favour the recent establishment and current spread of the Eurasian Collared Dove *Streptopelia decaocto* (Frivaldszky, 1838) in Dominican Republic. BioInvasions Record 7:95–99.

McFarland, K. P., J. D. Lloyd, S.J.K. Frey, P. L. Johnson, R. B. Chandler, and C. C. Rimmer. 2018. Modeling spatial variation in winter abundance to direct conservation actions for a vulnerable migratory songbird, the Bicknell's Thrush (*Catharus bicknelli*). Condor 120:517–529.

Mejía, D. A., M. M. Paulino, K. Wallace, and S. C. Latta. 2009. Great-tailed Grackle (*Quiscalus mexicanus*): a new species for Hispaniola. Journal of Caribbean Ornithology 22:112–114.

MIMARENA. 2019. Resolución que emite la lista roja de especies de fauna en peligro de extinción, amenazadas o protegidas de la República Dominicana (Lista Roja). Resolución No. 0017–2019. Ministerio de Medio Ambiente y Recursos Naturales de la República Dominicana, Santo Domingo.

Ovalles, P. J. 2011. Identificación de las causas de la deforestación y la degradación de los bosques en la República Dominicana. Programa REDDCCAD/GIZ en Centroamérica y República Dominicana.

Paryski, P., C. A. Woods, and F. Sergile. 1989. Conservation strategies and the preservation of biological diversity in Haiti. Pp. 855–878 in C. A. Woods (ed.), *Biogeography of the West Indies: Past, Present, Future*. Sandhill Crane Press, Gainesville, FL.

Paulino, M. M., D. A. Mejía, and S. C. Latta. 2010. A new review of the status of the Caribbean Flamingo (*Phoenicopterus ruber*) in the Dominican Republic and Haiti. Bulletin of the IUCN-SSC/Wetlands International Flamingo Specialist Group, Flamingo 18:62–66.

Paulino, M. M., D. A. Mejía, and S. C. Latta. 2013. First record of Great-tailed Grackle (*Quiscalus mexicanus*) breeding in the West Indies. Journal of Caribbean Ornithology 26:63–65.

Perdomo, L., and Y. Arias. 2009. Dominican Republic. Pp 171–178 in C. Devenish, D. F. Díaz Fernández, R. P. Clay, I. Davidson, and I. Yépez Zabala (eds.). Important Bird Areas Americas—Priority sites for biodiversity conservation. BirdLife International (BirdLife Conservation Series No. 16). Quito, Ecuador.

Quiroga, M. A., T. Hayes, C. Hayes, H. Garrod, L. Soares, S. Knutie, S. C. Latta, and D. L. Anderson. 2020. More than just nestlings: incidence of subcutaneous *Philornis* (Diptera: Muscidae) nest flies in adult birds. Parasitology Research. https://doi.org/10.1007/s00436-020-06696-2.

Raffaele, H., J. Wiley, O. Garrido, A. Keith, and J. Raffaele. 1998. *A Guide to the Birds of the West Indies.* Princeton University Press, Princeton, NJ.

Raffaele, H. A., J. Wiley, O. H. Garrido, A. Keith, and J. I. Raffaele. 2020. *Birds of the West Indies Second Edition* (Vol. 143). Princeton University Press, Princeton, NJ.

Rimmer, C. C., L. G. Woolaver, R. K. Nichols, E. M. Fernandez, S. C. Latta, and E. Garrido. 2008. First description of nests and eggs of two Hispaniolan endemic species: Western Chat-tanager (*Calyptophilus tertius*) and Hispaniolan Highland-tanager (*Xenoligea montana*). Wilson Journal of Ornithology 120:190–195.

Rimmer, C. C., P. L. Johnson, and J. D. Lloyd. 2017. Home range size and nocturnal roost locations of Western Chat-Tanagers (*Calyptophilus tertius*). Wilson Journal of Ornithology 129:611–615.

Sánchez Peña, R. 2013. Análisis de resultados de la aplicación de la metodología efectividad de manejo de Áreas Protegidas (METT) en República Dominicana: Comparación 2009–2012. Ministerio de Medio Ambiente y Recursos Naturales y Programa de las Naciones Unidas para El Desarrollo.

Satgé, Y., E. Rupp, A. Brown, and P. Jodice. 2020. Habitat modelling locates nesting areas of the Endangered Black-capped Petrel *Pterodroma hasitata* on Hispaniola and identifies habitat loss. Bird Conservation International 1–18.

Schreiber, E. A., and D. Lee. 2000. *Status and Conservation of West Indian Seabirds.* Society of Caribbean Ornithology, Special Publication #1, Ruston, LA.

Sly, N. D., A. K. Townsend, C. C. Rimmer, J. M. Townsend, S. C. Latta, and I. J. Lovette. 2010. Phylogeography and conservation of the endemic Hispaniolan Palm-Tanagers (Aves: Phaenicophilus). Conservation Genetics 11:2121–2129.

Sly, N. D., A. K. Townsend, C. C. Rimmer, J. M. Townsend, S. C. Latta, and I. J. Lovette. 2011. Ancient islands and modern invasions: disparate phylogeographic histories among Hispaniola's endemic birds. Molecular Ecology 20:5012–5024.

Stattersfield, A. J., M. J. Crosby, A. J. Long, and D. C. Wege. 1998. *Endemic Bird Areas of the World: Priorities for Bird Conservation.* BirdLife International, Cambridge.

Tang, Q., S. V. Edwards, and F. E. Rheindt. 2018. Rapid diversification and hybridization have shaped the dynamic history of the genus *Elaenia*. Molecular Phylogenetics and Evolution 127:522–533.

Townsend, A. K., C. C. Rimmer, S. C. Latta, and I. J. Lovette. 2007. Phylogeographic concordance of nuclear and mitochondrial gene genealogies in the single-island avian radiation of Hispaniolan Chat-tanagers (Aves: *Calyptophilus*). Molecular Ecology 16:3634–3642.

Townsend, J. M., E. Garrido, and D. A. Mejía. 2008. Nests and nesting behavior of Golden Swallow (*Tachycineta euchrysea*) in abandoned bauxite mines in the Dominican Republic. Wilson Journal of Ornithology 120:867–871.

Townsend, J. M., C. C. Rimmer, and K. P. McFarland. 2010. Winter territoriality and spatial behavior of Bicknell's Thrush (*Catharus bicknelli*) at two ecologically distinct sites in the Dominican Republic. Auk 127:514–522.

Townsend, J. M., C. C. Rimmer, S. C. Latta, D. A. Mejía, E. G. Garrido, and K. P. McFarland. 2018. Nesting ecology and nesting success of resident and endemic tropical birds in the Dominican Republic. Wilson Journal of Ornithology 130:849–858.

Woolaver, L. G., R. K. Nichols, E. S. Morton, and B.J.M. Stutchbury. 2013. Feeding ecology and specialist diet of critically endangered Ridgway's Hawks. Journal of Field Ornithology 84:138–146.

Woolaver, L. G., R. K. Nichols, E. S. Morton, and B.J.M. Stutchbury. 2013. Population genetics and relatedness in a critically endangered island raptor, Ridgway's Hawk *Buteo ridgwayi*. Conservation Genetics 14:559–571.

Woolaver, L. G., R. K. Nichols, E. S. Morton, and B.J.M. Stutchbury. 2015. Breeding ecology and predictors of nest success in the Critically Endangered Ridgway's Hawk *Buteo ridgwayi*. Bird Conservation International 25:385–398.

INDEX OF ENGLISH AND SCIENTIFIC NAMES

QUICK INDEX